around the world in 80 meatballs

Dedicated to my daughters, Beatrix Carlyon
and Clementine Hall, and Khass Yianni;
I wish there was a better expression than
'platonic love of my life' to describe what you
are to me, but that will have to suffice.

around the world in 80 meatballs

BUNNY BANYAI

Hardie Grant
BOOKS

Contents

Meatballs by dish type
6

Introduction
12

A guide to getting the most out of your balls
14

Meatball size guide
16

Recipes
20

Index
182

Acknowledgements
189

About the author
190

Meatballs by dish type

Soups, congees, broths/simmering sauces

PALESTINE Shorbat adas bil kofta 33
GREECE Youvarlakia 36
TÜRKIYE Ekşili köfte 52
ROMANIA Ciorba de perisoare 57
LITHUANIA Kotletai in dill-spiked broth 68
PHILIPPINES Misua with bola-bola 83
JAPAN Chanko nabe with tori dango 86
MEXICO Sopa de albondigas 109
THAILAND Jok moo 113
IRAN Ash-e anar 119
INDONESIA Bakso 127
CHINA Vermicelli meatball soup 130
ITALY Minestra maritata 139
CHINA Zhou rou wan 153
MALTA Pulpetti tal-laham and brodu tal-laham 155
LEBANON Shorba hamra 156
CHINA Gongwan 162
TIBET Tibetan meatball soup 178

Bakes

SYRIA Adele's koftas 34
CZECH REPUBLIC Mira's meatballs 43
TÜRKIYE Hasanpasha köfte 53
TÜRKIYE Izmir köfte 54
IRAQ Tepsi baytinijan 78
SERBIA Ćulbastije 85
PALESTINE Kafta and tahini bake with Palestinian salad 173

Stews and curries

PAKISTAN Kofta aalu 48
GHANA Ghanaian meatball stew 67
IRAN Koofteh berenji 115
MYANMAR A-thar-lohn-hin 116
IRAN Fesenjoon 118
CANADA Ragoût de boulettes 134
AFGHANISTAN Korme kofta 141

White sauces and dips

DENMARK Fiskefrikadeller 89
LEBANON Kibbeh labanieh 90
MOLDOVA Parjoale with mujdei 94
LEBANON Kafta with tarator sauce and tabbouleh 133
TÜRKIYE Fistkili kebab 149
SPAIN Albondigas Mama Pepa in white wine sauce 172
SWEDEN Kottbullar 175

Around the World in 80 Meatballs

Party/beer snack balls

CYPRUS Keftedes with fried potatoes 46
JAPAN Teriyaki tsukune 71
BELGIUM Boulets de Liège 77
PORTUGAL Almôndegas de bacalhau 82
BRAZIL Kibe 92
CAMBODIA Num pang with pork meatballs 97
LIBYA M'battan 110
FINLAND Lihapullat 112
ITALY Polpettine al limone 157
MALAYSIA Begedil 163
KOREA Goji-wanja-jeon 171

Gravy sauces

AUSTRALIA Rissoles with gravy and minted peas 39
NETHERLANDS Gehaktballen with hutspot 40
NORWAY Medisterkaker 58
UNITED KINGDOM Faggots/savoury ducks with gravy 101
LATVIA Kotlete in gravy 124
POLAND Klopsiki with cwikla z chrzanem 158

Tomato-based sauces

COLOMBIA Albondigas 30
ISRAEL Israeli-style meatballs 51
BULGARIA Kjufteta po Chirpanski 72
SERBIA Ćufte 100
ITALY Polpette in sugo 121
HUNGARY Fasirozott with nokedli 161
AUSTRALIA Porcupine meatballs 164
IRAN Kal leh gonjishki 167

Miscellaneous

GERMANY Frikadellen and rahmspinat 25
POLAND Pulpety with cold beet salad 26
MOROCCO Kefta mkaouara 29
FRANCE Boulette de bœuf 35
UKRAINE Kotleti 59
SOUTH AFRICA Oumense onder die komberse 64
HAITI Boulet with Haitian epis 74
TUNISIA Chebtiya 95
PAKISTAN Gola kabab with charred onions 106
BOSNIA Sogan dolma 128
AUSTRIA Faschierte laibchen 131
ALGERIA Kefta b'zeitoun 140
ITALY Polpette with melanzane alla sassarese 146
CHINA Lion's head meatballs with cabbage 150
CHINA Lion's head meatballs with thick sauce 152
RUSSIA Grechanyky with mushroom sauce 168

Meatballs by dish type

Around the World

in 80 Meatballs

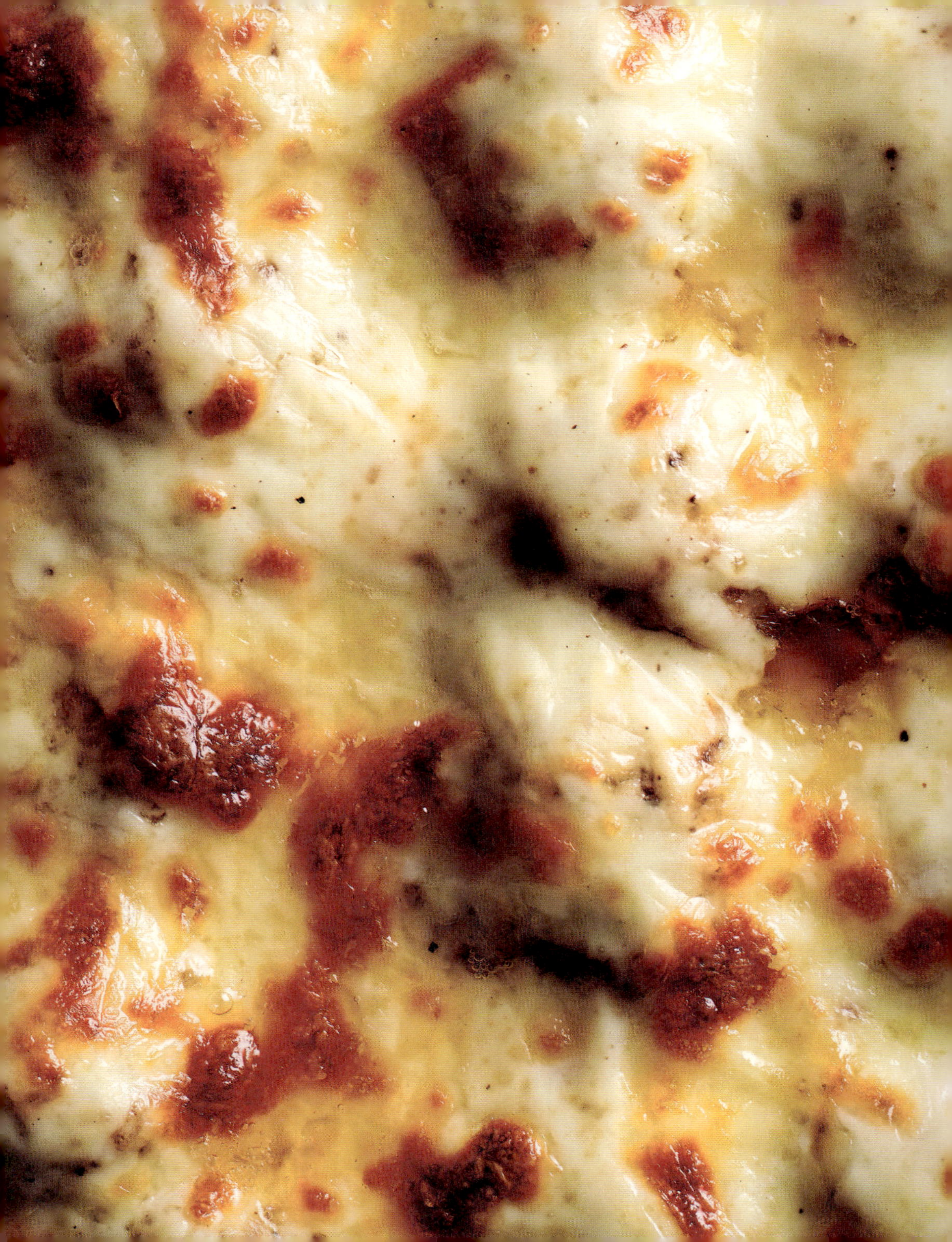

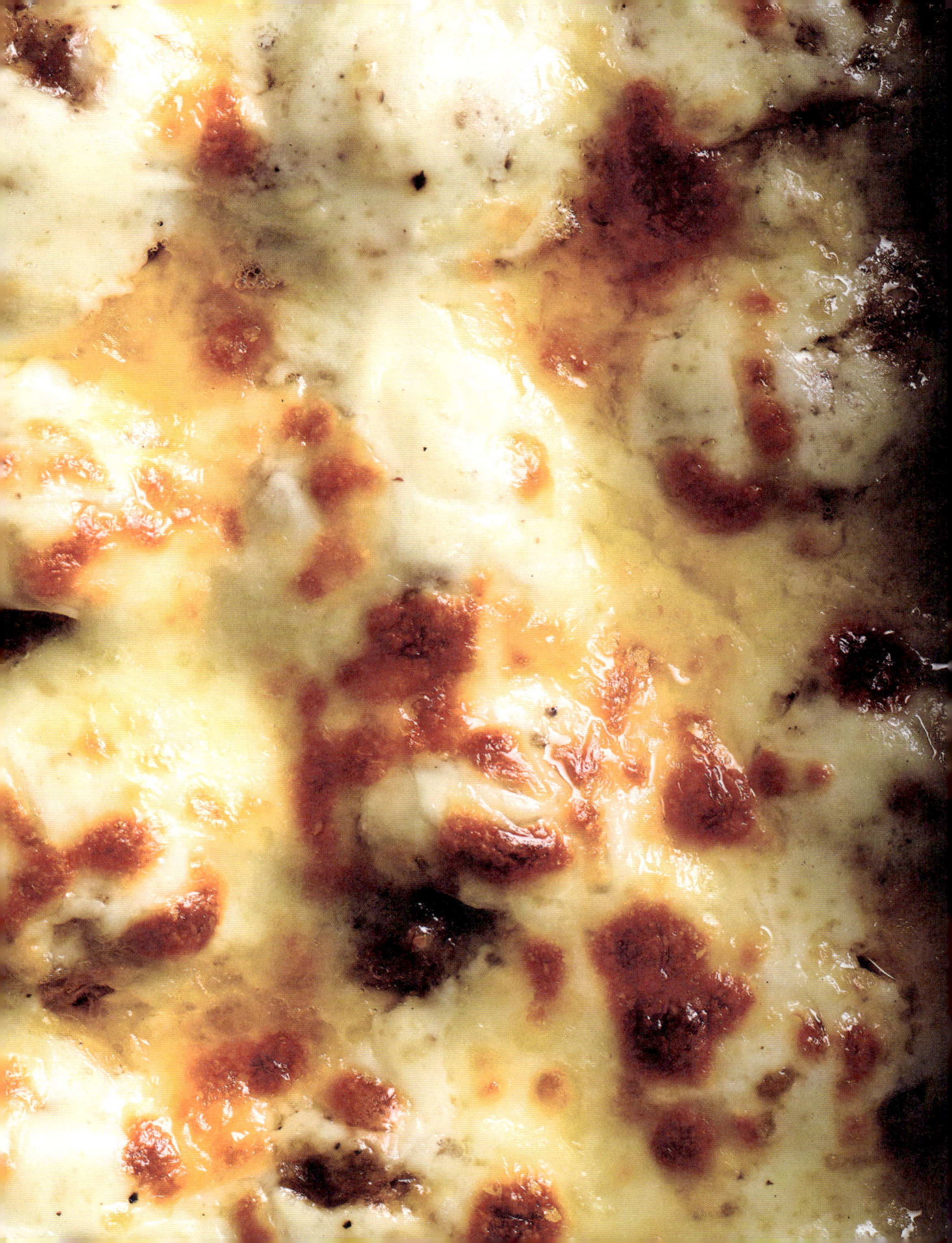

Introduction

The hardest thing about compiling a book of meatball recipes is working out when to start making ball jokes and, more importantly, when to stop.

Restraint is not my strong suit, so let's just get straight into it: I love balls. Fried balls. Baked balls. Cold balls. Hot balls. Scandi balls. Balkan balls. Asian balls. All the balls the world has to offer. And that's what this book is: a tour of the globe via the universally beloved meatball.

The magic of meatballs (I will refer to them as meatballs from here on in to avoid squandering your goodwill with a ceaseless volley of ball jokes) is that, should you wish, they can be eaten seven nights a week with scarcely a hint of repetition. In the mood for soup? There's a meatball recipe for that. Hearty potato bake beckoning? There's a meatball recipe for that, too. There is a meatball for every mood, every season and every season-within-a-season. There is even a recipe within these pages for a meatball commonly eaten during rainy weather in the Philippines: Misu with bola-bola (page 83).

A question many people asked me during the course of researching and writing this book was 'Are you sick of meatballs yet?' The answer, hand on heart, is no. The variety of recipes and the built-in appeal of any dish that spotlights the meatball meant that every single one felt like a treat, an adventure, a happy discovery. I wonder how I spent so much of my life unaware of the charms of Polish pulpety, Belgian boulette and Ghanaian meatball stew – all now permanent fixtures in my house.

The allure of meatballs is multidimensional. They don't require the deft, precise hand of a highly skilled chef; any shovel-handed buffoon can roll a gob of mince into a rustic ball. Their application knows no bounds: how do we get vegetables into the mouths of children who have a one-line list of safe vegetables? In a meatball. What do we give our loved ones after a painful tooth extraction? Soft, nurturing meatballs. What do we cook when cost-of-living expenses bite? Thrifty, flavoursome meatballs. And if that's not compelling enough evidence of their virtue, minced (ground) meat also helps to minimise food waste, as it utilises trimmings of meat that may otherwise be destined for the bin.

But, really, it's their global ubiquity that gives meatballs their icon status. Every corner of the planet has its own adorable twist on the meatball. Many countries, in fact, have a multitude of regional variations; Türkiye is said to have in excess of 200 varieties. To my mind, nothing you can serve at a dinner table better represents the interconnectedness of us all than the universally recognised, universally adored meatball in all its countless guises.

Within the pages of this book, you'll meet 80 variations on the meatball, from Japanese Chanko nabe with tori dango (page 86) to Greek Youvarlakia (page 36) and Norwegian Medisterkaker (page 58). You'll meet people who've graciously shared prized family recipes, passed down for generations. The spirit of these recipes is best summed up by Fernando Vidal Garrida, a Spaniard now living in Melbourne, who shared the recipe of his late, adored grandmother, Pepa:

'My grandmother didn't just pass on a recipe, but also the love that her parents and grandparents had transmitted to her. Love, in the form of a ridiculous little ball. Sometimes, when I prepare the meatballs now, I can almost feel my grandmother hugging me around the waist. Cooking the meatballs is a journey through space and time, straight to her; it is a date for both of us, and the only way I have left to feel her by my side. Eating meatballs, for me, is almost like the Communion, or Eucharist.'

Amen to that.

A guide to getting the

These recipes could be described as 'appealingly rustic', with most of them born out of necessity before becoming beloved family recipes, and all of them reflective of the ingredients readily available in the region of their origin. They range in difficulty from 'a labrador could make them' to 'a labrador could make them with the assistance of a very competent adult'. Only a couple of recipes require anything beyond rudimentary kitchen skills, and all are very much within the capabilities of the home cook. Sogan dolma (page 128) require a bit of playing around with onions, and M'battan (page 110) a bit of potato play. Both recipes are absolutely worth that little bit of extra work. All the ingredients can be found within the international aisles of major supermarkets, and Asian, Middle Eastern and Indian grocers.

While every contributor to this book has their own preferred way of working with the meat mixture, there are a few tricks that can be applied to all recipes.

- When shaping the meatballs, have a small bowl of water next to the mixture. Dip your hands in the water between balls, to avoid your hands becoming a sticky, unmanageable mess. You can also lightly oil your hands to achieve the same result. Gloves are a good idea if you've got longer nails, or don't fancy a prolonged bout of handwashing post roll. You can also use an ice cream scoop, but hands are better.

- Using your hands to combine the meat mixture also produces a superior result, unless the recipe specifies using a food processor. Again, use gloves if you're a bit squeamish about skin-to-meat contact.

- Refrigerating your meatball mix for an hour or so helps firm it up and makes for a more robust ball. Keeping your meat cool during prep is also important; some recipes even ask you to partially freeze the mince prior to cooking, as this stops the fat from melting and breaking down.

- When a recipe calls for minced (ground) chicken, it's best to go with thigh meat, or a mix of thigh and breast; breast alone results in a dry ball. There are very few recipes that specify a particular fat content in the meat because, let's be honest, these are meatballs, not nuclear submarines; we don't want to get bogged down in finicky sums. You can bet the nonnas, yiayias and omas of the world certainly don't.

- In most cases, you can switch proteins if desired: substitute beef for lamb; pork for chicken or turkey.

- For vegetarian versions, you can substitute minced (ground) meat with any number of plant-based alternatives. It may require a little experimentation to find the right substitute for each recipe, and measurements may need adjusting to account for differences in texture and fat content. Textured vegetable protein (TVP) works well in recipes that call for beef. Tofu and shiitake mushroom mince is easy to make and works very well with Asian-leaning flavours.

most out of your balls

Where an authentic family recipe is presented, few adjustments have been made. Many of these recipes have been coaxed onto paper for the very first time, having passed through generations via the 'watch-and-learn' method; the very notion of nailing down quantities is anathema to many old-school cooks.

As such, you may want to make tweaks of your own. Your version may become the beloved recipe passed down future generations, just as so many of the recipes you'll encounter here have been. Feel free to use them as inspiration; meatballs do not generally require the absolute precision of, for example, baked goods, though when it comes to cooking technique and recommended temperatures, it's best to pay attention. Many of the recipes are continually changing and evolving within the families they reside; some are even prepared differently each time they're cooked. Fernando Vidal Garrida recalls his grandmother making meatballs differently for every family member, according to their personal preferences.

A note on authenticity: this is *always* hotly contested territory, as a cursory glance at the comments section of any 'authentic' recipe will quickly inform you. People with a shared ethnic background can have *vastly* different notions of what a certain dish should and should never include. Most of the recipes in this book are family recipes, and what is authentic to them may not be to you. Please keep this in mind while reading.

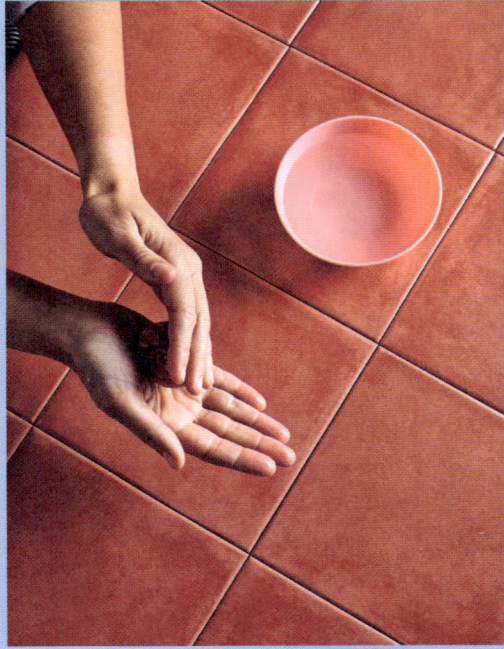

A guide to getting the most out of your balls

Meatball size guide

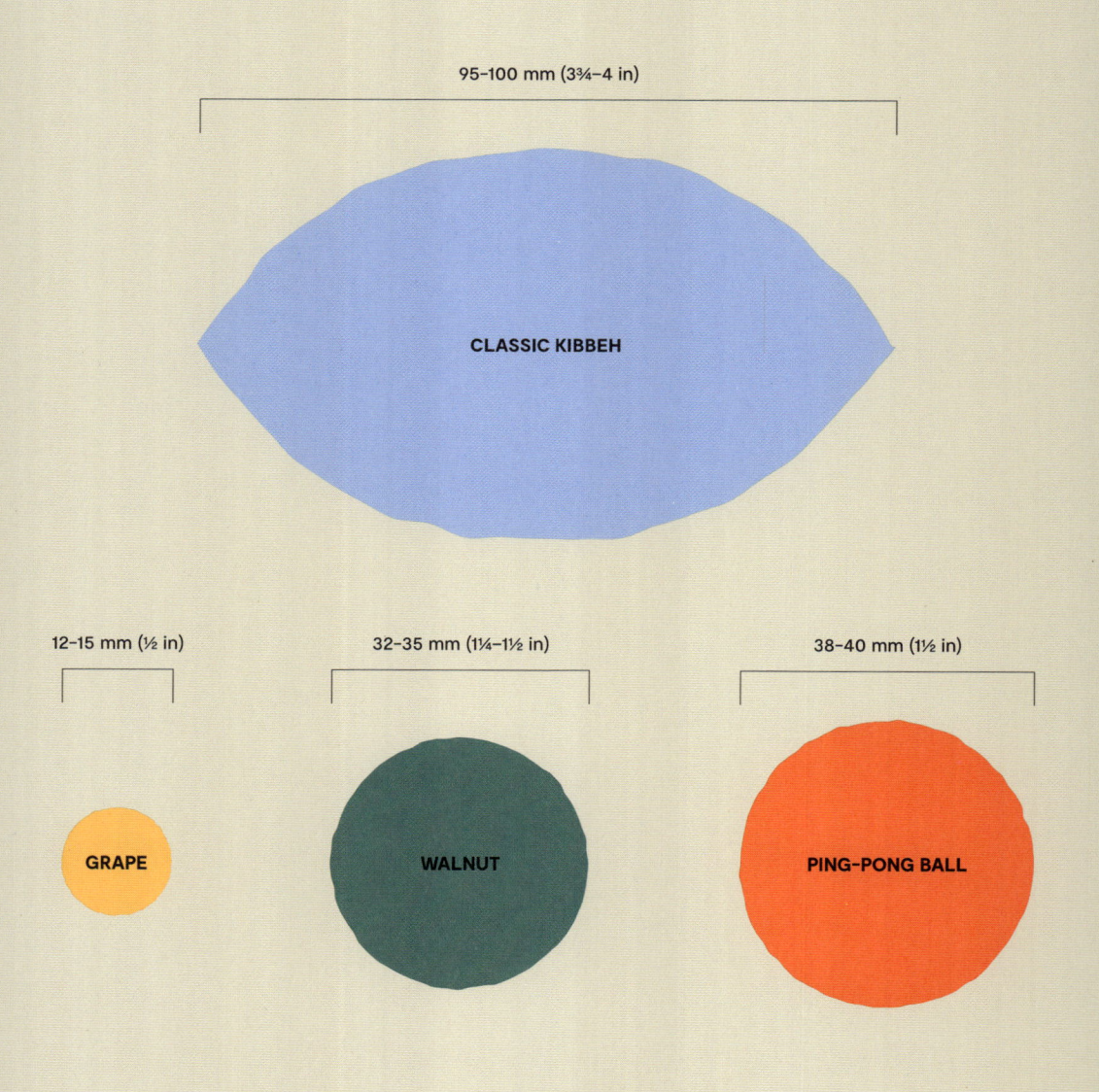

95–100 mm (3¾–4 in)

CLASSIC KIBBEH

12–15 mm (½ in)

GRAPE

32–35 mm (1¼–1½ in)

WALNUT

38–40 mm (1½ in)

PING-PONG BALL

43–45 mm (1¾ in)

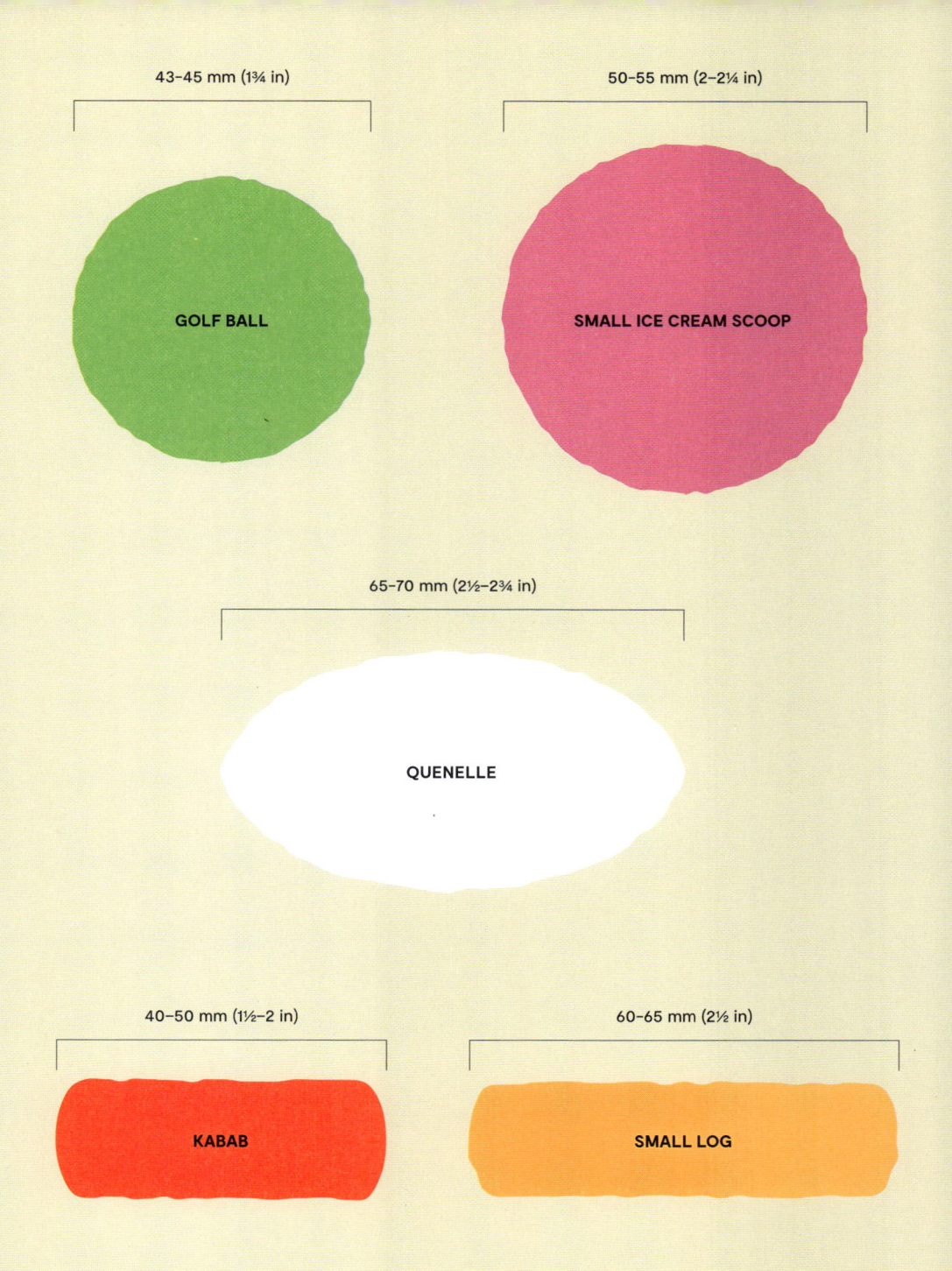

GOLF BALL

50–55 mm (2–2¼ in)

SMALL ICE CREAM SCOOP

65–70 mm (2½–2¾ in)

QUENELLE

40–50 mm (1½–2 in)

KABAB

60–65 mm (2½ in)

SMALL LOG

And now,
to the kitchen –

balls to the wall.

01
—

20

1.	**GERMANY**	Frikadellen and rahmspinat	25
2.	**POLAND**	Pulpety with cold beet salad	26
3.	**MOROCCO**	Kefta mkaouara	29
4.	**COLOMBIA (CARIBBEAN REGION)**	Albondigas	30
5.	**PALESTINE**	Shorbat adas bil kofta	33
6.	**SYRIA**	Adele's koftas	34
7.	**FRANCE**	Boulette de bœuf	35
8.	**GREECE**	Youvarlakia	36
9.	**AUSTRALIA**	Rissoles with gravy and minted peas	39
10.	**NETHERLANDS**	Gehaktballen with hutspot	40
11.	**CZECH REPUBLIC**	Mira's meatballs	43
12.	**CYPRUS**	Keftedes with fried potatoes	46
13.	**PAKISTAN**	Kofta aalu	48
14.	**ISRAEL**	Israeli-style meatballs	51
15.	**TÜRKIYE**	Ekşili köfte	52
16.	**TÜRKIYE**	Hasanpasha köfte	53
17.	**TÜRKIYE**	Izmir köfte	54
18.	**ROMANIA**	Ciorba de perisoare	57
19.	**NORWAY**	Medisterkaker	58
20.	**UKRAINE**	Kotleti	59

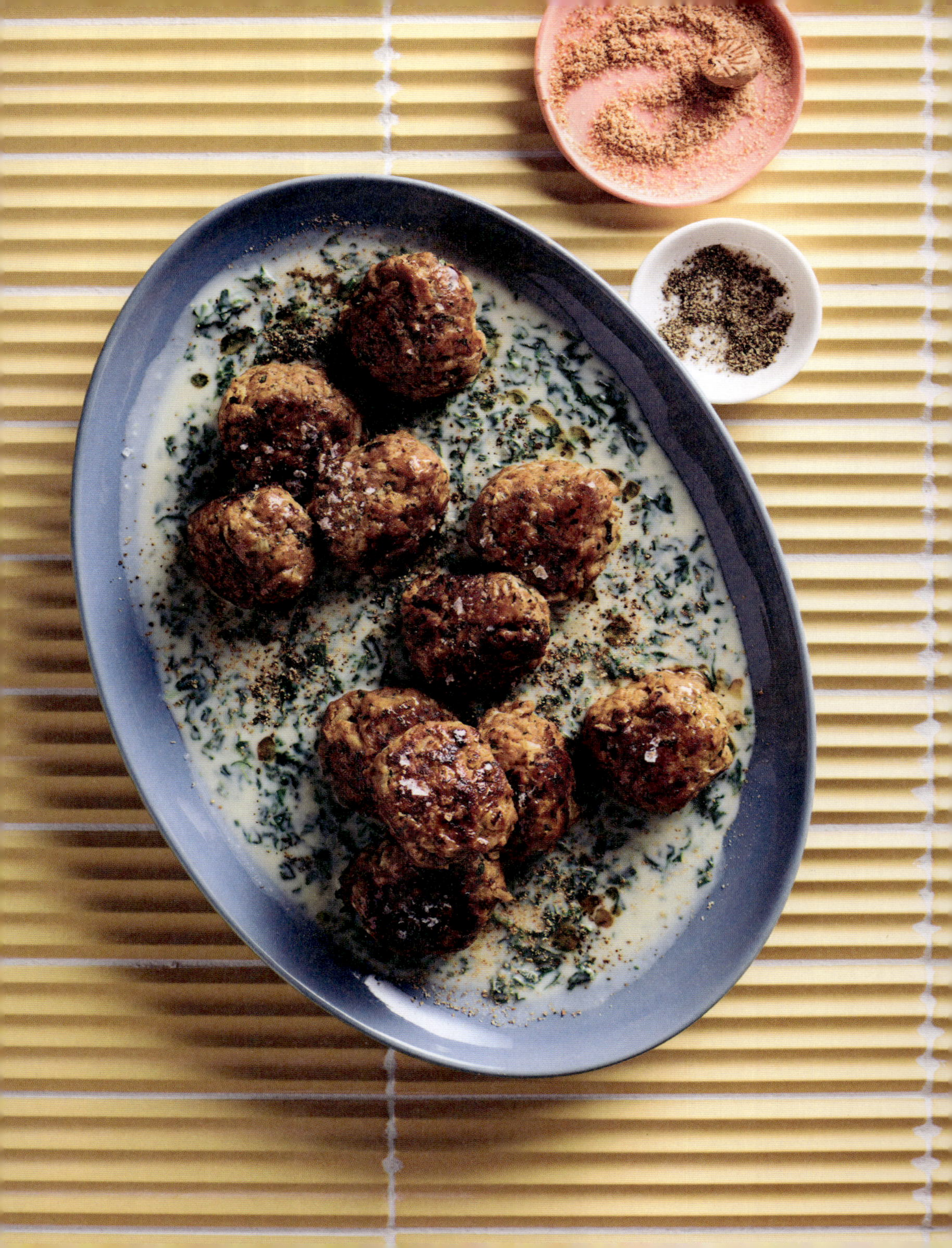

01
GERMANY

Were it not for my lovely friend Claudia Schneider, the custodian of this recipe, a home-cooked meal may never have passed my lips between the ages of twenty and thirty. Instead of limited variations on 'McMeals', I dined on cheese kransky and sauerkraut, schnitzel and mashed potato, and frikadellen with creamed spinach.

For this, I can thank Claudia's great-aunt Kathi, who lived with Claudia's family in the tiny town of Boppard, in the Rhineland region of Germany. Kathi cooked many old family recipes, eventually passing them down to Claudia. The family gathered for a hot lunch every day after school let out at 1 pm (don't get too jealous, kids – school started at 7.30 am), and these terrific frikadellen were frequently on the menu.

Claudia migrated to Australia in the nineties, and says, 'Collecting family recipes became important to me; the physical distance felt very pronounced in the early years, and food was a connection to home.' In time, Claudia's meatballs became a favourite with her Australian husband Anthony's family, replacing the rissoles that were previously a staple of all family gatherings.

Frikadellen and rahmspinat
MEATBALLS AND CREAMED SPINACH

SERVES 4–6

- **Meatballs**

1 day-old bread roll or piece of baguette, or 40 g (1½ oz/½ cup) fresh or 2 tablespoons dry breadcrumbs
100 ml (3½ fl oz) warm water or full-cream (whole) milk
1 onion, finely chopped
2 garlic cloves, finely chopped
2 tablespoons finely chopped parsley
500 g (1 lb 2 oz) minced (ground) meat, half pork and half beef, or just beef
1 egg
2 teaspoons dijon mustard
1 teaspoon salt
1 teaspoon sweet paprika
freshly cracked black pepper
ghee or olive oil, for pan-frying

- **Creamed spinach**

1 bunch English spinach, washed
2 tablespoons salted butter
2 tablespoons plain (all-purpose) flour
125 ml (4 fl oz/½ cup) full-cream (whole) milk
½ garlic clove, chopped
salt and freshly cracked black pepper, to taste
freshly grated nutmeg, to taste

To make the meatballs, soak the bread in the warm water or milk for 10 minutes. This makes the meatballs fluffy and light on the inside and crispy on the outside. Squeeze the soaked bread firmly and transfer it to a large bowl. If you are using fresh or dry breadcrumbs instead, just add them to your bowl without soaking.

Add all the remaining meatball ingredients to the bowl and mix well. Form into twelve meatballs, flattening each meatball slightly.

Heat the ghee in a cast-iron or other heavy-based frying pan over a medium heat. Fry the meatballs in batches until they are brown and crispy, about 5–6 minutes on each side. Keep warm in a low oven until ready to serve.

While the meatballs are cooking, prepare the creamed spinach. Bring a pot of salted water to the boil, add the spinach and cook for about 5 minutes. Drain, reserving the cooking liquid. Finely chop the cooked spinach and set aside.

Melt the butter in a saucepan over a low heat and stir in the flour. Cook for 2–3 minutes, stirring continually. Add the milk and 125 ml (4 fl oz/½ cup) of the reserved spinach cooking liquid and whisk over a low heat until smooth. Add the chopped garlic and simmer for about 5 minutes, then add the chopped spinach. Season with salt, pepper and nutmeg.

Serve the meatballs hot with the creamed spinach on the side.

- **Note**

Claudia sometimes adds chopped pickles and different kinds of herbs to the meatballs.

02
POLAND

This book is about celebrating the things that unite rather than divide us. With that said, I'm going to put forth a controversial opinion: pulpety deserve more than a little of the limelight hogged by their Swedish cousin, Kottbullar (page 175). I love kottbullar, but I will be buried with a bowl of pulpety.

Unlike its Polish sister-dish, klopsiki, where the meatballs are typically fried, pulpety are simmered in broth and usually served with boiled potatoes and a side salad of cold beetroot (beets) or sauerkraut. If you've got junior mouths to feed, mashed potato is the better option. This dish is unabashedly hearty, but works a treat in both the cooler and warmer months, the tang of the beetroot cutting nicely through the richness of the pulpety.

Pulpety with cold beet salad

SERVES 6

- **Cold beet salad**

3 beetroot (beets)
1 apple
2 dill pickles, coarsely grated
1 small red onion, finely chopped
1 tablespoon vegetable oil
1 tablespoon lemon juice
salt and freshly cracked black pepper, to taste

- **Meatballs**

2 tablespoons salted butter
1 onion, finely minced
500 g (1 lb 2 oz) minced (ground) pork
500 g (1 lb 2 oz) minced (ground) beef
4 garlic cloves, finely chopped
4 slices bread, blitzed to coarse crumbs (see Note)
2 tablespoons finely chopped parsley, plus extra to garnish
2 tablespoons finely chopped dill
1 egg
1 teaspoon salt
½ teaspoon freshly cracked black pepper
1 litre (34 fl oz/4 cups) chicken broth
4 bay leaves
6 whole black peppercorns
6 whole allspice berries
8 slices dried porcini mushroom
2 tablespoons plain (all-purpose) flour

- **To serve**

boiled or mashed potatoes

To prepare the cold beet salad, bring a large saucepan of water to the boil and cook the beetroot whole for 30 minutes, or until softened but still slightly crunchy. Drain and leave to cool for 15 minutes, then peel and coarsely grate them.

To prepare the meatballs, melt the butter in a frying pan over a medium heat and sauté the onion until golden brown around the edges. Combine the meat, garlic and bread in a large bowl, then add the sautéed onion, parsley, dill, egg, salt and pepper and mix until combined.

Bring the broth to a simmer in a saucepan with the bay leaves, peppercorns, allspice berries and mushrooms over a medium heat. Form the meat mixture into even balls about 5 cm (2 in) in diameter. Drop the raw balls into the simmering broth and simmer over a low heat for 15 minutes. Take one out and cut it open to check if it's cooked through. Once cooked, take the meatballs out and strain the broth through a fine-mesh sieve into a clean saucepan.

In a small bowl, whisk the flour with 180 ml (6 fl oz) cold water. Return the broth to the stove and heat through gently. Add the flour slurry, stir well and bring to the boil. Taste and adjust the seasoning if necessary. Set aside until you're ready to serve.

To finish the salad, grate the apple and combine with the grated beetroot, dill pickle and onion in a bowl. Add the vegetable oil and lemon juice, stirring thoroughly. Adjust the seasoning with salt and pepper to taste. Chill the salad in the refrigerator for about 30 minutes before serving.

When you're ready to serve, return the meatballs to the sauce and heat through over a low heat. Serve with boiled or mashed potatoes and the cold beet salad. Garnish with parsley.

- **NOTE**

The beauty of this recipe is that you can use any bread you have on hand; it doesn't have to be stale, fresh, white or dark. I love Khorasan bread for its sweet, buttery depth.

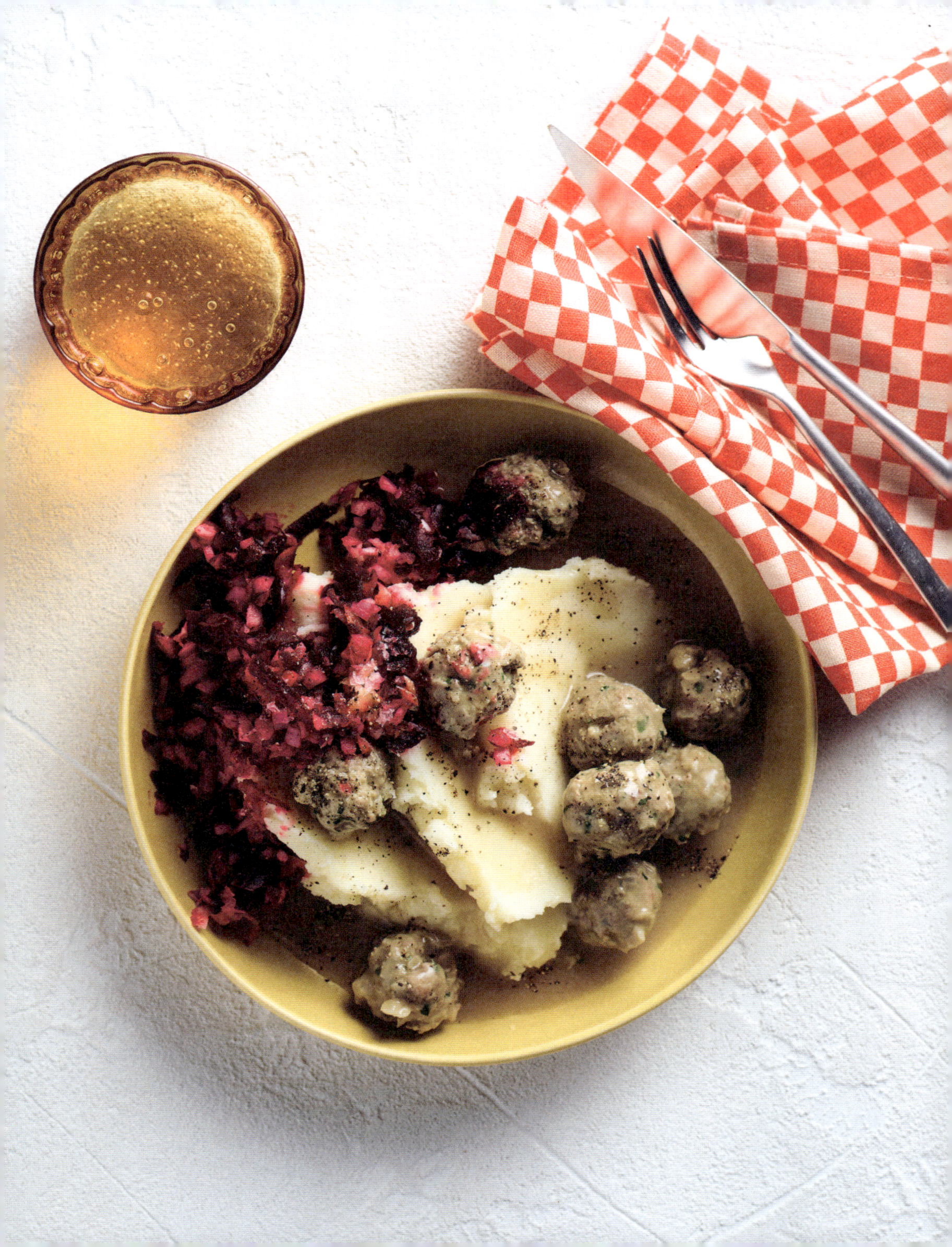

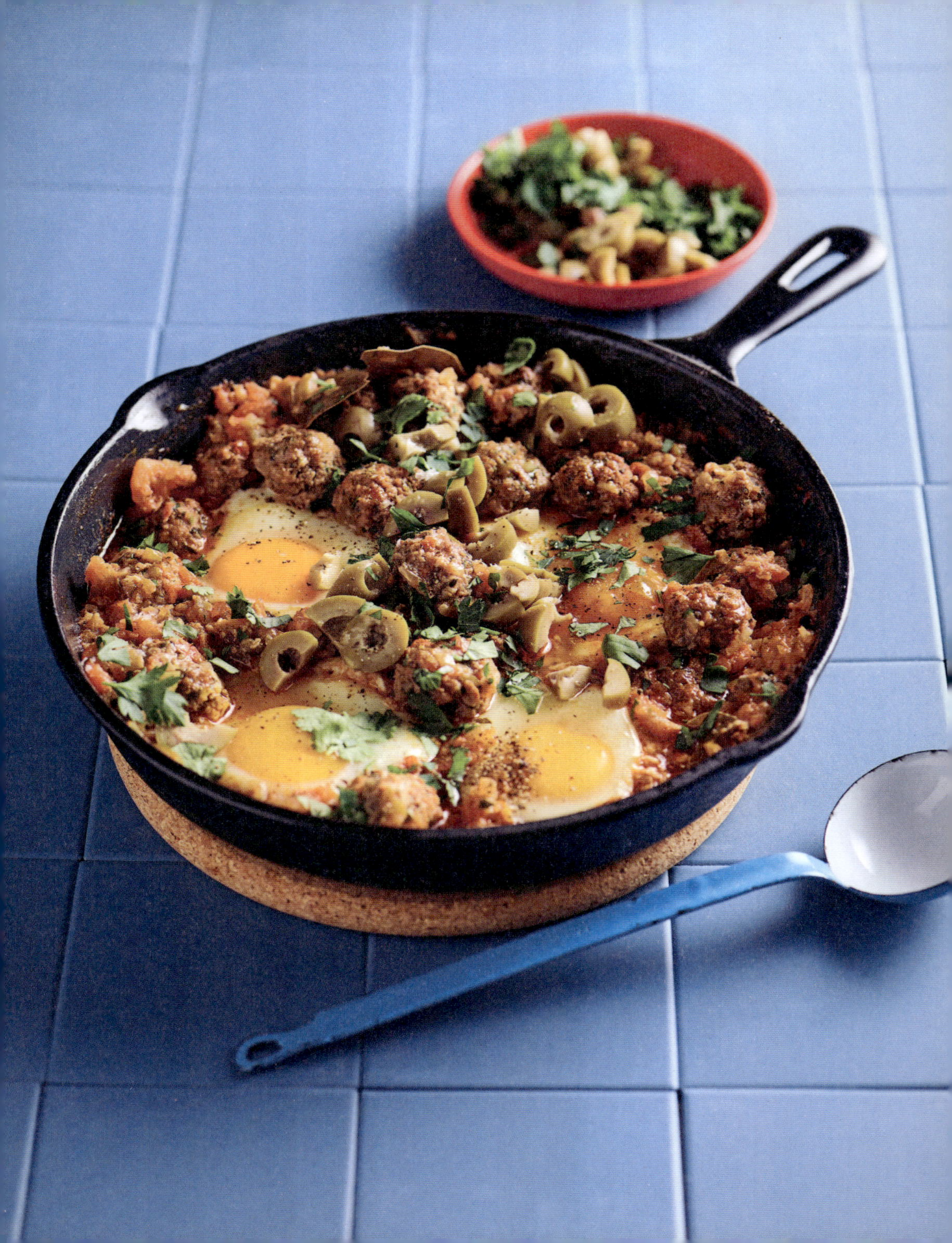

03 MOROCCO

Who in their right mind hasn't occasionally dreamt of hightailing it to Morocco and wiling away their days in their own private riad? Alas, I cannot manifest this into reality for you, but I can at least transport your mouth to Marrakech via this richly fragrant meatball tagine. A few things to note: the cooking time for the sauce varies greatly depending on the tomatoes you're using, so keep a close eye on it while it's simmering and be guided more by what you see rather than the suggested times. While a tagine is not essential – a large pan also works – when using a tagine, be sure to place a heat diffuser over the heat source to create a barrier between the heat and the tagine. This is important whether you are using an electric cooktop or a gas stove.

Kefta mkaouara
MEATBALL AND EGG TAGINE

SERVES 4

- **Meatballs**

500 g (1 lb 2 oz) minced (ground) lamb
1 small onion, finely chopped
3 tablespoons finely chopped coriander (cilantro) leaves
3 tablespoons finely chopped parsley
1 teaspoon ground cumin
1 teaspoon paprika
1 teaspoon salt
¼ teaspoon freshly cracked black pepper
¼ teaspoon ground cinnamon
¼ teaspoon ground turmeric

- **Tomato sauce**

60 ml (2 fl oz/¼ cup) olive oil
1 large onion, finely chopped
1 green capsicum (bell pepper), finely chopped
3–4 garlic cloves, finely chopped
1 kg (2 lb 3 oz) tomatoes, peeled, seeded and chopped (see Notes)
1 teaspoon paprika
1 teaspoon ground cumin
1 teaspoon salt
¼ teaspoon freshly cracked black pepper
2 tablespoons finely chopped parsley
2 tablespoons finely chopped coriander (cilantro) leaves
1 bay leaf
¼ teaspoon cayenne pepper, or to taste

- **To finish**

green olives, to taste
4 eggs
parsley and coriander (cilantro) leaves

To make the meatballs, combine all the ingredients in a large bowl. Shape into grape-sized balls, then cover and set aside.

For the sauce, heat the oil in a frying pan or tagine over a medium–low heat and sauté the onion and capsicum for 3 minutes. Add the garlic and sauté for 1 minute. Add all the remaining ingredients, except the cayenne pepper, and stir to combine. Bring to a simmer, then cover and allow to cook over a low heat for 20–30 minutes, or until the tomatoes have softened.

Using a spoon or spatula, crush the tomatoes until you have a sauce-like consistency. Add the cayenne pepper, cover and cook for another 20–30 minutes, stirring occasionally. Add a dash of water for a smoother consistency, if desired.

Add the meatballs to the sauce and cook for another 15 minutes, ensuring the meatballs are fully cooked through. Add the green olives to taste.

Gently crack the eggs into the sauce, being careful not to break the yolks. Cover the pan again and simmer until the yolks have begun to set and the whites have firmed up.

Sprinkle with fresh parsley and coriander and serve hot.

- **NOTES**

To peel, score a cross in the base of the tomato. Put in a heatproof bowl and cover with boiling water. Leave for 30 seconds, then transfer to cold water and peel the skin away from the cross.

To seed, cut the tomato in half and scoop out the seeds with a teaspoon.

04
COLOMBIA (CARIBBEAN REGION)

Gabriel Ospina learned to cook via phone calls to his mother while she was at work. 'My mother worked very hard in her own business, so when I needed to prepare a meal, I would call her and she would guide me through the process.' Gabriel's mother was from a small town in the northern part of Colombia, by the Caribbean Sea, and this recipe, a childhood favourite of Gabriel's, represents that regional influence. Gabriel has made small adaptations to the dish as an adult, which reflect his time living in Bogotá and various towns on the Caribbean coast. One of the most important is his treatment of the meat: 'I marinate it in the spices for 24 hours, which intensifies the flavour and richness, and adds depth and complexity.' Even with Gabriel's minor tweaks, he says, 'The essence of my mother's cooking always remains, and every time I prepare it, I'm transported back to those times when I would call her for cooking instructions.'

Albondigas

SERVES 4–6

- **Meatballs**

500 g (1 lb 2 oz) minced (ground) beef with 30% fat
1 onion, finely chopped
4 garlic cloves, minced
1 red capsicum (bell pepper), finely chopped
3 ripe tomatoes, peeled and diced
2 eggs, lightly beaten
40 g (1½ oz) crustless white bread, soaked in full-cream (whole) milk or water
2 tablespoons finely chopped coriander (cilantro) leaves
1 teaspoon ground cumin
1 teaspoon sweet paprika
1 teaspoon fines herbes (thyme, rosemary, basil)
1 teaspoon dried Italian herbs
salt and freshly ground black pepper
vegetable oil, for pan-frying

- **Ahogada sauce**

1 onion, finely chopped
1 large tomato, grated or finely chopped
60 ml (2 fl oz/¼ cup) beef broth

- **To serve**

chopped coriander (cilantro)
steamed rice or green salad

In a large bowl, combine all the ingredients, except for the oil, and mix well, until fully incorporated. Cover the bowl with plastic wrap and refrigerate for at least 24 hours to allow the flavours to develop.

After resting, remove the meat mixture from the refrigerator and shape it into meatballs about the size of golf balls.

Heat the oil in a large frying pan over a medium–high heat and fry the meatballs in batches until golden brown on all sides and cooked through, about 8–10 minutes. Remove the cooked meatballs from the pan and set them aside.

To the same pan, add the onion and grated tomato for the sauce and sauté for 4–5 minutes over a medium heat, or until the onion is softened and fragrant. Pour in the beef broth and stir well to deglaze the pan and create a flavourful sauce. Simmer for another few minutes until it has thickened slightly – enough to coat the meatballs.

Return the cooked meatballs to the pan, turning to coat them in the ahogada sauce. Allow to simmer for 2 minutes for the meatballs to absorb the flavours, then serve hot, garnished with fresh coriander, with some steamed rice or a green salad on the side.

- **NOTE**

For instructions for how to peel tomatoes, see Notes on page 29.

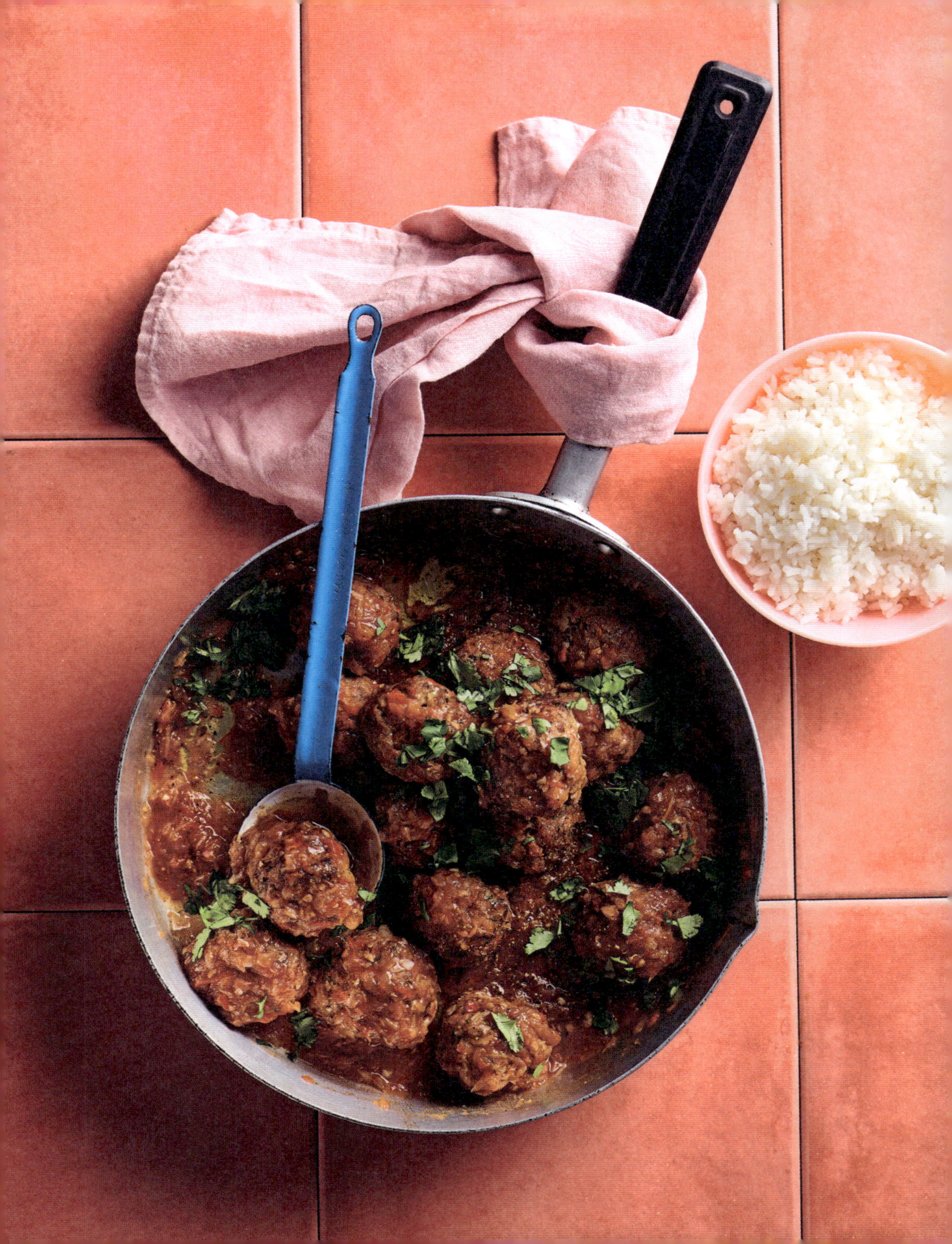

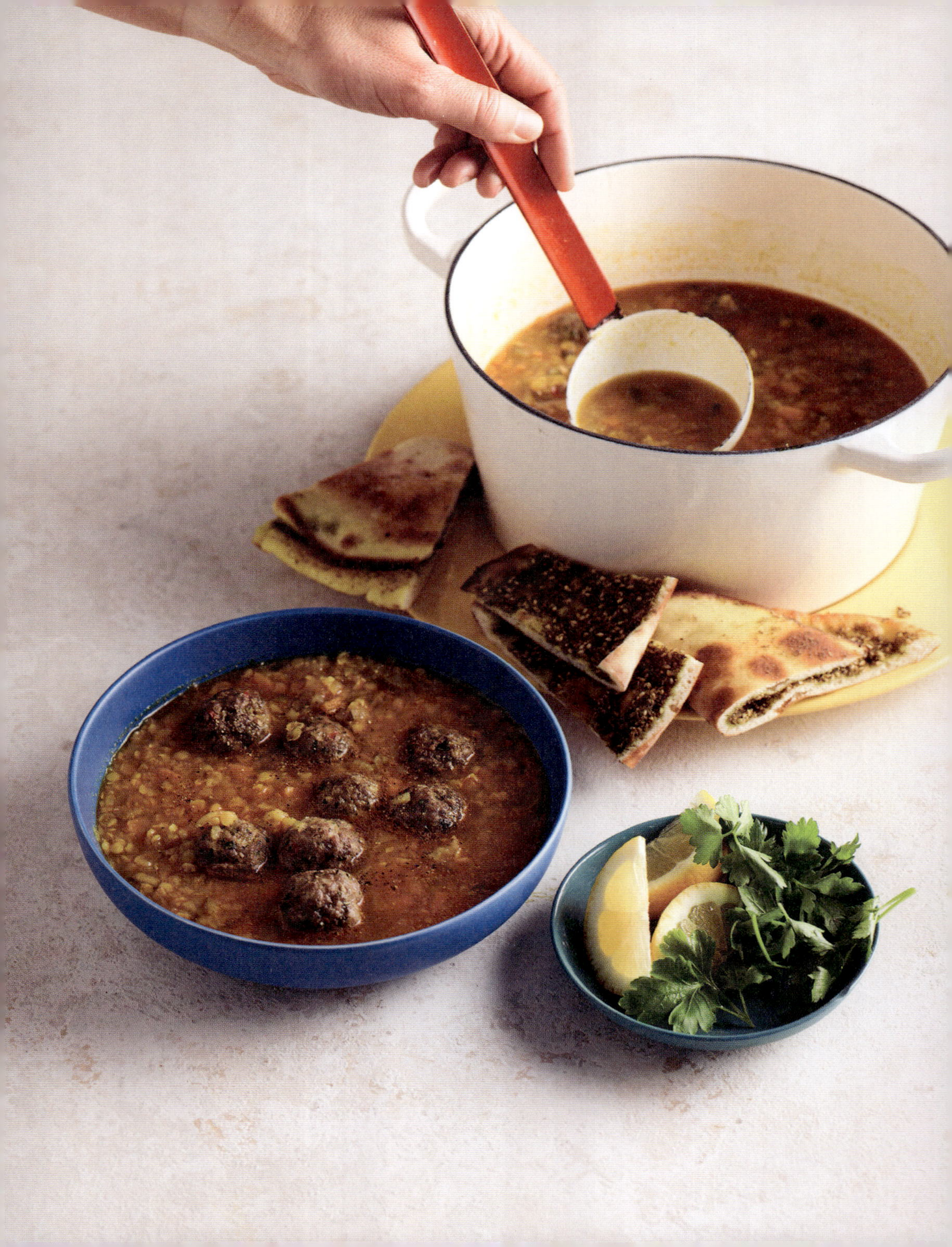

05
PALESTINE

Born in the village of Anabta, near Jerusalem, Najwa Marouf's recollections of childhood mealtimes make a compelling case for delving deeper into the region's cuisine. 'We would have a rich dairy breakfast with fresh seasonal fruits, a hot lunch with meat or seafood with seasonal vegetables, salads and stews, and a light dinner, mostly soups in winter,' she recalls. The recipe that Najwa shares here is for a lentil soup with meatballs, or shorbat adas bil kofta, and, frankly, it deserves a far greater degree of global recognition than it currently enjoys. 'Everyone in the US who tried my recipes always asked me to write them down so they could make it at home for themselves,' says Najwa. Let that be all the motivation you require to try this soup stat.

Shorbat adas bil kofta
LENTIL SOUP WITH MEATBALLS

SERVES 8

● **Lentil soup**

1 tablespoon olive oil
1 onion, finely chopped
1 carrot, diced
1 zucchini (courgette), diced
½ teaspoon ground cumin
½ teaspoon ground turmeric
½ teaspoon paprika
½ teaspoon freshly cracked black pepper
250 g (9 oz/1 cup) red lentils, rinsed and soaked in water for 20 minutes, then drained
2.5 litres (85 fl oz/10 cups) beef broth, bone broth or boiling water
salt and freshly cracked black pepper, to taste
fresh parsley or coriander (cilantro) leaves, to garnish (optional)
lemon wedges, to serve

● **Meatballs**

1 kg (2 lb 3 oz) minced (ground) beef or lamb
250 g (9 oz) chopped mixed red onion and spring onion (scallion)
125 g (4½ oz) parsley, finely chopped
3 tablespoons chopped coriander (cilantro) leaves, mint or basil leaves
125 g (4½ oz) fresh breadcrumbs
1 red capsicum (bell pepper), roasted, seeds and membranes removed
1 teaspoon whole black peppercorns
1 teaspoon salt

Start by making the soup. Heat the olive oil in a large saucepan over a medium heat. Add the onion, carrot and zucchini and cook until softened, about 15 minutes. Add the spices and cook for another 3 minutes until fragrant. Stir in the lentils, ensuring they are well coated with the spices and vegetables.

Add the beef broth and bring to the boil, then reduce the heat to low and simmer, partially covered, for 1 hour, or until the lentils are extremely tender. Taste and adjust the seasoning if needed. Use a handheld blender to partially blend the soup for a creamier texture, if you like.

For the meatballs, preheat the oven to 200°C (390°F). Combine all the ingredients in a food processor and blend until well mixed. Shape the mixture into meatballs, using about 1 tablespoon of the mixture for each one. Place on a baking tray lined with baking paper and cook in the oven for 7–8 minutes.

Add the meatballs to the lentil soup and simmer over a low heat for another 10 minutes.

Serve the soup hot, garnished with fresh parsley or coriander, and lemon wedges on the side.

● **Notes**

Najwa advises serving the soup with a Palestinian staple: freshly baked bread smothered with olive oil and za'atar. She says, 'It's the most common snack for Palestinians – we have it with breakfast, in school lunchboxes and as a go-to snack.'

Najwa also makes a gluten-free version of the meatballs, subbing out the breadcrumbs for 1 boiled and mashed potato.

06
SYRIA

Let's be very honest here: Australia circa 1970 was something of a culinary dystopia, with your standard dinner typically comprising forlorn mounds of overcooked vegetables and a rubbery lamb chop. Perhaps intuiting what awaited, Rob Makdissi's mum, Adele, brought along her grandmother's kofta recipe when she immigrated to Australia in 1970 from Habnimra, a small agrarian village in the southern mountains of Syria. Rob and his siblings grew up on this dish, which he describes as 'typical, traditional village-style kofta', and thus were spared the usual dinnertime privations suffered by their Anglo-Australian peers. Adele's only adaptation of the family recipe has been the inclusion, some years ago, of a capsicum (bell pepper) paste mixed into the meat, a boisterous tweak warmly received by her brood. The recipe has otherwise remained unchanged for seventy years, and Rob's family still regularly enjoy these koftas, serving them with unleavened bread or white rice. Pickles are also considered an essential side dish, 'cornichons preferred!'

Adele's koftas

SERVES 6–8

dash of olive oil
6 potatoes, cut into 1.5 cm (½ in) thick slices
8 tomatoes, cut into 1.5 cm (½ in) thick slices
cornichons, to serve

● **Koftas**

1 kg (2 lb 3 oz) minced (ground) lamb shoulder
1 onion, finely chopped
1 small bunch parsley, finely chopped
1 red capsicum (bell pepper), blended into a paste (see Note)
1 teaspoon salt
1 teaspoon vegetable stock (bouillon) powder

Preheat the oven to 180°C (360°F).

Combine all the ingredients for the koftas in a large bowl and mix with your hands. Form the mixture into patties approximately 6 cm (2½ in) in diameter and flatten slightly (the mixture should make 12–15 koftas).

Heat a dash of olive oil in a frying pan over a medium heat and fry the potato slices until they are half-cooked.

To a deep ovenproof dish, add a layer of tomato slices. Top with a layer of potato slices, then add a layer of koftas. Repeat the layering process one more time, ending with a layer of kofta patties.

Pour 125 ml (4 fl oz/½ cup) water into the ovenproof dish. Bake for 30 minutes.

Serve the baked koftas hot with a side of cornichons.

● **Note**

If you prefer, you can use store-bought roasted red capsicum (bell pepper) paste instead.

07
FRANCE

Newcastle chef Nic Poelaert may have impressive credentials (stints in Michelin-starred restaurants, a period working with Gordon Ramsay in his flagship restaurant and a slew of accolades at the helm of his own venues), but what do you think he asks his maman to cook when back home in Cappelle-Brouck, France? Boulette de bœuf, naturellement. These are simple little babies – a cinch to prep and even easier to eat, particularly when doused in a bath of tomato sauce (ketchup) and served with fries, as is customary in the Poelaert family. Of course, Nic being a chef of some renown, he does have a few suggestions for how to make these boulette a little more bougie (see Notes). Take the high road or the low road; either way, c'est si bon.

Boulette de bœuf
BEEF AND POTATO MEATBALLS

SERVES 4

1 large onion, finely chopped
400 g (14 oz) minced (ground) beef
4–5 potatoes, boiled and mashed
2 garlic cloves, minced
2 eggs, lightly beaten
½ bunch parsley, chopped
¼ teaspoon freshly grated nutmeg
plain (all-purpose) flour, for coating
500 ml (17 fl oz/2 cups) vegetable oil, plus extra for pan-frying
salt and freshly cracked black pepper

● **To serve**
French fries
tomato sauce (ketchup)

Heat about ½ tablespoon of vegetable oil in a frying pan over a medium heat and brown the onion, then set aside.

In a large bowl, mix the beef, mashed potato, browned onion, garlic, egg, parsley, nutmeg, salt and pepper until well combined.

Shape the mixture into meatballs about the size of golf balls, then roll them in flour to coat. Heat the oil in a saucepan until it reaches 180°C (360°F) on a cooking thermometer, then fry the meatballs for 10 minutes, or until golden and cooked through. Remove and place on paper towels to drain the excess oil.

Serve the meatballs hot with fries and tomato sauce.

● **Notes**
Nic's tips for posh balls: 'If you have a mincer at home, use it to mince 350 g (12½ oz) of osso bucco meat with 50 g (1¾ oz) bone marrow for a richer flavour. Try using smoked garlic for something different, too.'

08
GREECE

Chicken soup, aka Jewish penicillin, is arguably the most famous culinary cure for the common cold, but a strong case can also be made for Greek youvarlakia, a meatball and rice soup in a lemony broth. Think of it as 'Greek Benadryl'. Jon Pandoleon's mother, Cathy, from Meteora (famous for its jaw-dropping hilltop monasteries), liked to whip up a batch of youvarlakia whenever the family was felled by winter lurgies. Jon, the current custodian of the family business, Melbourne's iconic Laikon Deli, says, 'The velvety texture of the lemon emulsion, or avgolemono, perfectly complements the rich meatballs.' Indeed, it's a marvel of smooth heartiness as well as a formidable flu opponent. 'She never used measuring tools,' says Jon of his mother, a common refrain among the contributors to this book, 'and she learned to make it just by watching her own mother.' Jon notes that there are infinite variations on youvarlakia, including a version cooked in tomato sauce instead of lemon broth, and a Cretan spin incorporating mint and other fresh local herbs.

Youvarlakia
LEMONY MEATBALL SOUP

SERVES 4

- **Meatballs**

60 ml (2 fl oz/¼ cup) olive oil, plus extra for drizzling
500 g (1 lb 2 oz) minced (ground) beef
200 g (7 oz/1 cup) white long-grain rice
1 onion, grated
1 egg
25 g (1 oz/¾ cup) parsley, chopped
35 g (1¼ oz/¾ cup) mint, chopped
2 teaspoons salt
1 tablespoon ground white pepper

- **Avgolemono**

2 eggs, separated
juice of 2 lemons

- **To serve**

crusty bread
lemon wedges

Make a broth by adding 2 litres (68 fl oz/8 cups) water to a large stockpot with the olive oil and a pinch of salt. Bring to the boil, then reduce the heat to a simmer while you prepare the meatballs.

Combine all the ingredients for the meatballs in a large bowl. Mix thoroughly until everything is well incorporated. Shape the mixture into meatballs about the size of golf balls.

Bring the broth to a simmer and carefully add the meatballs using a spoon. Cook for 20–30 minutes over a medium heat, or until the meatballs are cooked through.

For the avgolemono, whisk the egg whites until fluffy. Add the yolks and lemon juice to the egg whites and mix thoroughly.

Once the meatballs are cooked, take a ladle of the hot broth and slowly whisk this into the avgolemono mixture. Add the broth gradually, whisking continuously to avoid curdling. Repeat with another ladle of broth, ensuring the mixture is well combined.

Pour the avgolemono mixture back into the stockpot with the meatballs, stirring continuously. Turn off the heat, cover with the lid and let the soup rest for 10 minutes to thicken.

Serve the soup hot with plenty of crusty bread, lemon wedges and a drizzle of olive oil.

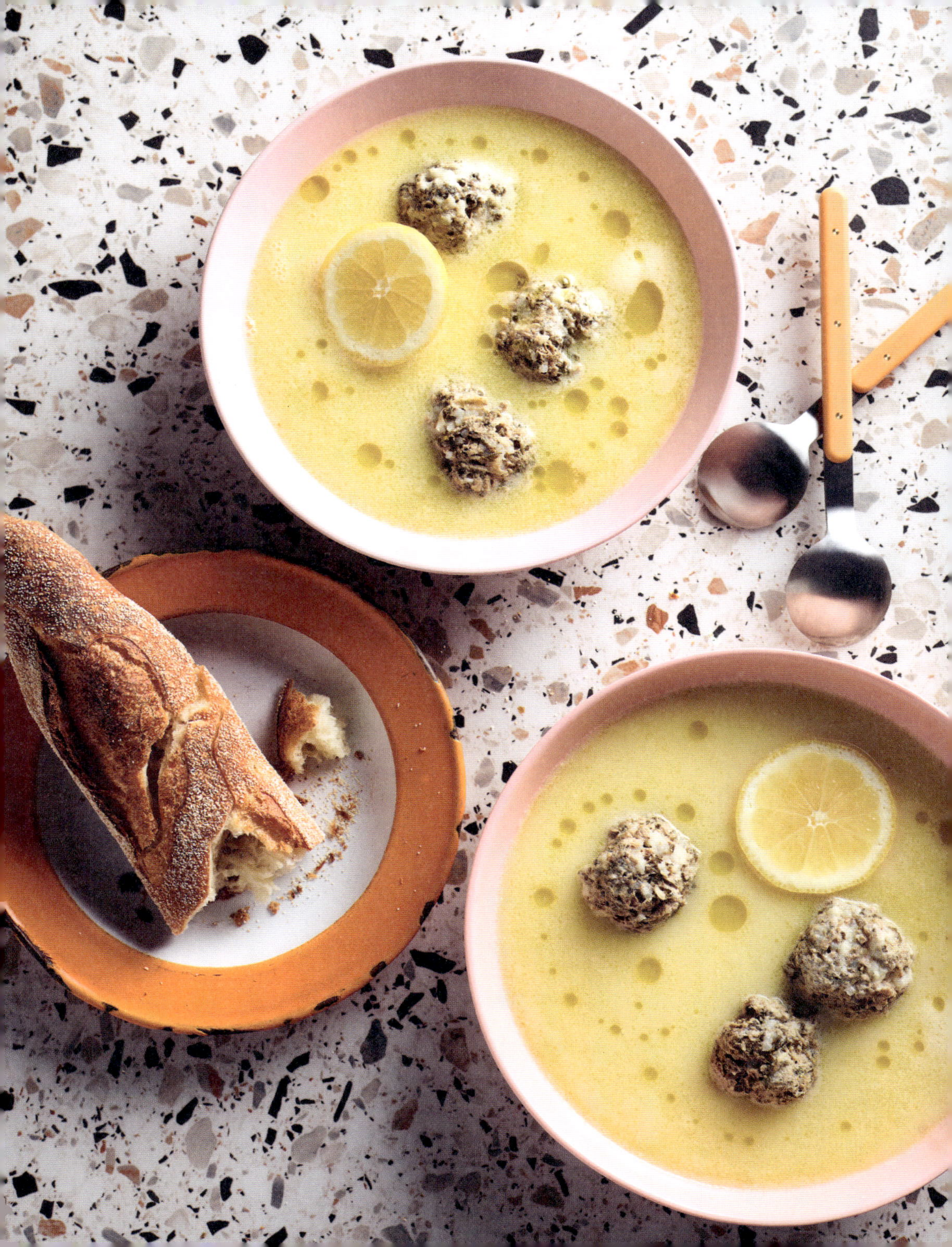

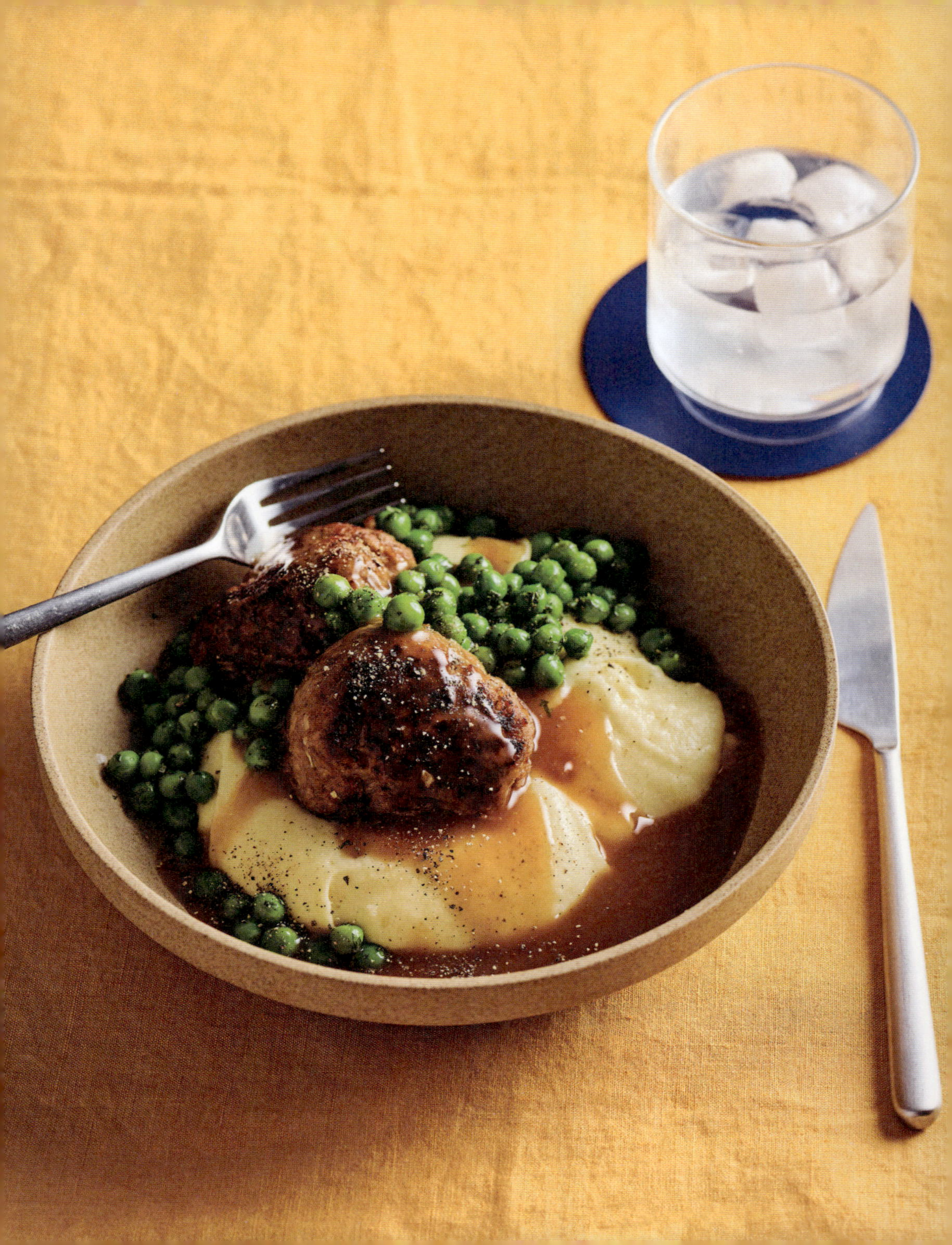

09 AUSTRALIA

Everyone knows the only person allowed to pass judgement on your family is you, and the same might be said for the cuisine of your homeland. As an Australian citizen, I can tell you that these meatballs – known as rissoles in Australia and New Zealand, and often presenting in a slightly more burger-shaped guise – are about as subtle and sophisticated as a fart in an elevator, which is to say: they are not likely to find their way on to the menu of any fine dining establishment.

But boy, are they good; what they lack in elegance, they make up for with pure force of personality. It's the mustard and Worcestershire sauce that delivers the bold, umami flavour here. Add ½ teaspoon of Vegemite to the mix if you want to go the whole nine yards on the Australia theme.

Rissoles with gravy and minted peas

SERVES 4–6

900 g (2 lb) minced (ground) beef
2 eggs
1 onion, finely chopped
80–120 g (2¾–4½ oz/1–1½ cups) dry breadcrumbs
80 ml (2½ fl oz/⅓ cup) tomato sauce (ketchup)
1 tablespoon Worcestershire sauce
1 tablespoon finely grated garlic
1 tablespoon dried herbs of your choice (such as sage, parsley, thyme)
1 teaspoon mustard
2 tablespoons plain (all-purpose) flour, for dusting
2 tablespoons oil
1 packet brown meat gravy mix
260 g (9 oz/2 cups) frozen baby peas
salted butter, to taste
chopped fresh mint, to taste
salt and freshly cracked black pepper, to taste
mashed potato, to serve

In a large bowl, combine the beef, eggs, onion, breadcrumbs, tomato sauce, Worcestershire sauce, garlic, dried herbs, salt, pepper and mustard. Mix everything together until well combined using your hands. Shape the mixture into four to six round balls, then dust them with flour.

Heat the oil in a heavy-based frying pan over a high heat until very hot. Place the rissoles in the pan, making sure not to overcrowd them. Cook until browned and slightly crispy on one side, then flip them over and cook on the other side. Reduce the heat to medium and continue cooking until the rissoles are cooked through, about 3–4 minutes per side, depending on their size. Be careful not to overcook them.

While the rissoles are cooking, prepare the gravy according to the packet instructions.

For the minted peas, bring a small saucepan of water to the boil and simmer the peas for 4 minutes. Drain and return the peas to the pan. Stir in some butter, chopped mint and some salt and pepper to taste.

Serve the rissoles with mashed potato, the gravy and the minted peas.

● **Note**
Grate half a zucchini (courgette), or 1 small zucchini, into the mixture for additional moisture. These rissoles are also fantastic the day after, served in a white bread and tomato sauce (ketchup) sandwich.

10 NETHERLANDS

Olga Zegers's grandparents owned a bakery in Leiden in the south of the Netherlands, and with nine children to feed, gehaktballen was a dinnertime staple, cheap, delicious and easily produced on a large scale. Their daughter Petronella, Olga's mum, inherited the recipe, and Olga, now a vegetarian, can't help but get a little misty recalling the gehaktballen she grew up on. 'It's the nutmeg that make these distinctly Dutch,' she says. 'Nutmeg was worth its weight in gold in the seventeenth century, when the Dutch started trading spices, and we are very partial to it.' The gehaktballen are served with hutspot, an aptly cosy name for a dish that consists of mashed potato, carrots and onion, and finished off with a gravy made from the juices the meatballs are fried in. While there are other worthy contenders for Best Dutch Ball (bitterballen, kaas gehaktballen), to my mind, this is the simplest and most nurturing of the bunch.

Gehaktballen with hutspot
DUTCH MEATBALLS WITH MASH

SERVES 4

● **Meatballs**
- 250 g (9 oz) minced (ground) beef
- 250 g (9 oz) minced (ground) pork
- 1 teaspoon salt
- ½ teaspoon freshly grated nutmeg
- ¼ teaspoon freshly cracked black pepper
- 1 egg
- 25 g (1 oz/⅓ cup) fresh breadcrumbs
- ½ onion, finely chopped
- 100 g (3½ oz) salted butter
- 250 ml (8½ fl oz/1 cup) boiling water or beef stock
- 1 tablespoon plain (all-purpose) flour, mixed with a little water until smooth to make a slurry

● **Hutspot**
- 5 large floury potatoes, peeled and cut into large chunks
- 6 large carrots, peeled and cut into large chunks
- 2 large onions, chopped
- 125 ml (4 fl oz/½ cup) full-cream (whole) milk (optional)
- salt and freshly cracked black pepper, to taste
- chopped parsley, to garnish

In a large bowl, combine the beef, pork, salt, nutmeg, pepper, egg, breadcrumbs and onion. Mix thoroughly until all the ingredients are well incorporated. Shape the mixture into meatballs about the size of golf balls.

Brown the butter in a large frying pan over a medium–low heat. Reduce the heat to low and add the meatballs to the pan. Fry for about 10 minutes on each side, turning them occasionally to ensure they are evenly browned and cooked through. Remove the meatballs from the pan and place on paper towel to drain the excess oil.

To make the gravy, drain most of the butter from the pan. Add the boiling water to the pan and whisk to combine with the pan juices. Add the flour slurry, whisking for another 2 minutes, or until the gravy has thickened.

To make the hutspot, while the meatballs are frying, place the potato, carrot and onion in a large saucepan and cover with water. Bring to the boil, then reduce the heat and simmer for 20 minutes, or until the vegetables are tender.

Drain the vegetables, reserving a little of the cooking water. Mash the vegetables to your preferred consistency, adding a little of the reserved water or the milk, if desired, to make the mixture smoother. Season to taste with salt and pepper and garnish with chopped parsley.

Divide the mashed vegetables between serving bowls. Make a well in the middle of the mash and add the cooked meatballs. Top with the gravy and serve.

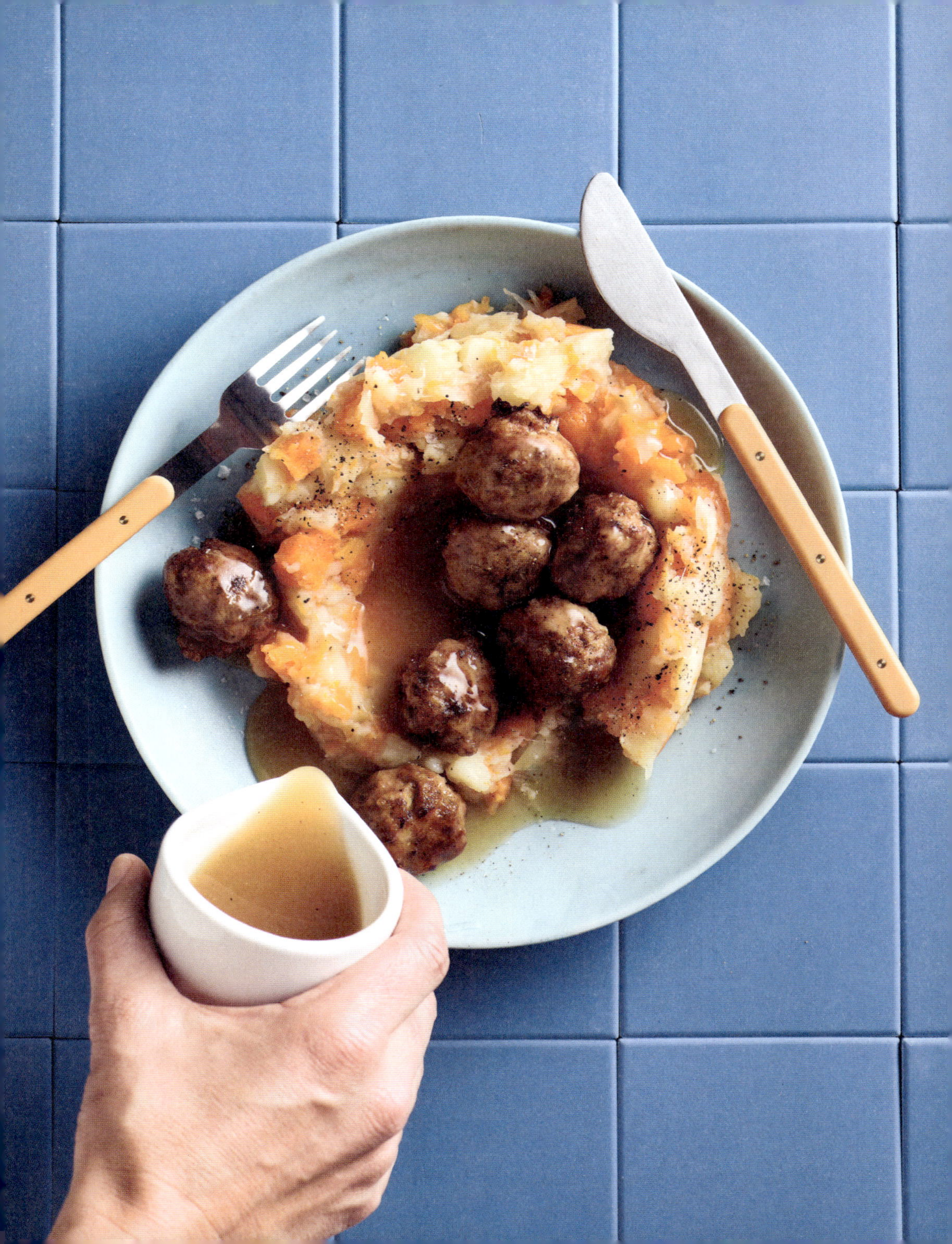

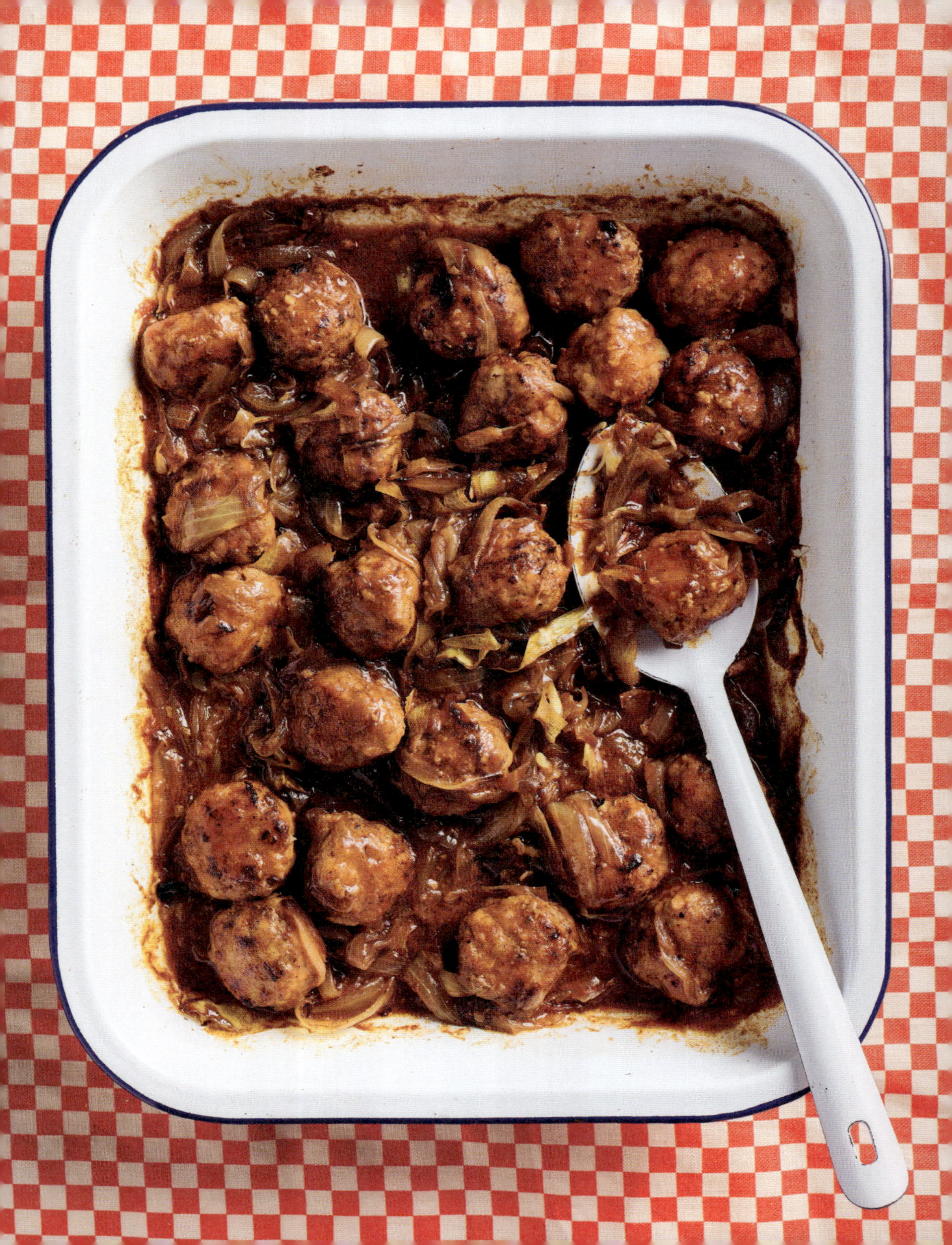

11
CZECH REPUBLIC

Rachelle Unreich's late mother, Mira, made an indelible impression on everyone she encountered, and this can be attributed to her uniquely spritely spirit. As a survivor of four concentration camps, Mira – who lost almost her entire family to the Nazis – was able to reflect on her experiences and say, 'In the Holocaust, I learned about the goodness of people.' The love of life that Mira had in such abundance is evident in the recipe Rachelle shares here. Czech-born Mira used to prepare these meatballs for Rachelle and her siblings, based on the memory of a dish she had enjoyed as a child. 'She claimed to hate cooking, but she certainly loved feeding people,' recounts Rachelle, 'and though a long way from her birthplace, she ensured that the feeling of her early childhood family meals could be felt once more.' These meatballs give all of us a chance to experience a little of the Mira magic for ourselves, and their simple, homely pleasure reminds us that, as Mira used to tell Rachelle, 'the happiness is near!'

Mira's meatballs

SERVES 4–6

350 g (12½ oz) minced (ground) dark chicken
350 g (12½ oz) minced (ground) veal or beef
1 onion, grated
1 egg
1 small challah roll or hamburger roll
vegetable oil, for pan-frying
1 onion, sliced
1 tablespoon plain (all-purpose) flour or gluten-free flour, plus extra for dusting
1 tablespoon chicken stock (bouillon) powder
1 tablespoon sweet paprika

Combine the chicken and veal in a dish. Add the grated onion and the egg into the mixture.

Briefly run the bread roll under water, peel off the outer layer of crust, squeeze out excess water, and grate it into the mixture. (If you're using gluten-free bread, skip the wetting step to avoid the bread going too mushy.) Mix the ingredients thoroughly to ensure even distribution then shape the mixture into small balls roughly the size of small ice cream scoops. Roll each ball in flour to coat.

Heat the vegetable oil in a frying pan over a medium heat and sauté the sliced onion for 10–15 minutes, or until nicely caramelised. Remove from the pan, add the meatballs and fry over a medium–high heat until evenly browned. Transfer the browned meatballs to an ovenproof dish. Place the caramelised onion on top of the meatballs in the dish.

Preheat the oven to 150°C (300°F). In a cup, mix the flour with a bit of hot water to make a slurry. Stir the slurry, chicken stock (bouillon) powder and paprika into 250 ml (8½ fl oz/1 cup) water. Add the sauce mixture to the frying pan. Reduce the heat to low and cook, stirring occasionally, until it thickens. Pour the thickened sauce over the meatballs and bake for 1 hour (uncovered).

Serve the meatballs warm, directly from the ovenproof dish.

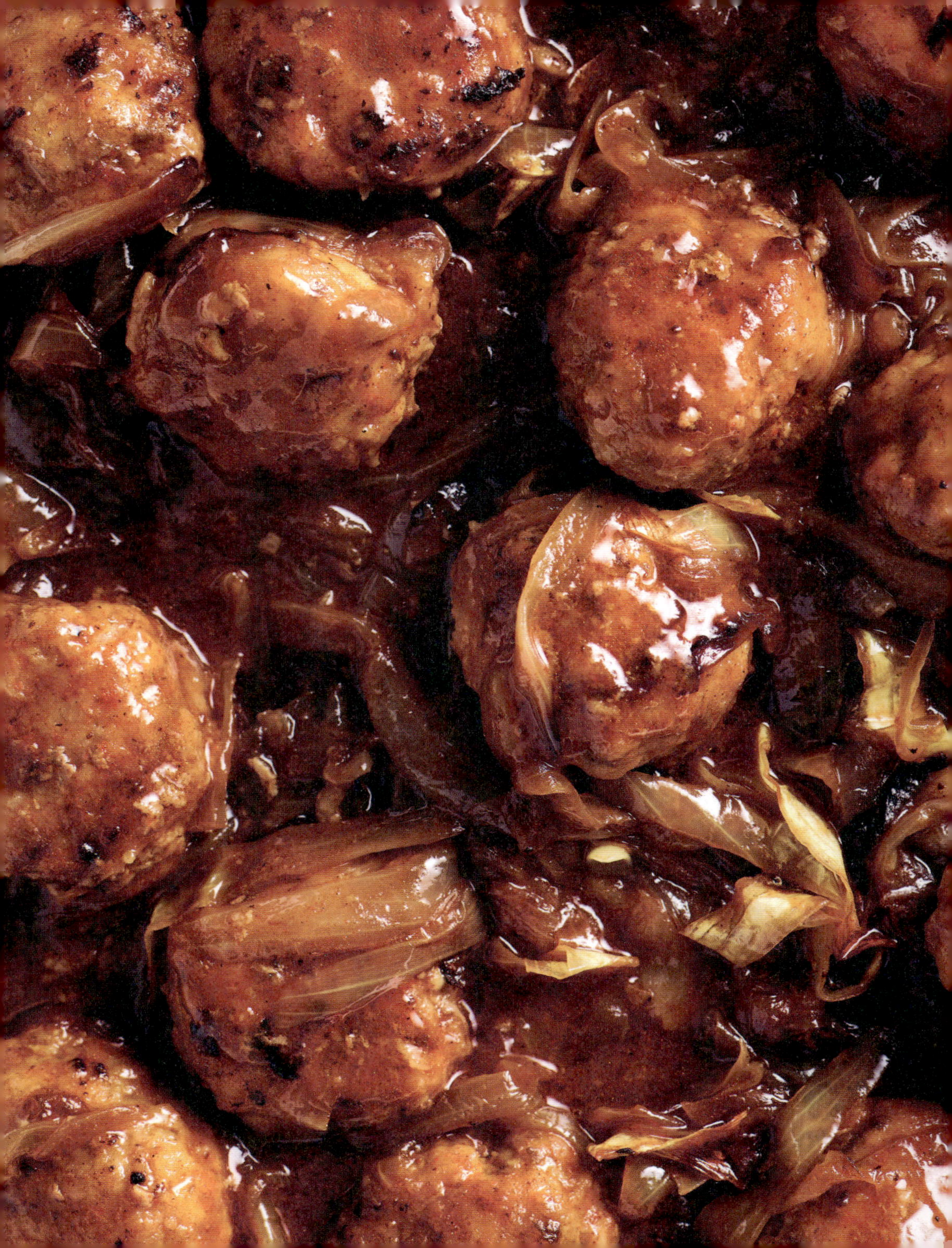

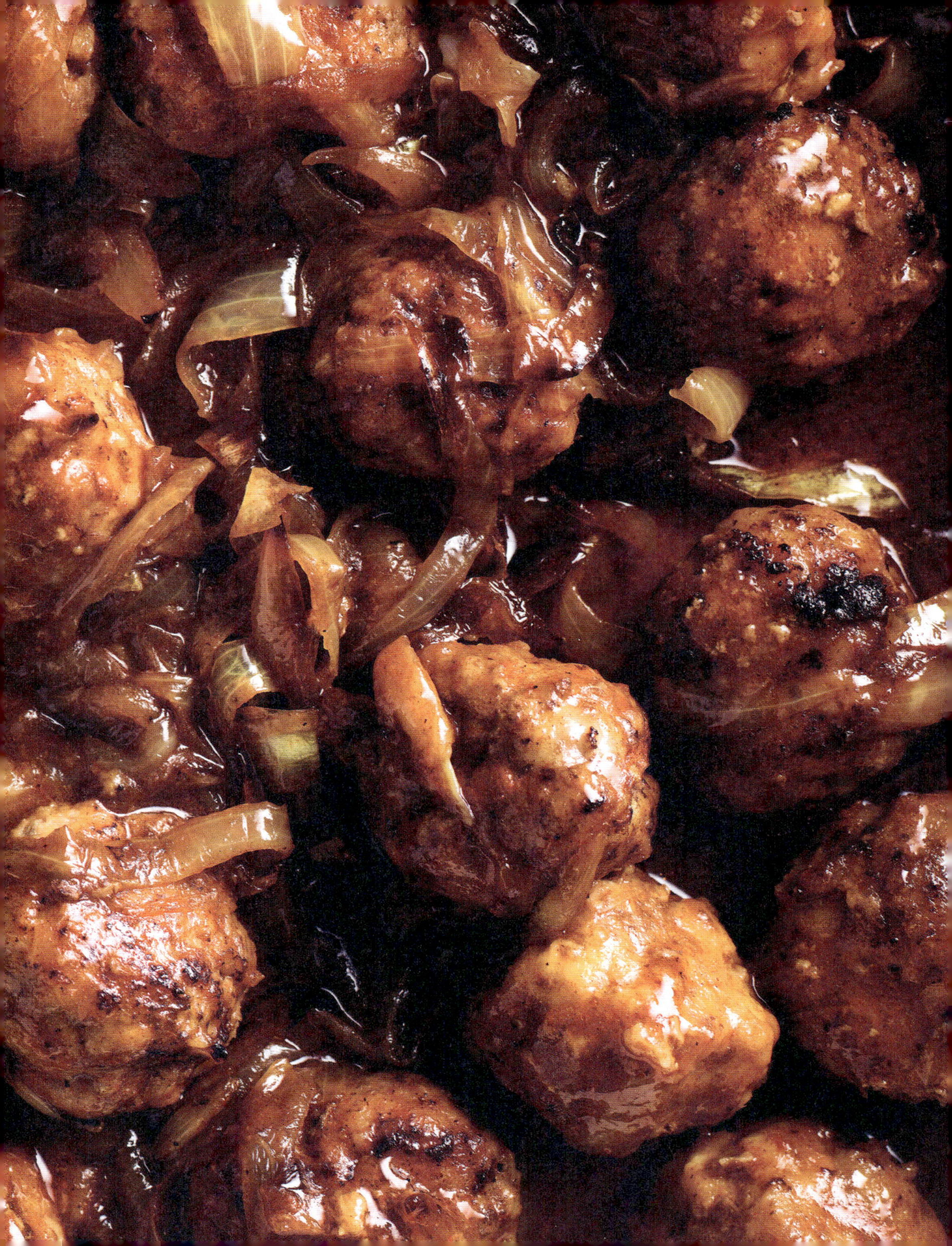

12
CYPRUS

I think we can all agree that where after-school snacks are concerned, a plate of lovingly prepared meatballs compares favourably to a packet of raw jelly (gelatin dessert) crystals. Stacy Korkou and I are the same age, but while I was pouring sugar pellets down my gullet come 3.30 pm, Stacy was sitting down to warm keftedes cooked by her yiayia, Eleni, a migrant from Paphos, Cyprus – the very place where, according to Greek mythology, Aphrodite came ashore after being born into the sea foam. It's an apt association, given the passionate response these meatballs incite in all who try them. Stacy's version of Eleni's keftedes is so authentic that Cypriot friends, on eating it for the first time, are convinced a yiayia must have prepared it. 'It's the best feeling,' she says. 'I know that I'm keeping a family recipe alive, and it won't be forgotten.' Stacy likes to serve Eleni's keftedes with fried potatoes and a Greek salad (see Notes), which are the standard accompaniments in Cyprus.

Keftedes with fried potatoes

SERVES 4–6

- **Keftedes**

500 g (1 lb 2 oz) minced (ground) beef
1 large onion, finely diced
2 potatoes, grated and excess liquid squeezed out
7 g (¼ oz/¼ cup) parsley, finely chopped
1½ teaspoons dried mint
½ teaspoon ground cinnamon
1 teaspoon salt
½ teaspoon freshly cracked black pepper
2 eggs
40 g (1½ oz/½ cup) fresh breadcrumbs, soaked in water and squeezed dry
vegetable oil, for pan-frying

- **Potatoes**

4–6 potatoes, cut into wedges
vegetable oil, for deep-frying
salt, to taste
dried oregano, for sprinkling (see Notes)

- **To serve**

Greek salad (see Notes)

To prepare the keftedes, combine all the ingredients in a large bowl and mix until well combined. Shape the mixture into meatballs about the size of golf balls.

Pour vegetable oil into a frying pan to a depth of 3 cm (1¼ in) and heat over a high heat. Pan-fry the meatballs in batches until they are browned on all sides and cooked through, about 10–15 minutes. Place the cooked meatballs on paper towels to drain the excess oil. Transfer to a baking tray, cover with aluminium foil and keep warm in a low oven while you prepare the potatoes.

To prepare the potatoes, heat the vegetable oil for deep-frying in a deep frying pan or saucepan over a medium–high heat. Fry the potato wedges until they are cooked through but not browned. Drain on paper towels and allow to cool. Remove the pan from the heat but don't discard the oil.

Once cooled, fry the potatoes again in the same oil until crisp and golden brown. Drain on paper towel and sprinkle with salt and dried oregano.

Serve the potatoes immediately, alongside the keftedes.

- **Notes**

To make a simple Greek salad, toss iceberg lettuce, tomatoes, feta and onion together in a bowl and drizzle with olive oil and white balsamic vinegar.

Look out for the beautiful bunches of dried Greek oregano you can find in specialty Italian grocers; the flavour is far superior to the jarred variety.

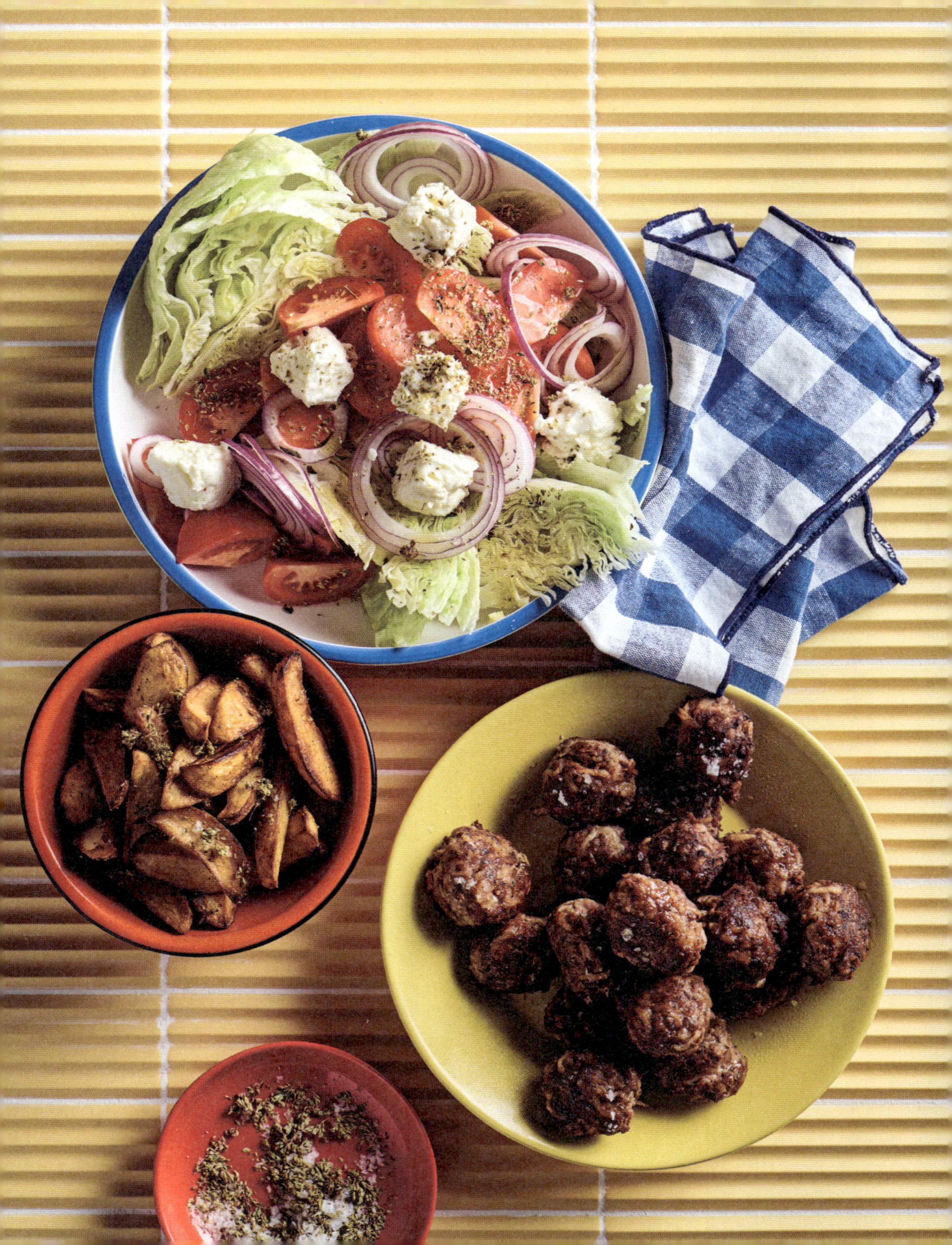

13 PAKISTAN

One of the most welcome surprises while researching this book was the discovery that Pakistan is positively teeming with premium meatball offerings; narrowing recipes down to just two proved a wrench. Rohail Akhtar Baig does not hesitate to label these koftas 'the best in the world'. Rohail's beloved mother, Seema Akhtar, from Karachi, is the creator of this Kofta aalu recipe. 'I vividly remember watching my mother prepare this tomato and meatball stew in our cosy kitchen. I would stand on my tiptoes, peeking over the counter to catch a glimpse of the magic happening in the pot. Mum would let me help by stirring the pot a few times, a task I took very seriously. She always said that adding the green chillies and coriander (cilantro) at just the right moment was the secret to the perfect flavour. The warmth and love she put into every dish made it taste extra special.'

Kofta aalu
MEATBALL AND POTATO CURRY

SERVES 6–8

● **Meatballs**

1 kg (2 lb 3 oz) minced (ground) lean beef (10% fat)
1 tablespoon ginger-garlic paste
1 tablespoon white poppy seeds, finely ground
1 teaspoon garam masala
1 tablespoon salt, or to taste
2 teaspoons chilli powder (optional)
1 tablespoon desiccated (shredded) coconut, or coconut powder
finely chopped coriander (cilantro) leaves (optional)
4 green chillies, finely chopped
3 cm (1¼ in) piece ginger, finely chopped
1 garlic clove, finely chopped
1 onion, finely chopped
2 tablespoons vegetable oil, for pan-frying

● **Chana pulao**

60 ml (2 fl oz/¼ cup) canola or sunflower oil, or ghee
1 onion, sliced
1 tablespoon cumin seeds
3 teaspoons salt
6 whole cloves
2 whole black cardamom pods
1 cinnamon stick
2–3 whole green chillies (optional)
500 g (1 lb 2 oz) cooked chickpeas (drained weight)
400 g (14 oz/2 cups) basmati rice, washed and soaked in water for at least 30 minutes, then drained

Combine all the ingredients for the meatballs, except for the oil, in a large bowl until evenly incorporated. Shape the mixture into meatballs about the size of golf balls. Arrange the meatballs in a steamer basket or on a steaming rack and steam the meatballs for 10–15 minutes, or until they are cooked through. They should be firm and no longer pink inside.

Heat the vegetable oil in a frying pan over a medium heat. Carefully put the steamed meatballs into the hot oil and fry for 5 minutes, or until they are golden brown and crispy on all sides, turning occasionally to ensure even cooking. Remove the meatballs from the pan and place on paper towels to drain the excess oil.

To prepare the chana pulao, heat the canola oil in a stockpot, add the sliced onion and fry until golden, about 10 minutes. Add the cumin seeds, salt, cloves, cardamom pods, cinnamon stick and green chillies, if using. Fry these for a few more minutes until the onion turns a dark gold.

Add the chickpeas and rice to the pot with 750 ml (25½ fl oz/3 cups) water and bring to the boil, stirring occasionally without breaking the rice. Cook over a high heat until most of the water has been absorbed, about 8 minutes, then secure a tight-fitting lid onto the pot and reduce the heat to its lowest setting. Steam for 10–15 minutes. You can wrap the lid in a clean tea towel (dish towel) to absorb more steam, which will give you fluffier rice. Gently fluff up the rice with a slotted spoon or fork immediately after steaming, even if you do not intend to serve it immediately.

- **Tomato sauce**

60 ml (2 fl oz/¼ cup) canola or sunflower oil
4–5 tomatoes, chopped
3 teaspoons salt
1 teaspoon freshly cracked black pepper
2 potatoes, peeled and cubed
1 tablespoon chilli powder
4 green chillies, finely chopped
finely chopped coriander (cilantro) leaves

To make the tomato sauce, heat the oil in a saucepan over a medium heat. Add the tomatoes, salt and pepper. Cover with a lid and cook until the tomatoes turn into a puree, about 5–7 minutes. Add the cubed potato, cover and cook for another 10–15 minutes, or until the potato is tender. Add the chilli powder and mix well. Add the green chilli to the pan and stir to combine.

Gently add the fried meatballs to the sauce. Stir everything well, ensuring the meatballs are coated with the tomato mixture. Before removing the pan from the stove, add the coriander and stir once more to combine.

Serve the meatballs hot with the chana pulao.

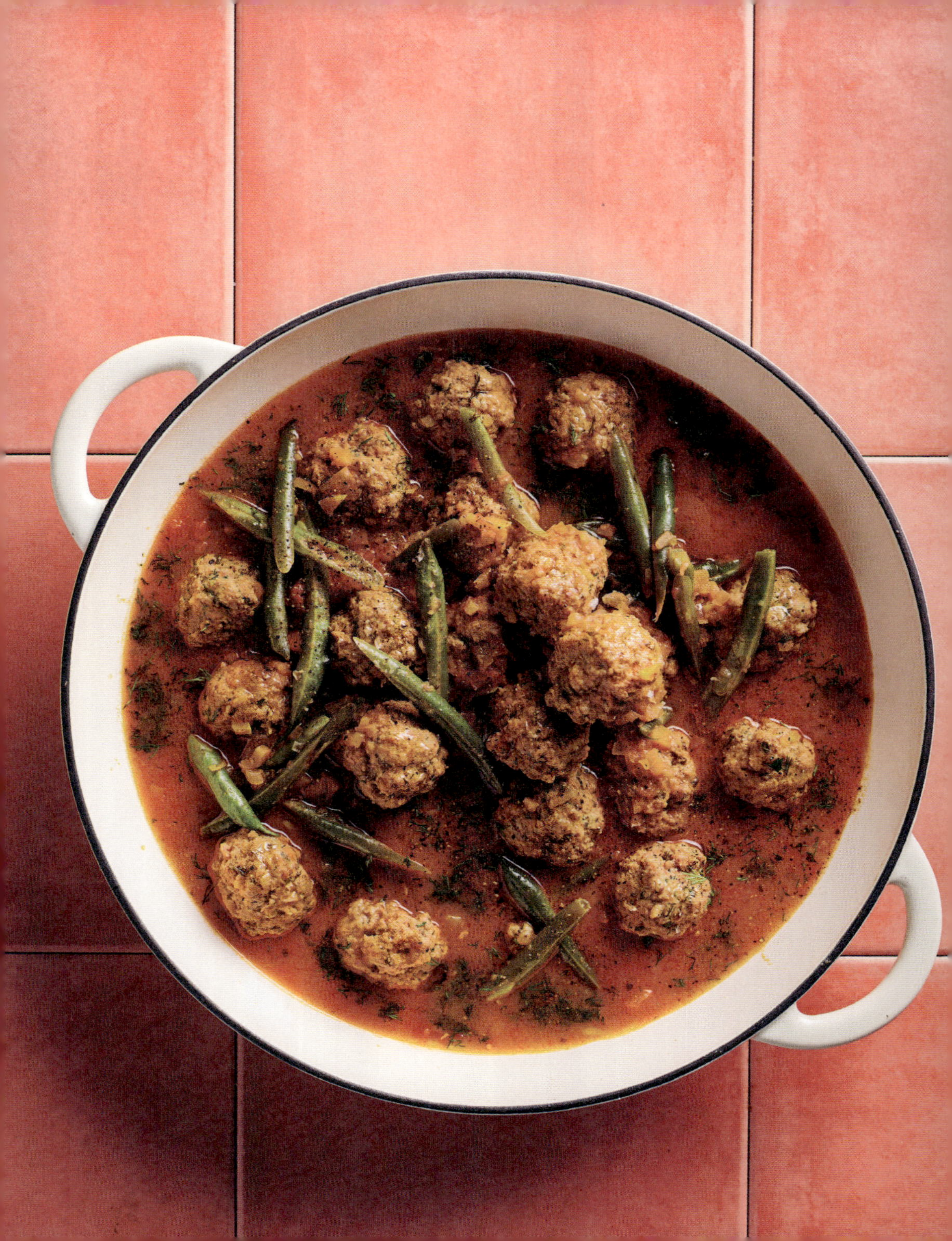

14

ISRAEL

A meatball recipe can reveal a lot about the creator. Siberian-born author Lee Kofman, who moved to Odessa at twelve, Israel at eighteen, and settled in Australia in her late twenties, is abundantly warm-natured and generous, just like her meatballs. Lee developed this recipe, reminiscent of the ones she enjoyed as a student in Tel Aviv, for a multicultural cooking class she initiated while employed as a social worker at a community services organisation. 'It was actually the most popular of all the dishes we cooked,' says Lee, reaffirming my belief that meatballs have achieved a level of global adoration even Taylor Swift might envy. Lee's children, excessively picky eaters, are always receptive to her meatballs; she likes to serve them on mashed potato or steamed white rice, and notes the sauce is packed with vegetables, lending it an uncommon air of virtue, and making the task of getting greens into young mouths that much easier.

Israeli-style meatballs

SERVES 4–6

- **Meatballs**

600 g (1 lb 5 oz) minced (ground) beef
40 g (1½ oz/½ cup) fresh breadcrumbs
½ bunch parsley, chopped
½ bunch dill, chopped
5 garlic cloves, minced
2 eggs
1 teaspoon Israeli chicken soup powder or 1 chicken stock (bouillon) cube
1 teaspoon sweet paprika
1 teaspoon garlic salt or granules
freshly cracked black pepper

- **Sauce**

2–3 tablespoons olive oil
1 onion, finely chopped
2 carrots, finely chopped
200 g (7 oz) tinned chopped tomatoes
1 litre (34 fl oz/4 cups) chicken stock (fresh or from powder/cube)
1 tablespoon tomato paste (concentrated puree)
1 teaspoon sweet paprika
freshly cracked black pepper, to taste
200 g (7 oz) green beans, trimmed and halved
½ bunch dill, chopped

- **To serve**

steamed white rice or mashed potato

To make the meatballs, combine all the ingredients in a large bowl until evenly incorporated.

Shape the mixture into meatballs about the size of golf balls, then chill them in the fridge for 30 minutes. Bring them back to room temperature prior to cooking.

Heat the olive oil in a large, wide saucepan over a medium heat and sauté the onion and carrot until soft, about 5–7 minutes. Add the chopped tomatoes, chicken stock and tomato paste and bring to the boil. Reduce the heat and add the paprika and black pepper. Mix thoroughly.

Carefully place the meatballs in the sauce, ensuring they are submerged. Cover the pan and simmer for 10 minutes, then add the green beans and chopped dill and continue simmering until the beans are tender, about 15 minutes.

Serve the meatballs and sauce on steamed white rice or mashed potato.

15
TÜRKIYE

Türkiye has bestowed upon the world a fantastic abundance of köfte recipes, so it's only right that, when asked to provide a recipe, Basak Dizman Thompson gave three, each with their own distinct profile. Immigrating to Adelaide in 2014 after meeting her Australian husband in Istanbul, Basak says particularly close to her heart is her grandmother Munufe's recipe for Ekşili köfte. 'It takes me straight back to summers in Çorlu, Tekirdağ, and the comforting smell of the sour meatball soup emanating from her kitchen while my siblings and I played in the garden.' Making it now for friends and family, Basak says that 'everyone who tries it reacts with delight at its unique flavour' and seeing her daughter enjoy it with the same excitement she experienced as a child always warms her heart.

Ekşili köfte
TURKISH MEATBALL SOUP

SERVES 4

- **Meatballs**

350 g (12½ oz) minced (ground) beef
50 g (1¾ oz/¼ cup) short-grain rice, boiled for 5 minutes then drained
1 onion, grated
1 egg
plain (all-purpose) flour, for coating
salt and freshly cracked black pepper

- **Vegetables**

1 tablespoon olive oil
2 carrots, sliced
1 celery stalk, diced
2 small potatoes, diced
1.75 litres (60 fl oz/7 cups) hot water
salt, to taste

- **Egg-lemon mixture**

1 egg yolk
juice of 1 lemon

- **To serve**

crusty bread

To make the meatballs, combine all the ingredients in a large bowl until evenly incorporated. Shape the mixture into small meatballs the size of grapes. Roll the meatballs in flour and set aside.

For the vegetables, heat the oil in a large, deep saucepan over a medium heat. Sauté the carrot until it starts to soften, then add the celery, potato and hot water. Add salt to taste and bring to the boil.

Gently add the floured meatballs to the boiling water and leave them to cook for about 25 minutes without stirring too much initially, to avoid breaking the meatballs.

In a bowl, whisk together the egg yolk and lemon juice. Once the soup has been cooking for 20 minutes, take a ladle of the hot soup and slowly whisk it into the egg-lemon mixture to temper it. Slowly pour the tempered mixture back into the pot while stirring gently. Let the soup cook for another 10–15 minutes uncovered, or until the meatballs and vegetables are fully cooked.

Serve with crusty bread.

16
TÜRKIYE

The Middle Eastern meatball version of a cottage pie – because the only thing better than cottage pie is meatball cottage pie.

Hasanpasha köfte
MEATBALL AND POTATO CASSEROLE

SERVES 4–6

- **Meatballs**

500 g (1 lb 2 oz) minced (ground) beef
1 onion, grated
60 g (2 oz/¾ cup) fresh breadcrumbs
1 egg
2 garlic cloves, grated
1 teaspoon ground allspice
large pinch of dried thyme
salt and freshly cracked black pepper

- **Mashed potatoes**

1 large or 3 medium potatoes, boiled until tender
3 teaspoons salt
½ teaspoon freshly grated nutmeg
1 teaspoon white pepper
125 ml (4 fl oz/½ cup) full-cream (whole) milk
1–2 heaped tablespoons salted butter
60 g (2 oz/½ cup) grated cheddar, plus extra for topping

- **Sauce**

1 tablespoon olive oil
2 tablespoons tomato paste (concentrated puree)

Preheat the oven to 180°C (360°F).

To make the meatballs, combine all the ingredients in a large bowl until evenly incorporated. Shape the mixture into meatballs about the size of golf balls, then shape them into small bowls by pressing in the middle of each ball with your finger. Arrange the meatballs in an ovenproof dish. Bake the meatballs for 20–25 minutes, until partially cooked.

While the meatballs are cooling, mash the boiled potatoes until smooth, then add the salt, nutmeg, white pepper, milk, butter and cheese. Mix well, until you get a smooth, creamy consistency. Use a piping (icing) bag fitted with a plain nozzle to fill the partially cooked meatballs with the mashed potato mixture.

Heat the olive oil in a small saucepan over a medium heat. Add the tomato paste and cook until it starts to smell fragrant. Add 375 ml (12½ fl oz/1½ cups) water and stir until the sauce thickens to your preferred consistency. Pour the sauce over the meatballs and bake for 10–15 minutes.

Remove the meatballs from the oven and sprinkle with extra grated cheese. Return to the oven and bake for another 5 minutes, or until the cheese is melted and golden brown.

Serve straight from the oven.

17
TÜRKIYE

Named for the city of Izmir in western Türkiye, this classic Turkish comfort dish – another blessed meatball–potato union – is simple to prepare and easier again to love.

Izmir köfte
BAKED MEATBALLS IN TOMATO SAUCE

SERVES 4

375 ml (12½ fl oz/1½ cups) vegetable oil
3 large potatoes, peeled and cut into wedges
2 tomatoes, cut into wedges
3–4 green capsicums (bell peppers), chopped
3 garlic cloves

- **Meatballs**

500 g (1 lb 2 oz) lean minced (ground) beef
1 onion, grated
3 tablespoons day-old or panko (Japanese) breadcrumbs
1 egg
1 teaspoon salt
½ teaspoon freshly cracked black pepper
2 teaspoons ground cumin

- **Sauce**

2 tablespoons olive oil
1 tablespoon tomato paste (concentrated puree)
2 tomatoes, finely chopped
500 ml (17 fl oz/2 cups) hot water
salt and freshly cracked black pepper

Heat the vegetable oil in a saucepan over a medium-high heat and deep-fry the potato wedges in the hot oil until they are slightly golden, about 4 minutes. Set aside on paper towel to drain the excess oil. Retain the oil in the saucepan.

For the meatballs, combine all the ingredients in a large bowl until evenly incorporated. Take walnut-sized portions of the mixture and shape into long, thin meatballs (you should have 11–12 pieces).

Place the pan with the oil back over a medium heat and, once hot, fry the meatballs until lightly browned on both sides. Do not overcook them, as they will continue cooking in the oven.

To make the sauce, heat the oil in a small saucepan, add the tomato paste and cook for a few minutes over a medium heat. Add the chopped tomatoes, hot water and some salt and pepper to taste. Let the sauce simmer for 10 minutes, or until it thickens. If you like, you can blend it for a smoother texture.

Preheat the oven to 180°C (360°F). In a deep ovenproof dish, layer the fried potatoes and meatballs. Add the tomato wedges, green capsicum (bell pepper) and garlic cloves to the dish. Pour the prepared tomato sauce over everything, then bake for about 30 minutes, or until the vegetables are cooked through and the flavours are well combined.

Remove the dish from the oven and let it sit for a few minutes before serving. Serve hot, ensuring each portion includes a mixture of meatballs, potato and vegetables.

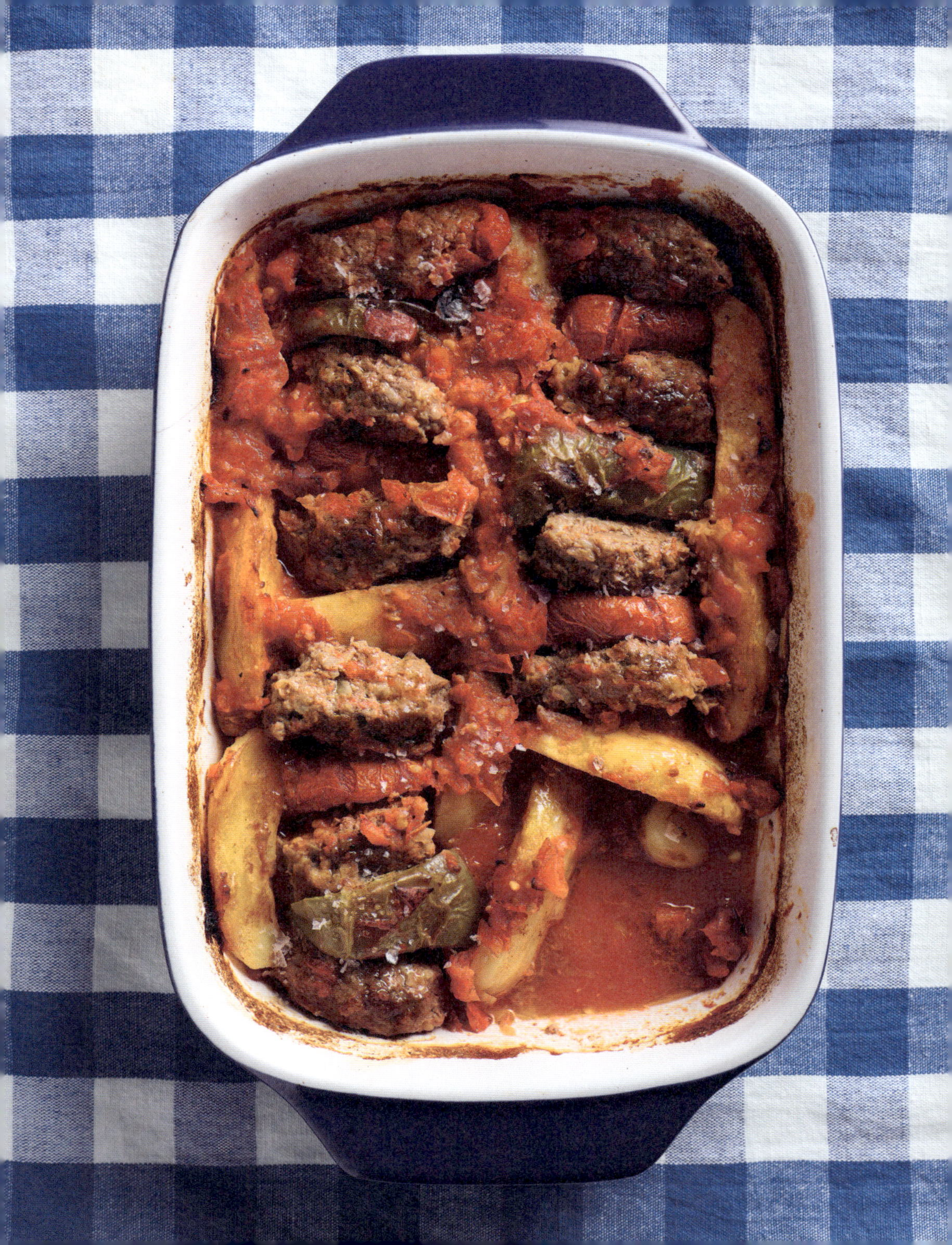

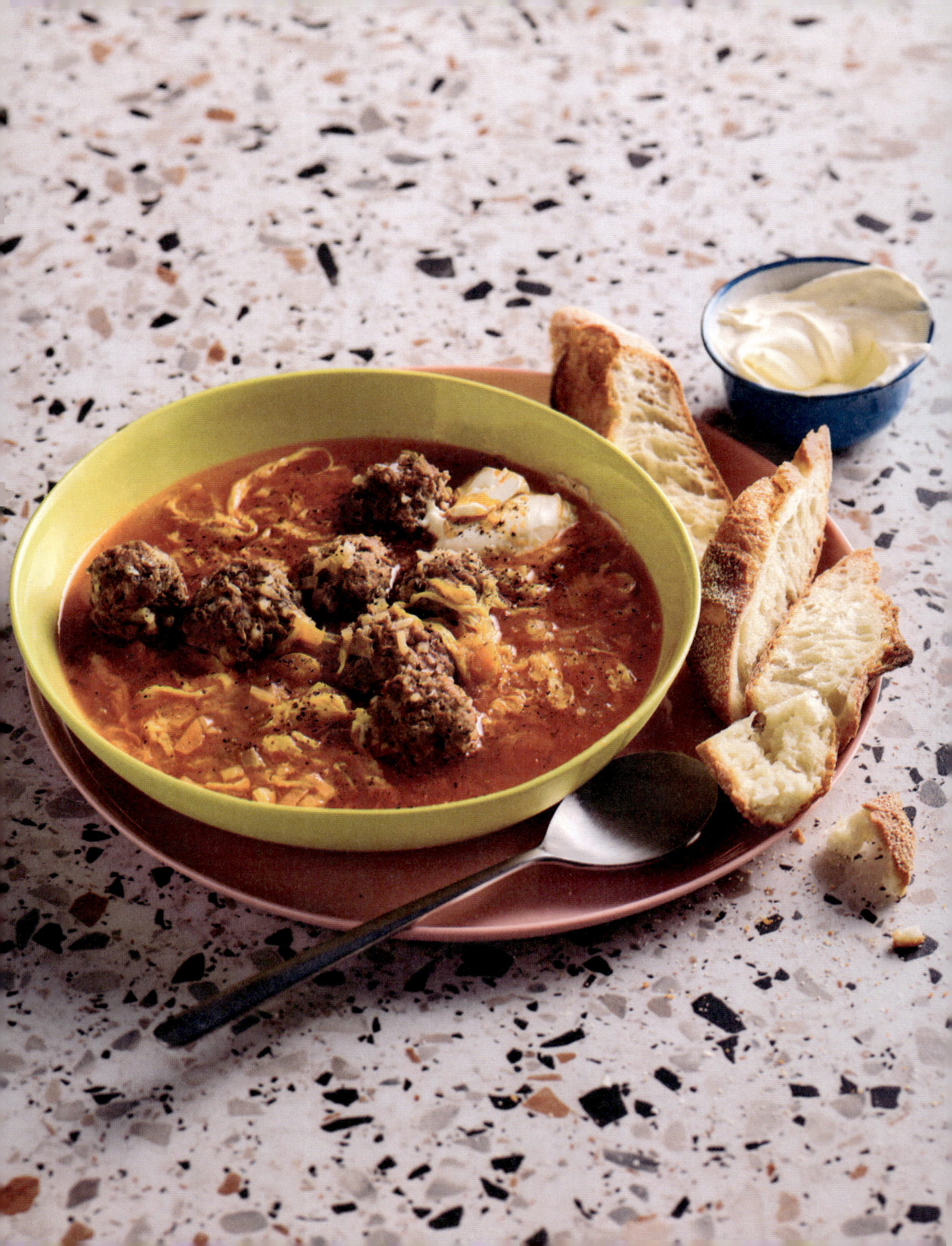

18
ROMANIA

Poor old Transylvania. It's famous for one thing, and one thing only: the fictional creation Dracula, and the real-life jerk on whom he was based, Vlad the Impaler.

This is a shame, as Transylvania also has much to offer the meatball afficionado, among them this rustic meatball soup. Frank Banyai, aka my dad, hails from Bistrița, deep in the Transylvanian region of Romania. Frank was born in the dark days of World War II, raised by a single mother who frequently served up ciorba, the word simply meaning 'vegetable soup', minus the meatballs; circumstances were tough, and meatballs only made their way into the soup when charitable organisations donated the meat. After migrating to Australia in his early twenties, Frank was finally able to make the ciorba of his childhood the way God intended: with meatballs.

It's worth noting that there is no garlic in this recipe, so if you're courting a vampire, this is the soup with which to woo them.

Ciorba de perisoare
SOUR SOUP WITH MEATBALLS

SERVES 4

- **Soup**

2 tablespoons olive oil
1 large onion, chopped
2 large carrots, chopped
2 celery stalks, chopped
1 teaspoon salt
½ teaspoon freshly cracked black pepper, or to taste
2 tablespoons tomato paste (concentrated puree)
1 litre (34 fl oz/4 cups) chicken stock
½ teaspoon chicken stock (bouillon) powder
3 tablespoons lemon juice
2 tablespoons finely chopped lovage or parsley
1 egg, beaten
chopped parsley, to garnish

- **Meatballs**

450 g (1 lb) minced (ground) beef
1 egg
2 tablespoons finely chopped dill
2 tablespoons finely chopped parsley
50 g (1¾ oz/¼ cup) white long-grain rice
20 g (¾ oz/¼ cup) fresh breadcrumbs
1 teaspoon salt
½ teaspoon freshly cracked black pepper

- **To serve**

sour cream
crusty bread

For the soup, heat the olive oil over a medium heat in a medium–large pot. Add the onion, carrot and celery and fry until the onion softens, about 5 minutes. Add the salt, pepper and tomato paste, then the chicken stock and 1 litre (34 fl oz/4 cups) water, then remove from the heat.

To make the meatballs, combine all the ingredients in a large bowl until evenly incorporated. Shape into small meatballs, then refrigerate until ready to add to the soup.

Bring the soup to the boil, then add the meatballs and cook over a medium heat for 10–15 minutes, or until the meatballs are cooked through (they will rise to the surface of the soup once cooked). Season with the chicken stock (bouillon) powder, then add the lemon juice and lovage.

Slowly pour in the beaten egg, rapidly stirring in a clockwise direction for 1 minute. Cook for another minute, then remove from the heat and garnish with parsley.

Serve with a dollop of sour cream and fresh crusty bread.

19 NORWAY

Hakon Bergby, a Melbourne-based marketing guru who immigrated from Norway to Australia in 2009, has the healthiest complexion I have ever seen. I like to think his awesomely bronzed hue is a direct consequence of a steady boyhood diet of medisterkaker, aka Norwegian Christmas meatballs. Passed down through generations of his mother Torill's family, Hakon now makes these festive balls for his own children every Christmas. 'The smells, taste and atmosphere it evokes are of childhood Christmases, me and the other kids eagerly scoffing the food down in anticipation of the gifts that are handed out after dinner.' According to Hakon, every Norwegian family has their own version of medisterkaker, and it's an integral feature of traditional Christmas fare in and around Oslo.

Medisterkaker
NORWEGIAN PORK MEATBALLS

SERVES 4–6

- **Meatballs**

1 kg (2 lb 3 oz) minced (ground) lean pork with 20% beef suet (see Notes), chilled
3 teaspoons salt
500 ml (17 fl oz/2 cups) full-cream (whole) milk, chilled
50 g (1¾ oz) potato starch or cornflour (cornstarch)
¾ teaspoon freshly cracked black pepper
½ teaspoon freshly grated nutmeg
¼ teaspoon ground ginger or ½ teaspoon grated fresh ginger
salted butter, for greasing

- **To serve**

gravy
mashed potato

Add the pork and salt to a large bowl and mix by hand until the meat becomes sticky. You can test the stickiness by taking a pinch between two fingers.

Gradually add the cold milk to the meat, mixing thoroughly after each addition. When about two-thirds of the milk has been added, mix in the potato starch and spices. Continue to mix well while adding the remaining milk.

Take tablespoons of the mixture and roll it into balls.

Lightly grease a frying pan with butter then place over a medium heat and fry the meatballs until they are golden brown and cooked through.

To serve, ladle the meatballs and gravy over mashed potato.

- **Notes**

Beef suet can be purchased from your butcher – just ask.

Hakon advises making your gravy from scratch and trying to get your hands on some lingonberry sauce at an international deli (failing that, it can be reliably found in the IKEA food store).

20
UKRAINE

Let's let food critic Larissa Dubecki have the first word here: 'No one ever accused Ukrainian food of honouring the healthy eating pyramid and these kotleti – aka "ground cutlets" – are no exception (hello, double cream!).' There's not much Larissa hasn't sampled in the course of her professional life as a restaurant critic and food writer, so you best pay attention when she says her grandmother's kotleti are the perfect combination of thrifty and delicious. Larissa's Ukrainian connection comes via her Lviv-born father; for an authentic Uki experience, she suggests wearing a headscarf tucked under your chin while you cook and grinding the meat yourself.

Kotleti

SERVES 6–8

• Meatballs
- 5 slices day-old white bread, crusts removed, roughly torn
- 250 ml (8½ fl oz/1 cup) thick (double/heavy) cream or full-cream (whole) milk
- 500 g (1 lb 2 oz) minced (ground) pork
- 500 g (1 lb 2 oz) minced (ground) beef
- 1 large onion, finely chopped
- 1 egg, beaten
- 15 g (½ oz/½ cup) herbs of your choice (such as dill, thyme, parsley, oregano), chopped
- 2 teaspoons salt (see Notes)
- 2 teaspoons freshly cracked black pepper (see Notes)
- olive oil, for pan-frying

• To serve
- cooked buckwheat
- sauerkraut

Soak the torn bread in the cream for 5 minutes.

In a large bowl, combine the pork and beef, onion, egg, soaked bread, herbs, salt and pepper and mix well until evenly incorporated. Wet your hands and form the mixture into kotleti (patties).

Heat the olive oil in a heavy-based frying pan over a medium heat. Add the patties, being sure not to overcrowd the pan. Fry for 4 minutes on each side, turning only once to allow a caramelised crust to form.

Once the patties are cooked through and have a golden crust, remove them from the pan and place on a serving plate.

Serve hot with cooked buckwheat and sauerkraut.

• Notes
Adjust the salt and black pepper according to your taste preferences. If you want to test for seasoning, cook a little bit of meatball mixture in a frying pan, taste and adjust the seasoning as needed.

Larissa notes, 'These meatballs are even better the next day, and perfect for kids' lunchboxes – if you can keep your own mitts off them.'

21

40

21. SOUTH AFRICA Oumense onder die komberse 64

22. GHANA Ghanaian meatball stew 67

23. LITHUANIA Kotletai in dill-spiked broth 68

24. JAPAN Teriyaki tsukune 71

25. BULGARIA Kjufteta po Chirpanski 72

26. HAITI Boulet with Haitian epis 74

27. BELGIUM Boulets de Liège 77

28. IRAQ Tepsi baytinijan 78

29. PORTUGAL Almôndegas de bacalhau 82

30. PHILIPPINES Misua with bola-bola 83

31. SERBIA Ćulbastije 85

32. JAPAN Chanko nabe with tori dango 86

33. DENMARK Fiskefrikadeller 89

34. LEBANON Kibbeh labanieh 90

35. BRAZIL Kibe 92

36. MOLDOVA Parjoale with mujdei 94

37. TUNISIA Chebtiya 95

38. CAMBODIA Num pang with pork meatballs 97

39. SERBIA Ćufte 100

40. UNITED KINGDOM Faggots/savoury ducks with gravy 101

21
SOUTH AFRICA

However hungry you are, you've probably never considered chowing down on your nan. While 'Oumense onder die komberse' literally translates as 'grandma under the blanket', I can assure you that no ground-up grandmothers are required for this recipe – nor any blankets. The 'grandma' is beef, the 'blanket', cabbage leaves, and if you can get past the mildly macabre recipe name, it's a belter.

You can use whichever part of the cabbage you like, but the traditional South African way is to use the outer leaves. Cabbage-wrapped meatballs are a much-loved dish in South Africa, drawing on both Cape Dutch and Cape Malay influences: when prepared in the traditional Cape Malay fashion, the meatballs are cooked in a mutton stew.

Oumense onder die komberse
CABBAGE MEATBALLS

SERVES 6

2 slices white bread, soaked in full-cream (whole) milk
700 g (1 lb 9 oz) minced (ground) beef
1 large onion, finely chopped
15 g (½ oz/½ cup) parsley, finely chopped
1 teaspoon freshly grated nutmeg
¼ teaspoon ground cinnamon
1½ teaspoons salt
¼ teaspoon freshly cracked black pepper
1 egg, beaten
plain (all-purpose) flour, for coating the meatballs
8–10 cabbage leaves (preferably outer leaves), washed
3 tablespoons salted butter
1 tablespoon olive oil
250 ml (8½ fl oz/1 cup) beef stock
steamed white rice, to serve
wholegrain mustard, to serve

Squeeze the soaked bread to remove excess milk. In a large bowl, combine the soaked bread, beef, onion, parsley, nutmeg, cinnamon, salt, pepper and beaten egg using your hands, until evenly incorporated. Shape the mixture into meatballs, then roll them in the flour to coat.

Bring a saucepan of water to the boil, add the cabbage leaves and cook for 5 minutes, then drain thoroughly. Do not refresh in cold water.

Preheat the oven to 200°C (390°F).

In a frying pan, heat the butter and olive oil over a medium heat. Fry the meatballs until browned all over, seasoning with salt and black pepper as you cook. Avoid packing them too tightly in the pan.

Remove the meatballs from the pan and set aside on paper towels to drain the excess oil. Pat dry the cabbage leaves with paper towels. Wrap each meatball in a cabbage leaf and arrange them in a greased ovenproof dish. Pour the beef stock into the bottom of the dish and bake for 20 minutes.

Serve the cabbage-wrapped meatballs over steamed white rice. Top with any leftover juices from the ovenproof dish and serve with wholegrain mustard.

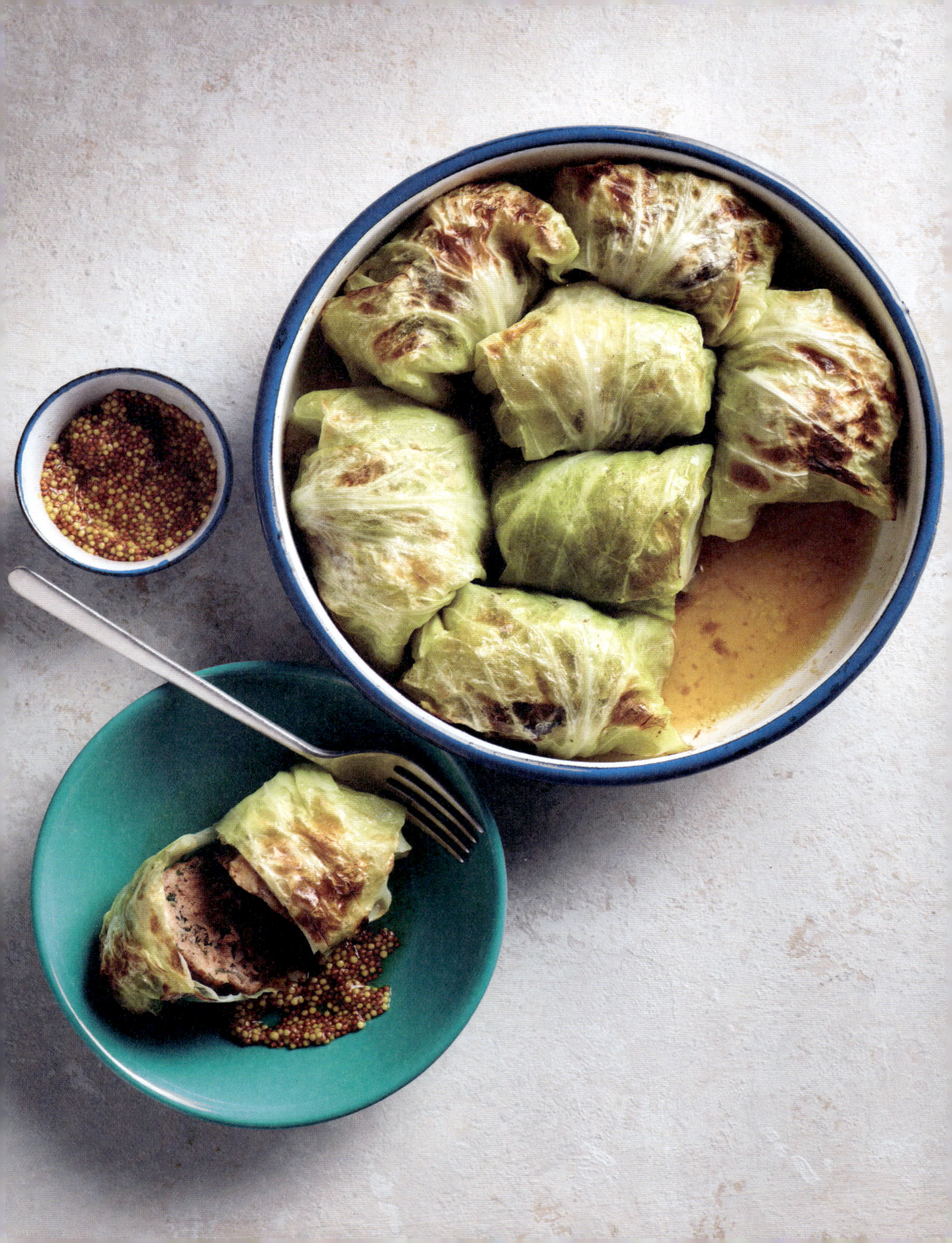

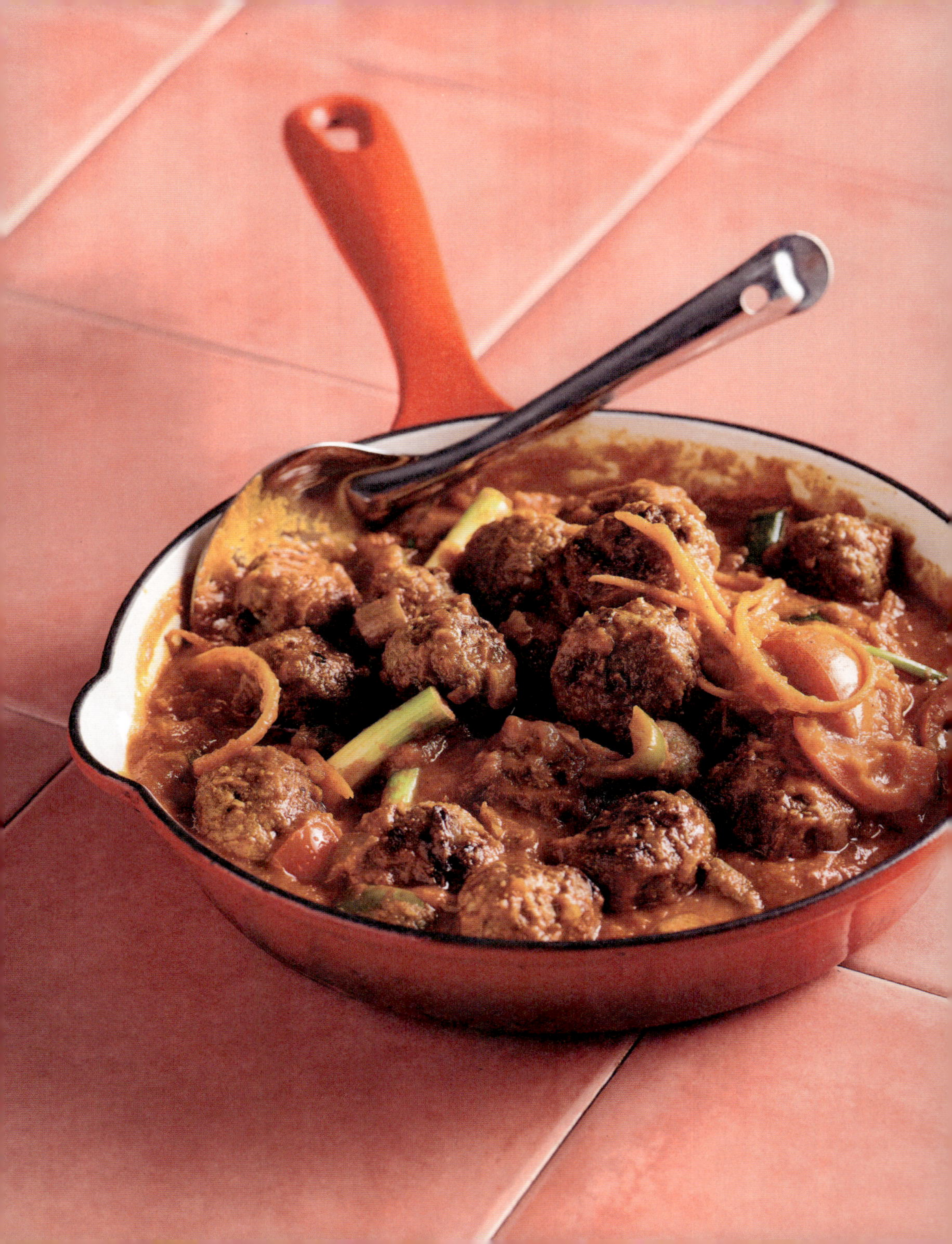

22
GHANA

If the litmus test for a dish's appeal is in the saliva output of the cook and those around them, this meatball stew succeeds handsomely. Ghanaians are fond of a stew, and it stands to reason; they're very, very good at them. Of particular importance here is the addition of that extra onion at the end, which brings a deeply satisfying element of crunch. There are a few (simple) steps to this recipe, so if you're short on time, sub out the homemade sauce for a store-bought version. It will pack less of a punch, but with so many other diva ingredients hitting the high notes, it's not a terrible compromise. Traditionally, Ghanaian stews are served with a starch such as sweet potatoes, rice or plantains.

Ghanaian meatball stew

SERVES 8

- **Sauce**

1–2 tablespoons vegetable oil
2 large onions, finely chopped
2 garlic cloves, finely chopped
1 tablespoon chopped fresh ginger
2–3 habanero chillies, chopped, to taste
1.2 kg (2 lb 10 oz) tinned chopped tomatoes

- **Meatballs**

850 g (1 lb 14 oz) minced (ground) beef
1 large onion, grated (including juices)
1 egg
2 beef or vegetable stock (bouillon) cubes
1 teaspoon garlic powder
1 tablespoon all-purpose seasoning
½ teaspoon salt
½ teaspoon freshly cracked black pepper
vegetable oil, for pan-frying

- **Stew**

2 tablespoons vegetable oil
3 onions, chopped
170 g (6 oz) tomato paste (concentrated puree)
1 tablespoon smoked paprika
2 tablespoons hot curry powder
1 teaspoon salt
1 carrot, grated or curled
4 mixed-colour capsicums (bell peppers), chopped
6 spring onions (scallions), chopped
2 beef or vegetable stock (bouillon) cubes

For the sauce, heat the oil in a frying pan over a medium–low heat and lightly fry the onion for 1–2 minutes. Add the garlic and ginger and fry for another 1–2 minutes. Add the chillies and tinned tomatoes and bring to a gentle boil, then reduce the heat to low and simmer for 10 minutes. Remove from the heat and allow to cool slightly, then blend the mixture until smooth using a hand-held blender.

To make the meatballs, combine the beef, onion (including juices), egg, stock cubes, garlic powder, all-purpose seasoning, salt and pepper in a bowl. Shape the mixture into meatballs about the size of golf balls. Heat the vegetable oil in a deep frying pan over a medium heat and fry the meatballs, turning occasionally, until browned on all sides. Set aside on paper towels to drain the excess oil.

To make the stew, heat the vegetable oil in a stockpot over a medium heat. Add 2 chopped onions and sauté for 3 minutes. Add the tomato paste, paprika, curry powder and salt and cook for about 2 minutes. Stir in the blended tomato sauce, cover and simmer for 20 minutes over a medium heat. Gently add the meatballs and stir, then cover and simmer for another 10 minutes. Stir in the carrot, capsicum and spring onion. Add the stock cubes and cover, cooking over a low heat for a further 5 minutes. Add the remaining chopped onion and cook for 3–4 minutes, ensuring the onion doesn't completely soften.

Serve the meatballs and stew with a starch of your choice.

23
LITHUANIA

I wouldn't have thought I had a lot of room left in my overcrowded heart to so easily fold in yet another meatball recipe, but these Lithuanian kotletai are as easy to love as a kitten in a bonnet.

Fresh dill and parsley are the star players, which help make this dish that most elusive of combinations; hearty yet light. Traditionally served with white rice, I also like to ladle them over fluffy white quinoa. Pickled cucumbers on the side are not mandatory, but strongly recommended.

Kotletai in dill-spiked broth

SERVES 6–8

• Meatballs
450 g (1 lb) minced (ground) beef
450 g (1 lb) minced (ground) chicken
1 teaspoon ground cumin
1 teaspoon ground coriander
½ teaspoon freshly cracked black pepper
1 teaspoon garlic powder
2 teaspoons salt
3 garlic cloves, minced
1 large egg
30 g (1 oz/½ cup) dill, chopped
15 g (½ oz/½ cup) parsley, chopped
2 tablespoons olive oil

• Broth
1½ tablespoons olive oil
1 small onion, finely diced
2 garlic cloves, minced
500 ml (17 fl oz/2 cups) chicken or vegetable stock, plus extra if needed
salt and freshly cracked black pepper, to taste

• To serve
steamed rice

To make the meatballs, add the beef and chicken to a large bowl with the spices, garlic and egg, and half of the dill and parsley. Mix well, then shape the mixture into meatballs about the size of golf balls. Place on a baking tray lined with baking paper.

Heat the olive oil in a frying pan over a medium-high heat and fry 5–6 meatballs at a time until browned on the outside, about 2 minutes on each side. Set the meatballs aside.

To make the broth, heat the oil in a stockpot over a medium-high heat. Add the onion and garlic and sauté for about 5 minutes, or until soft. Add salt and pepper to taste, then stir for 15 seconds. Add the browned meatballs to the pot and stir gently to combine. Pour in the chicken stock and bring to the boil. Cover and turn the heat down to medium-low. Cook for 30 minutes, stirring occasionally. Add the remaining dill and parsley, and simmer, uncovered, for another 5 minutes, adding a little more stock if needed to create a loose consistency.

Serve hot with steamed rice.

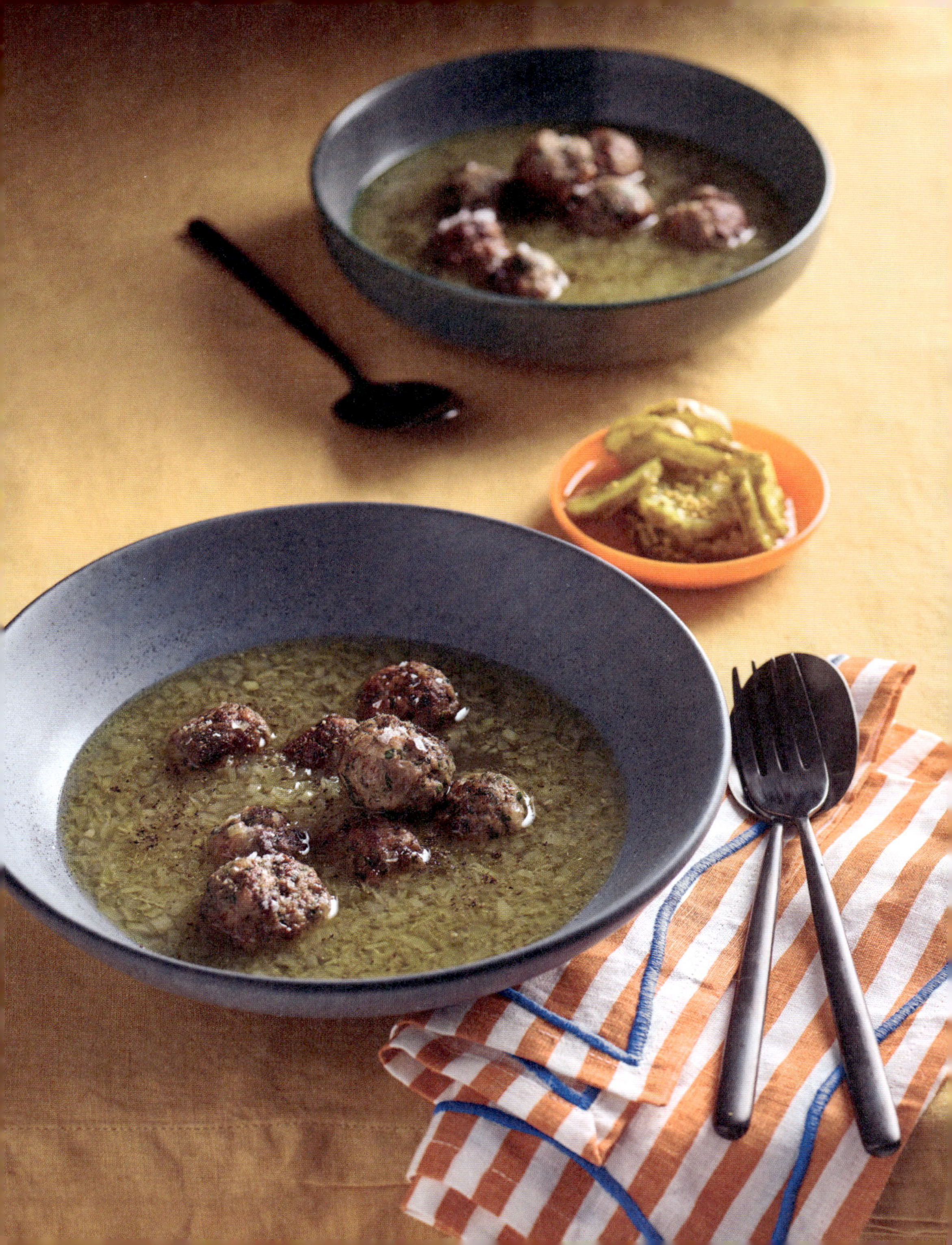

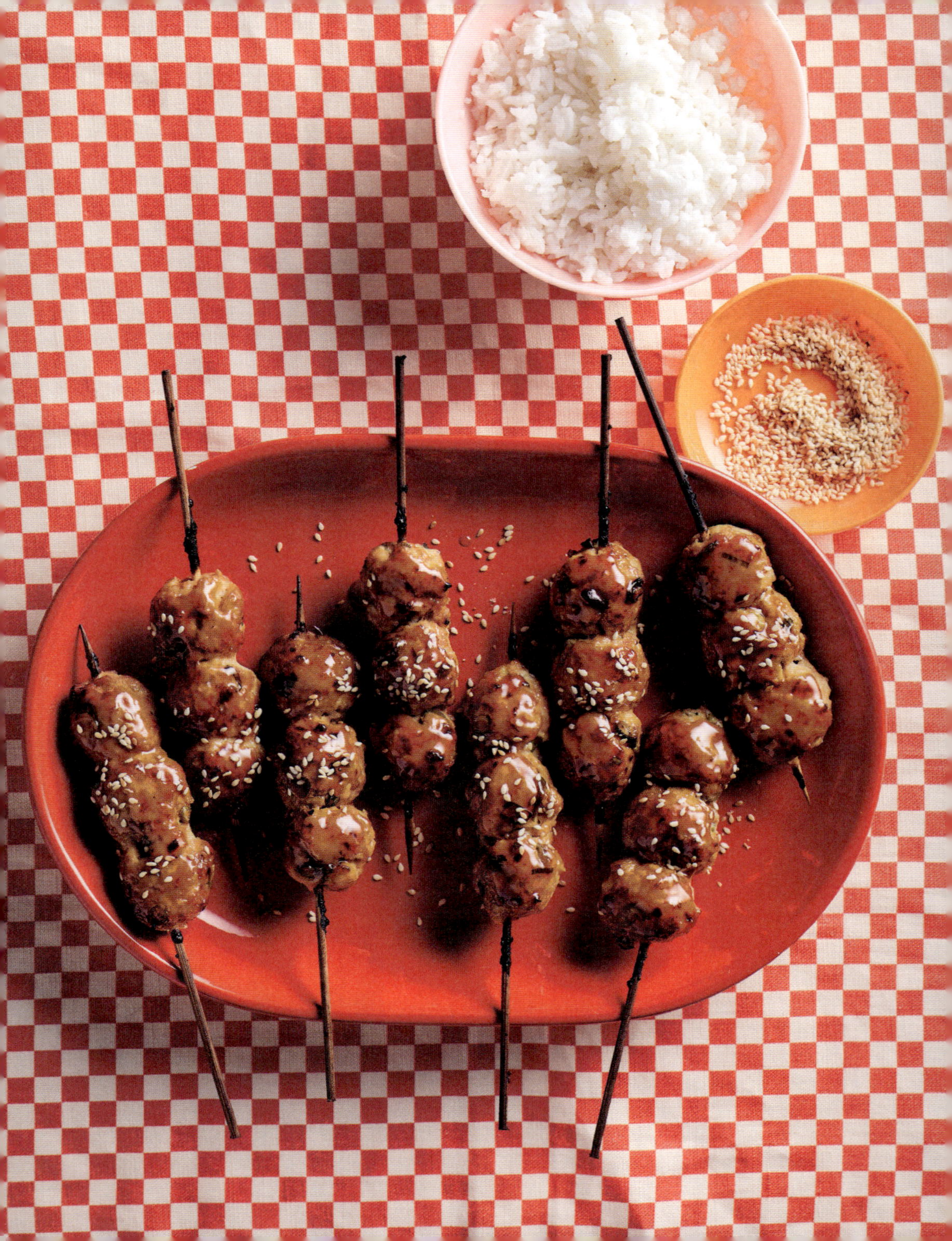

24
JAPAN

Very few kids turn up their noses at meatballs, no matter how inflexible their food preferences, and I'm going to go out on a limb and say no kids would reject a plate of these springy little teriyaki tsukune. Sweet but not sickly, they're given extra lightness and bounce with the addition of crumbled tofu. Undetectable taste-wise, the tofu helps to bind the mixture, and it's a great way to get a double hit of protein into picky eaters. I like to sprinkle them liberally with golden sesame seeds and finely chopped spring onion (scallion), with a little iceberg lettuce on top, but they're excellent with plain white rice, too.

Teriyaki tsukune
CHICKEN MEATBALLS WITH TERIYAKI SAUCE

SERVES 6

- **Meatballs**

300 g (10½ oz) firm tofu (see Note)
400 g (14 oz) minced (ground) chicken thigh
2 spring onions (scallions), thinly sliced
1 egg, at room temperature
1 teaspoon grated fresh ginger
½ teaspoon salt
⅛ teaspoon ground white pepper
1 tablespoon vegetable oil

- **Teriyaki sauce**

3 tablespoons light soy sauce
3 tablespoons mirin
3 tablespoons sugar
2 tablespoons rice vinegar
1½ teaspoons cornflour (cornstarch)

- **To serve**

steamed rice
toasted sesame seeds

Pat the tofu dry with paper towel and wrap it in another paper towel for 15 minutes to absorb any excess moisture.

While the tofu is drying, mix the sauce ingredients together in a bowl.

Once the tofu is dry, mash it into small pieces in a large bowl. Add the chicken, spring onion, egg, ginger, salt and pepper, and mix into the tofu.

Use a tablespoon to scoop out portions of the mixture and place on a plate.

Heat the oil in a large frying pan over a medium heat. Once the oil is almost smoking, add the meatballs, ensuring they do not touch (you may need to work in batches). Cook until the bottom of the meatballs have browned, about 6 minutes, then flip them over and brown the other side for 6 minutes. Cover the pan and cook for a further 3–6 minutes, or until the meat is cooked all the way through. If the meatballs brown too quickly, reduce the heat. Repeat until all the meatballs are cooked. Reduce the heat to low and pour the sauce over the meatballs. Simmer until the sauce is slightly reduced and thick, making sure the meatballs are thoroughly coated.

You can also cook these meatballs in the oven. Carefully thread the meatballs onto bamboo skewers that have been soaked in water for at least 1 hour. Pour the sauce over the meatballs and bake at 180°C (360°F) for 20 minutes, basting every 5 minutes with the sauce to ensure the meatballs are well glazed.

Serve with steamed rice and a scattering of lightly toasted sesame seeds.

- **Note**

Don't use silken tofu as a substitute for firm; it will make the mixture too difficult to work with.

25
BULGARIA

Chirpan, a town in south-central Bulgaria, is the birthplace of kjufteta po Chirpanski, and it's claimed that almost every household in the region has their own version of the dish. Chirpan is well known for its fertile land and agricultural production, and an abundance of vegetables in the sauce reflects the bounty of this region.

There are plenty of easy-to-incorporate adaptations you can make to this recipe to take the heat up or down (see Notes).

Kjufteta po Chirpanski
MEATBALLS IN TOMATO SAUCE

SERVES 4

- **Meatballs**

1–2 slices day-old bread
500 g (1 lb 2 oz) minced (ground) pork and beef
1 egg
1 bunch parsley, stems reserved for the sauce, leaves finely chopped
½ large onion, finely minced
2 garlic cloves, finely minced
1 teaspoon summer savory (optional; see Notes)
1 teaspoon freshly cracked black pepper
1 teaspoon salt
sunflower oil, for pan-frying
plain (all-purpose) flour, for coating

- **Sauce**

50 ml (1¾ fl oz) sunflower oil
½ large onion, finely chopped
1 carrot, finely chopped
2 celery stalks, finely chopped
1 bunch parsley, stems only, finely chopped
2 hot chillies (optional)
1 green capsicum (bell pepper), diced
1 potato, diced
1 teaspoon smoked paprika
1 teaspoon sugar
790 g (1 lb 12 oz) tinned crushed tomatoes
150 ml (5 fl oz) red wine
salt, to taste
chopped parsley, to serve

Start by making the meatballs. Soak the bread in a little water or milk to moisten it, then drain and squeeze out the liquid. Combine the meat, egg, soaked bread, chopped parsley, onion, garlic, summer savory (if using), pepper and salt in a large bowl. Mix by hand for about 5 minutes, then shape the mixture into meatballs about the size of golf balls, wetting your hands with cold water as you go to prevent the mixture from sticking.

Pour enough sunflower oil into a frying pan to cover the base of the pan then place over a medium heat. While the oil is heating, coat the meatballs in flour, tapping off the excess. Fry the meatballs for about 1 minute on each side until lightly browned, then set aside on a plate.

To a clean frying pan add the sunflower oil for the sauce and place over a medium heat. Add the onion, carrot, celery and parsley stems and sauté for 1–2 minutes, stirring continuously. Add the chilli at this point, if using.

Add the diced capsicum and potato and cook for another 1–2 minutes, stirring occasionally. Add the paprika, sugar, tomatoes and wine. Stir well and return the meatballs to the pan.

Cover the pan and bring the sauce to the boil over a high heat. Once boiling, reduce the heat, slightly open the lid and let it simmer over a low heat for 40 minutes. Stir occasionally, careful to avoid breaking the meatballs.

After 40 minutes, season with salt to taste and simmer for another 10 minutes over a low heat. Remove from the heat and add some finely chopped parsley, to serve.

- **Notes**

For an extra flavour boost, roast 2–3 hot peppers on the stove while frying the meatballs, then dice and add them to the sautéed onion.

Summer savory belongs to the mint family and can be found in most independent and organic grocers.

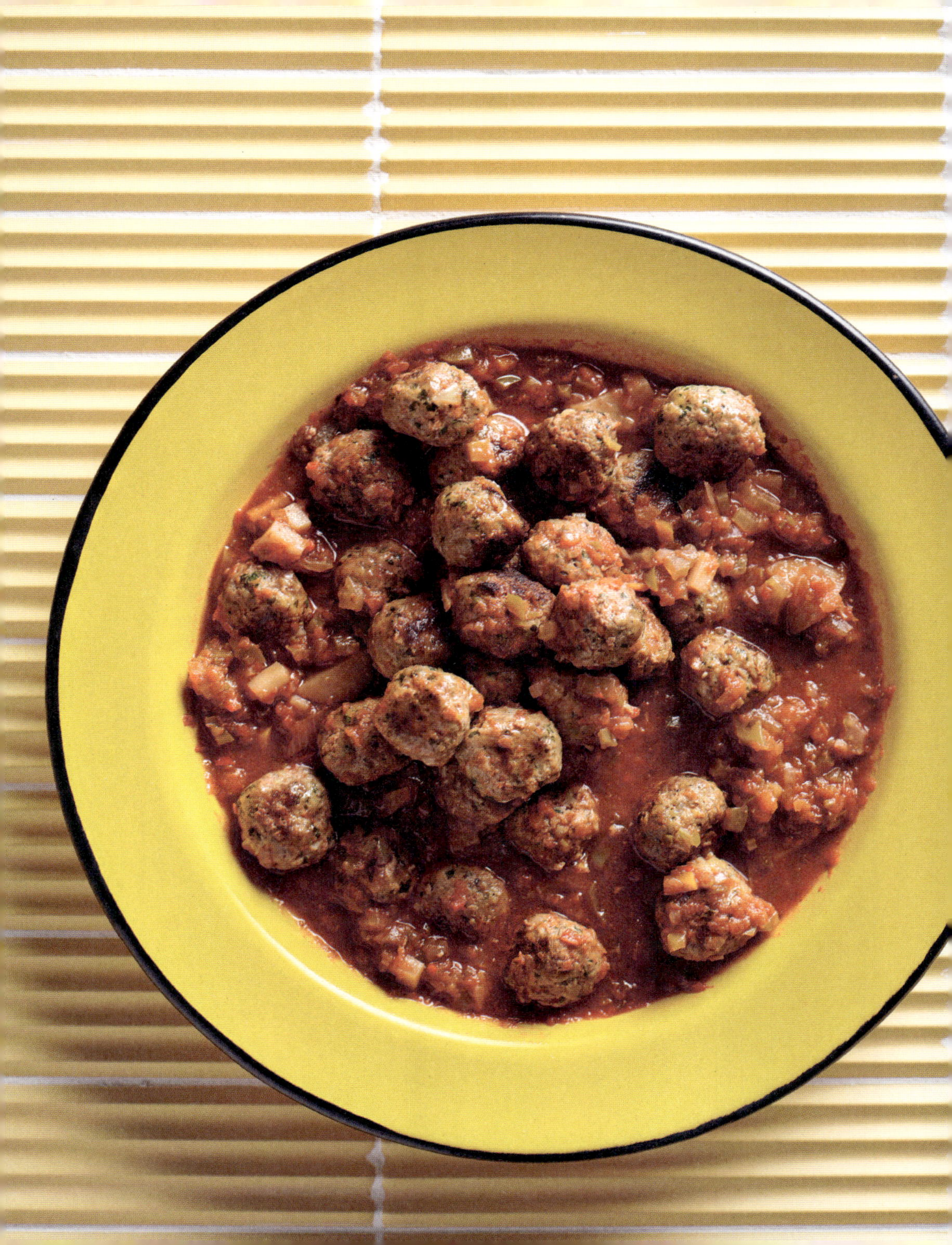

26
HAITI

Looking for a ball to really wake you up? Look no further than this wonderfully in-your-face boulet recipe. The key ingredient is Haitian epis, a marinade that serves as the basis of many Haitian recipes. Here, it's added not just to the sauce but to the meatball mixture, too, which produces a spicy, soaring symphony of a ball. It's most often served over steamed white rice, but if you have access to them, fried green plantains are the most authentic accompaniment. Boulet-vous coucher avec moi, ce soir? Oui, s'il vous plait.

Boulet with Haitian epis

SERVES 6–8

- **Haitian epis**

15 g (½ oz/½ cup) parsley, chopped
10 thyme sprigs
1 tablespoon whole cloves
5 garlic cloves
150 g (5½ oz/1 cup) mixed capsicum (bell pepper) and onion, chopped
120 g (4½ oz/1 cup) spring onion (scallion), chopped
2 tablespoons chopped basil
1 teaspoon salt
1 teaspoon freshly cracked black pepper
1–2 teaspoons cayenne pepper
250 ml (8½ fl oz/1 cup) olive oil
80 ml (2½ fl oz/⅓ cup) apple-cider vinegar
1 tablespoon chicken stock (bouillon) powder or 1 stock (bouillon) cube

- **Meatballs**

1 kg (2 lb 3 oz) minced (ground) beef
50 g (1¾ oz/⅓ cup) diced onion
2 large eggs, beaten
3 garlic cloves, minced
1 tablespoon chopped parsley
2 slices bread, soaked in water then drained
1 teaspoon sea salt flakes
½ teaspoon freshly cracked black pepper
75 g (2¾ oz/½ cup) plain (all-purpose) flour
375 ml (12½ fl oz/1½ cups) canola oil

To make the Haitian epis, place all the ingredients in a blender or food processor and blend until smooth but not liquefied. The texture should be similar to pesto. Refrigerate until ready to use. It will keep in an airtight container in the fridge for up to 1 week.

For the meatballs, combine the beef, onion, egg, 60 g (2 oz/¼ cup) Haitian epis, garlic, parsley, bread, salt and black pepper in a bowl and mix well. Scoop the mixture into balls, then roll each meatball in flour until coated on all sides. Set aside.

Heat the canola oil in a large frying pan to 175–200°C (345–390°F) and fry the meatballs in batches, about 5–7 at a time, for 6 minutes per side, or until golden brown. Place on paper towel to drain the excess oil. Repeat with the remaining meatballs.

- **Tomato sauce**

2 tablespoons olive oil
50 g (1¾ oz/⅓ cup) diced onions
1 tablespoon tomato paste (concentrated puree)
juice of 1 lemon
2 garlic cloves, minced, or 1 teaspoon dried minced garlic
1 tablespoon chopped fresh parsley or 2 teaspoons parsley flakes
salt and freshly cracked black pepper, to taste

For the sauce, heat the oil in a frying pan over a medium–low heat and cook the onion for 30–45 seconds. Stir in 3 tablespoons Haitian epis, then add the tomato paste and mix well. Add the lemon juice to deglaze, then stir in the minced garlic and 250 ml (8½ fl oz/1 cup) water. Reduce the heat to low, add the meatballs to the sauce and simmer for 5–8 minutes. Stir in the chopped parsley and adjust the seasoning if needed.

- **Notes**

Mixed capsicum (bell pepper) typically includes red, green and yellow varieties.

To increase the heat, include 1 teaspoon of chopped habanero chilli.

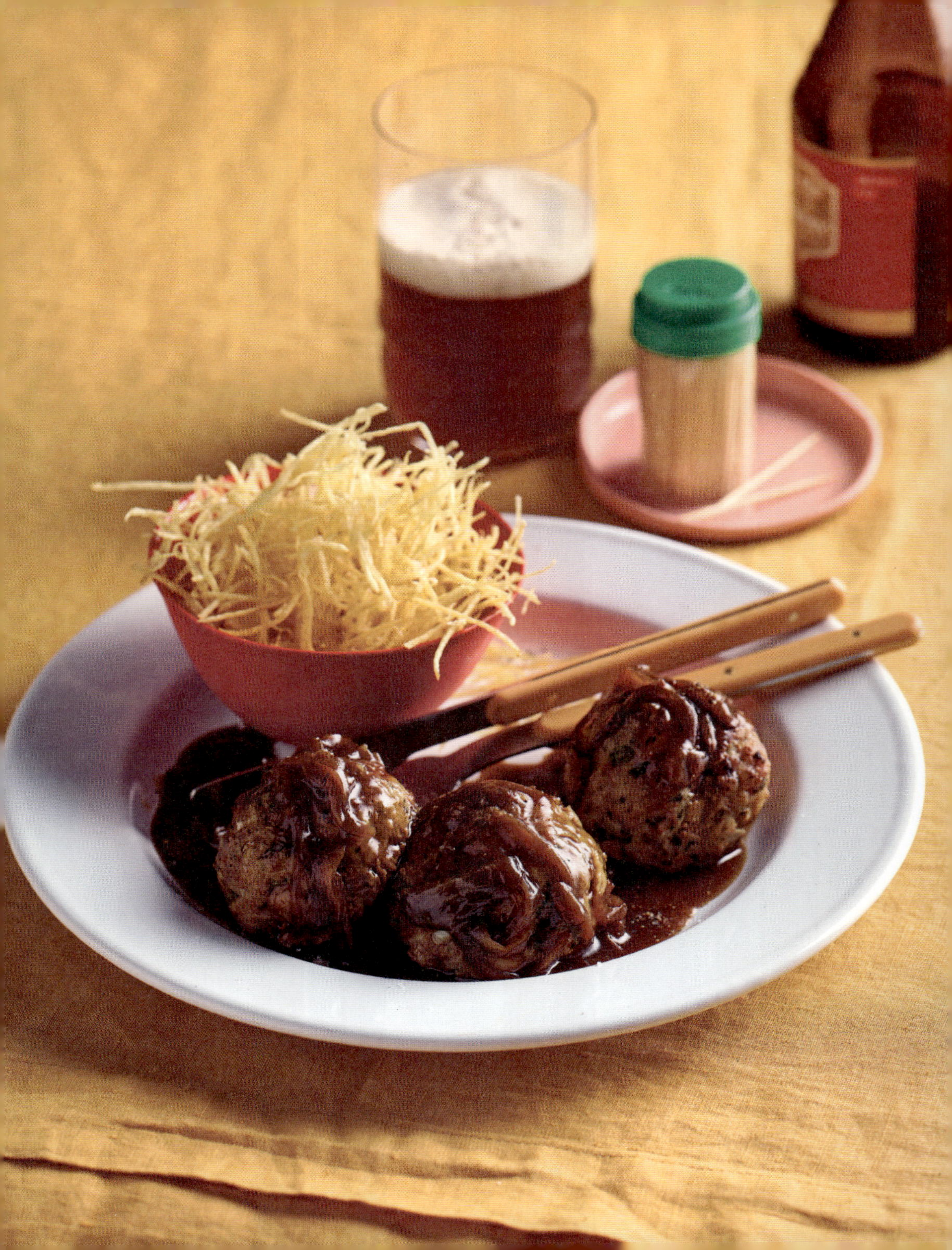

27
BELGIUM

It is a truth universally acknowledged that in a globetrotting recipe book you're going to encounter a couple of hard-to-find ingredients. This is one of those recipes, but don't be discouraged; while the star ingredient is sirop de Liège – not easily found outside of France and Belgium – a similar effect can be achieved with the far less elusive apple butter, or Dutch apple sauce.

Jean-Claude Faustein Deckers, a hairdresser who has owned salons in Paris and Mallorca, was born in Liège and spent childhood vacations with his seven siblings at the petit chateau of his grandmother, Eugenie. Boulets de Liège is one of Belgium's most beloved dishes, and Eugenie often made it for her formidably large brood of grandkids.

An added flavour kick comes care of the Belgian beer in the meatball mixture, and topped with a sweet, tangy onion gravy, it's easy to see how these attained their sweetheart status. Belgian beer is the standard side dish.

Boulets de Liège
BELGIAN MEATBALLS WITH ONION GRAVY

SERVES 6–8

- **Meatballs**

4 thick slices bread, crusts removed, soaked in full-cream (whole) milk
300 g (10½ oz) minced (ground) lean beef
700 g (1 lb 9 oz) minced (ground) pork
1 onion, finely chopped
1 large handful parsley, finely chopped
2 eggs
35 g (1¼ oz/⅓ cup) dry breadcrumbs
¼ teaspoon freshly grated nutmeg
salt and freshly cracked black pepper

- **Sauce**

2 tablespoons vegetable oil or beef dripping, plus extra for greasing
3 onions, halved and sliced into half-moons
4 thyme sprigs
3 tablespoons dark muscovado sugar
1 teaspoon red-wine vinegar
330 ml (11 fl oz) dark Belgian beer
650 ml (22 fl oz) beef stock
2 tablespoons sirop de Liège (or apple butter or Dutch apple sauce, if unavailable)
4 whole cloves
6 juniper berries
2 bay leaves
20 g (¾ oz) cornflour (cornstarch), dissolved in a little water
salt and freshly cracked black pepper, to taste

Preheat the oven to 200°C (390°F) and lightly grease a roasting tin with oil or dripping.

For the meatballs, gently squeeze out the soaked bread and combine it with the beef and pork, onion, parsley, eggs, breadcrumbs, nutmeg and some salt and pepper. Mix well.

Shape the mixture into 10–12 large meatballs. Place in the roasting tin and bake for 30–40 minutes. If preferred, you can make smaller, golf ball-sized meatballs. In this case, reduce the cooking time to 15–20 minutes.

To make the sauce, heat the vegetable oil in a frying pan over a medium heat and cook the onion and thyme until the onion is soft and starting to colour. Add the muscovado sugar and stir until the onion is caramelised, then deglaze the pan with the vinegar. Add the beer and beef stock and bring to the boil. Stir in the sirop de Liège, cloves, juniper berries and bay leaves. Season with salt and pepper to taste, cover the pan and simmer for 25 minutes.

Stir in the cornflour slurry to thicken the sauce and cook for a further 5 minutes.

Add the cooked meatballs to the sauce and allow to warm through for a couple of minutes before serving.

Serve with fried potatoes, a green salad and – age permitting – a glass of leftover Belgian beer.

28
IRAQ

I have a real soft spot for meatball bakes, given they generally feature the holy grail of veg, potatoes and meatballs, and don't necessitate the addition of any side dishes. This Iraqi recipe is homely, hearty and potatoey – all the ingredients to fill both the stomach and heart. Bonus points for the name, tepsi baytinijan, which rolls off the tongue like Rumi's rhyming couplets. (The same cannot be said for 'rissoles in gravy'.) Of note: while many children roundly denounce eggplant (aubergine), the charms of this dish are such that one twelve-year-old taste-tester declared it 'the yummiest thing ever', proving my point that there is nothing the meatball can't improve, including a jejune palate.

Tepsi baytinijan
EGGPLANT CASSEROLE

SERVES 4–6

- **Bake**

3 eggplants (aubergines), sliced lengthways
½ teaspoon curry powder
½ teaspoon ground cumin
½ teaspoon ground turmeric
½ teaspoon ground coriander
1 teaspoon salt, plus extra for sprinkling
½ teaspoon freshly cracked black pepper
2 onions, 1 diced, 1 sliced into rounds
1 green chilli
500 g (1 lb 2 oz) minced (ground) beef or lamb
3 tablespoons plain (all-purpose) flour or dry breadcrumbs
80 ml (2½ fl oz/⅓ cup) vegetable oil, plus extra if necessary
15 g (½ oz/½ cup) parsley leaves, plus extra to garnish
2 large potatoes, peeled and thinly sliced
1 red capsicum (bell pepper), cored and sliced into rounds
2 large tomatoes, sliced into half-moons

- **Sauce**

3 tablespoons tomato paste (concentrated puree)
juice of 1 lemon
2½ tablespoons pomegranate molasses
1 teaspoon salt
300 ml (10 fl oz) boiling water

- **To serve**

steamed white rice

Preheat the oven to 180°C (350°F). Grease a deep ovenproof dish and set aside.

Lay the eggplant slices on a flat surface and sprinkle with salt. Press the eggplant slices between two paper towels to squeeze out the moisture.

To a food processor, add the curry powder, cumin, turmeric, coriander, ½ teaspoon of salt, the pepper, diced onion and chilli, and blitz until well combined. Transfer to a bowl, add the meat and flour and mix well. Shape into small logs and set aside.

Heat 2 tablespoons of the vegetable oil in a frying pan over a medium-high heat. Fry 2–3 eggplant slices at a time, for a few seconds on each side, until golden brown, then set aside. Repeat until all the eggplant has been browned, adding more oil to the pan as necessary.

Heat the remaining oil in the pan over a medium heat and fry the meatballs for 4–5 minutes on each side, or until golden brown. Set aside.

To make the parcels, lay an eggplant slice flat, then place a meatball and a couple of parsley leaves in it. Roll up the eggplant to encase the meatball.

For the sauce, combine all the ingredients in a bowl with a pouring lip and mix until well combined.

To assemble the dish, lay the potato slices in the bottom of the ovenproof dish, followed by the capsicum and sliced onion. Pack in the eggplant parcels tightly and fill any gaps with the remaining meatballs. Cover the top with tomato slices and pour the sauce evenly over the dish. Cover the dish with aluminium foil and bake for 40–45 minutes. Remove the foil and bake for another 10 minutes to brown the top.

Serve with steamed white rice and extra parsley to garnish.

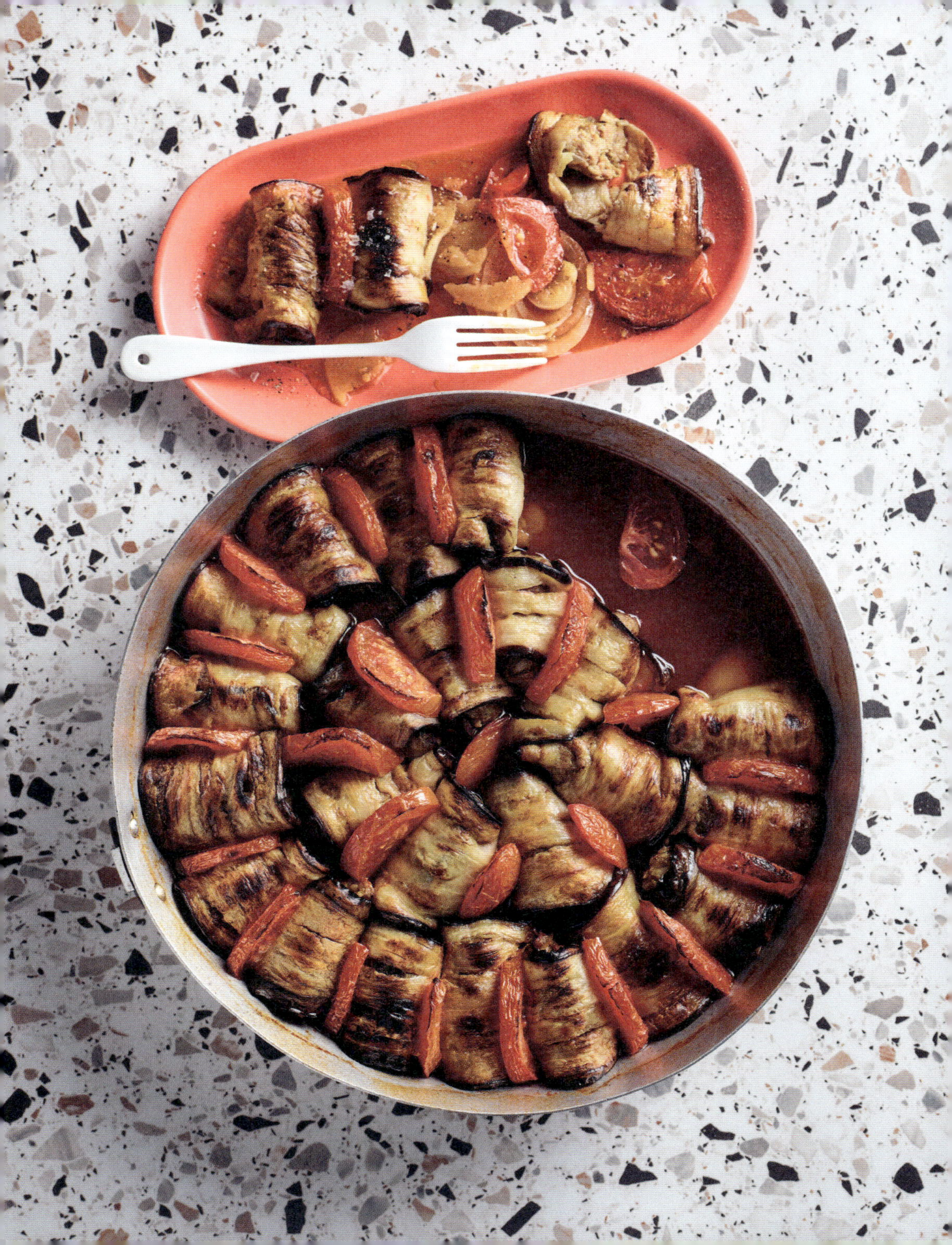

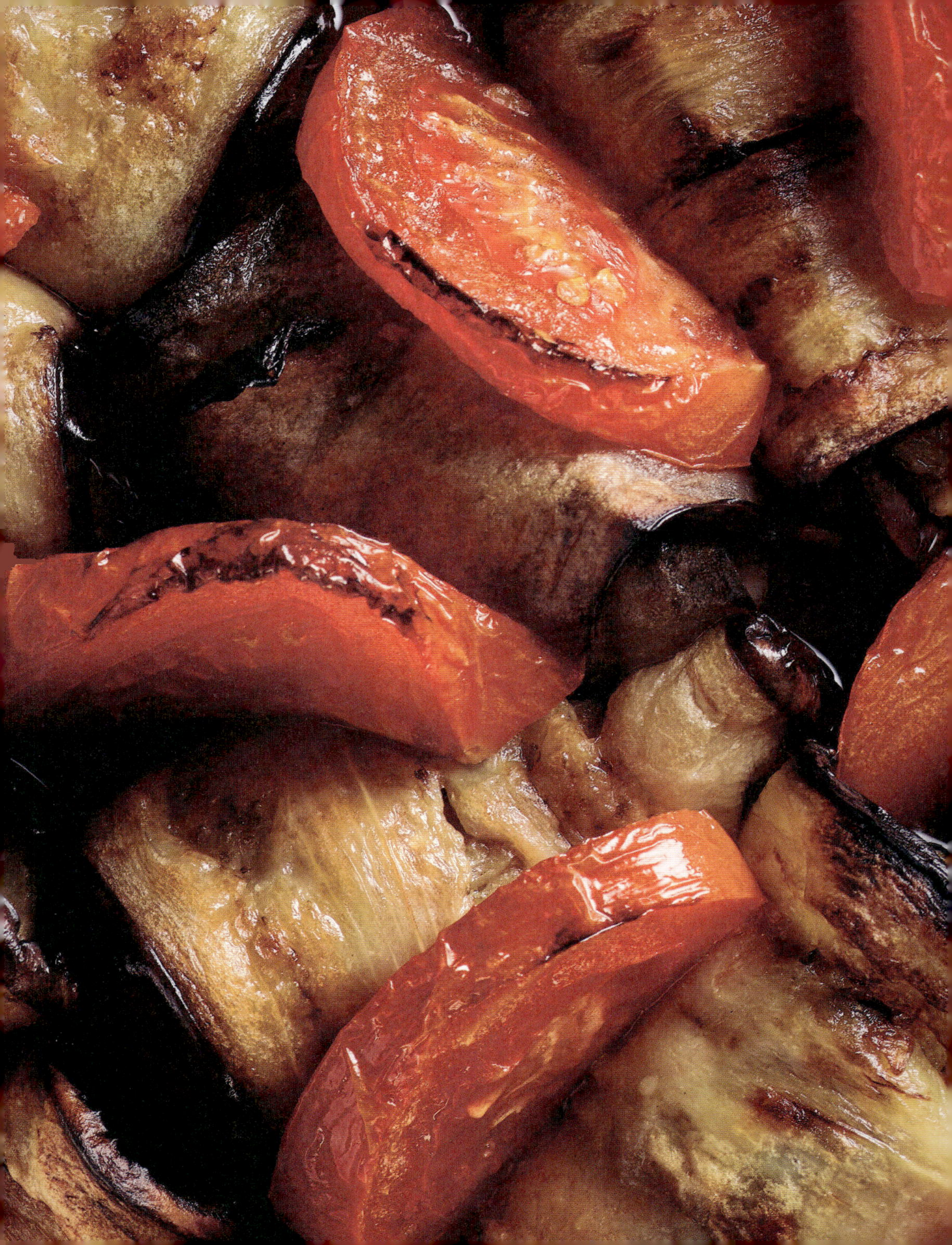

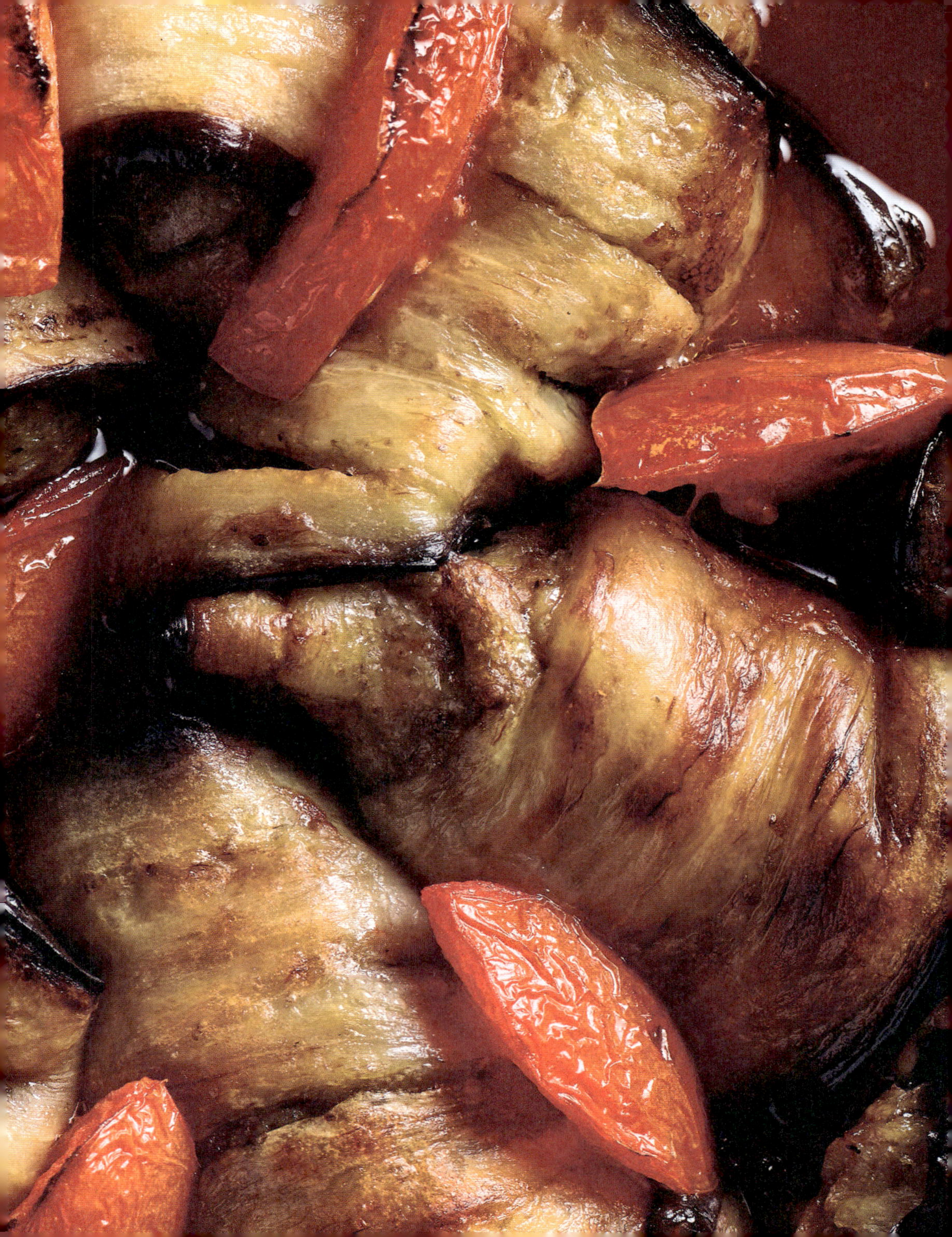

29
PORTUGAL

Bacalhau, or dried salt cod, is one of the oldest and most beloved cornerstones of Portuguese cuisine. In the fifteenth and sixteenth centuries, Portuguese sailors travelled with dried and salted cod, a long-lasting source of nutrition during lengthy voyages. They would have fared even better with a belly full of salt cod meatballs, now a standard feature on the table at most Portuguese gatherings.

If dried salt cod is not available, fresh cod also works well – you'll just need to experiment a bit with the salt content.

Almôndegas de bacalhau
COD BALLS

SERVES 4

- **Fish balls**

400 g (14 oz) red or white potatoes, unpeeled
280 g (10 oz) bacalhau (dried salt cod), preferably thick pieces, soaked overnight in water
3 large eggs
1 small onion, very finely chopped
2 tablespoons finely chopped parsley
1–2 tablespoons full-cream (whole) milk to loosen, if needed
vegetable oil, for deep-frying

- **To serve**

salad
crusty bread

Boil the potatoes until soft in their skins to prevent them from absorbing water. This should take about 25 minutes. Once boiled, peel the potatoes and mash or sieve them. Set aside.

Drain the cod from its soaking water and place in a large saucepan. Cover with fresh water and bring to the boil. Cook for 20 minutes, or until tender, then drain and set aside until cool enough to handle. Discard the skin and bones and flake the fish with your fingers or a fork to reduce it to threads. You can also mash the cod by placing the flaked cod inside a clean cloth, folding it and squeezing and pounding the contents with your fists.

Mix the cod with the mashed potato in a large bowl. Add the eggs, one by one, then add the onion and parsley. Taste and season with salt if needed. The mixture should be stiff enough to support a standing spoon. If it is too dry, add milk to loosen. Allow the mixture to cool completely. Shape the mixture into quenelles (egg-shaped ovals) using two tablespoons or roll it into 4 cm (1½ in) balls if you prefer.

Add 10–13 cm (4–5 in) of oil to a saucepan and heat to 190°C (375°F). Carefully lower each fish ball into the oil with a spoon and cook for 3–5 minutes, turning three or four times to ensure it browns evenly. Once cooked, remove the fish balls with a slotted spoon and drain on paper towel to absorb excess oil. Continue shaping and frying until all the mixture has been used.

Serve with salad and fresh crusty bread.

30
PHILIPPINES

Filipinos who reflect on their memories of this soupy hug of a dish often speak of eating it during rainy weather. It's that kind of recipe: as comforting as the sound of raindrops on a roof. Traditionally cooked with a type of extra-fine Chinese noodle called misua, easily found in Asian grocery stores, it works equally well with any type of thin rice noodle.

Misua with bola-bola is also usually made with patola, a green, cylindrical gourd commonly grown in South-East Asia, but you can substitute with zucchini (courgette), or simply leave it out.

Misua with bola-bola
MEATBALL NOODLE SOUP

SERVES 4

450 g (1 lb) minced (ground) pork
3 spring onions (scallions), sliced diagonally
1 large egg, lightly beaten
3 tablespoons plain (all-purpose) flour
½ teaspoon sea salt flakes
¼ teaspoon freshly cracked black pepper
1 tablespoon olive oil
2 garlic cloves, minced
80 g (2¾ oz/½ cup) onion, finely diced
2 litres (68 fl oz/8 cups) chicken stock
½ tablespoon fish sauce
170 g (6 oz) misua, or other thin rice noodles

Combine the pork, all but 1 tablespoon of the spring onion, the egg, flour, salt and pepper in a large bowl and mix well. Shape the mixture into meatballs about the size of golf balls. Set aside.

Heat the olive oil in a large saucepan over a medium–high heat. Add the garlic and diced onion and sauté until soft and fragrant, about 1–2 minutes.

Pour in the chicken stock and fish sauce, then bring to the boil. Once boiling, gently add the meatballs, one at a time, and cook for 10 minutes, or until the meatballs are cooked through.

Add the noodles and cook for about 3 minutes, stirring regularly, until the noodles are cooked.

Turn off the heat and serve the soup garnished with the remaining spring onion.

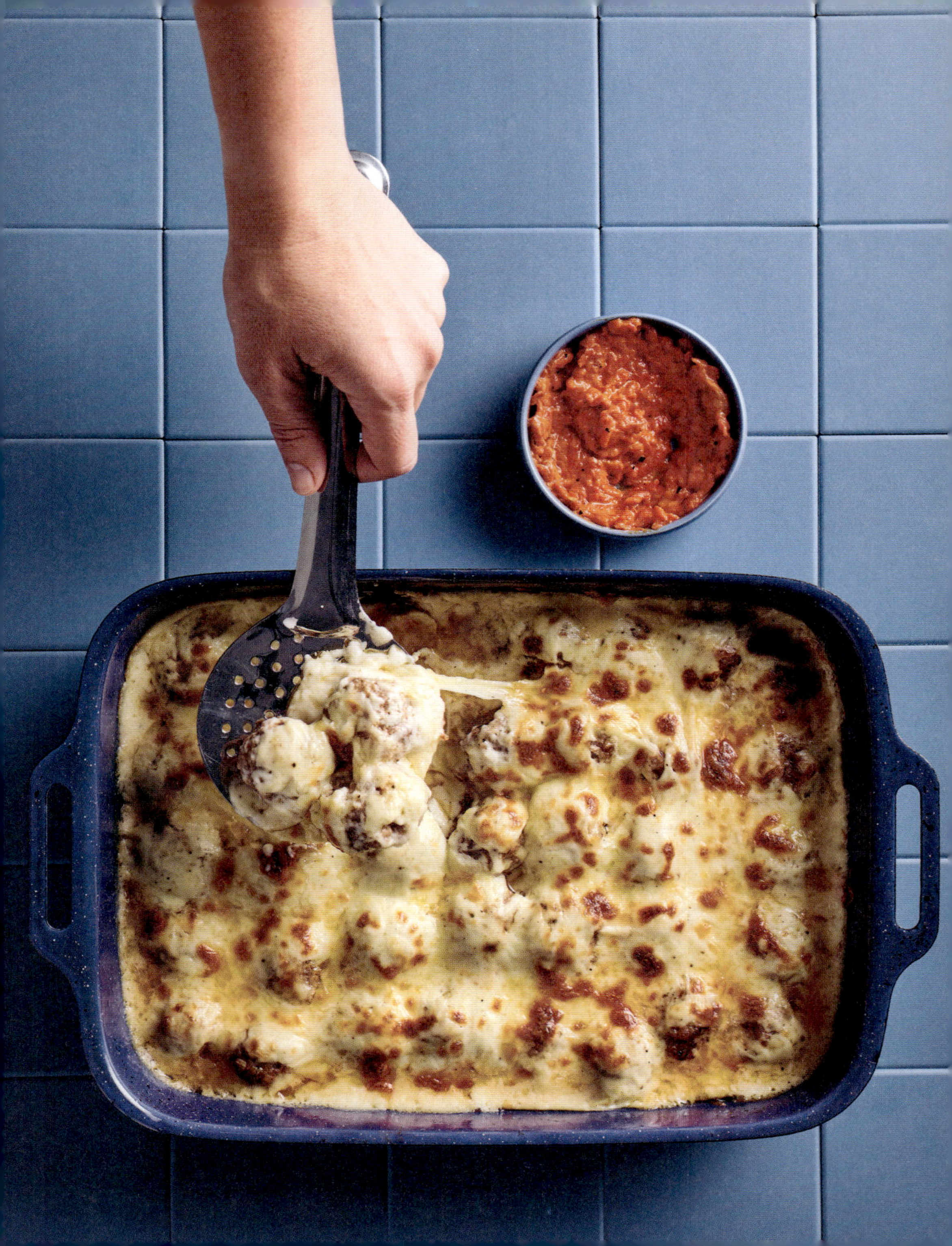

31
SERBIA

Thus far, cheese has not featured prominently in these recipes. All that is about to change with this dish – a melty marriage of meatballs and mozzarella made in heaven. Popular in south Serbia, it's also known as Djubastije. Traditionally served with mashed potato or a simple side salad, I like to throw some shredded cabbage in a bowl and toss it with a simple dressing of olive oil, mustard, lemon juice, apple-cider vinegar and salt and pepper.

This dish also pairs resoundingly well with ajvar (see Note), the brilliantly biting Balkan dip, typically consisting of roasted red capsicums (bell peppers), eggplant (aubergine), garlic and chilli.

Ćulbastije
MEATBALL BAKE WITH BECHAMEL SAUCE

SERVES 6–8

- **Meatballs**

500 g (1 lb 2 oz) minced (ground) beef
500 g (1 lb 2 oz) minced (ground) pork
1 large onion, minced
3 garlic cloves, grated
1 egg
60 g (2 oz) fresh or dry breadcrumbs
⅛ teaspoon freshly cracked black pepper
½ teaspoon sweet paprika
1 teaspoon vegetable stock (bouillon) powder or 1 vegetable stock (bouillon) cube
1 teaspoon salt
1 tablespoon vegetable oil

- **Bechamel sauce**

100 g (3½ oz) unsalted butter
80 g (2¾ oz) plain (all-purpose) flour
1 litre (34 fl oz/4 cups) full-cream (whole) milk
80 g (2¾ oz) grated mozzarella, plus extra for sprinkling
salt and freshly cracked black pepper, to taste

- **To serve**

garden salad

Combine all the meatball ingredients, except for the oil, in a large bowl until evenly incorporated. Shape the mixture into meatballs about the size of golf balls. Place the meatballs on a plate and refrigerate for about 30 minutes.

To make the bechamel sauce, melt the butter in a saucepan over a medium heat. Stir in the flour and cook until it starts to brown, about 1 minute, being careful not to burn it. Pour in the milk, stirring well to scrape any flour from the bottom and side of the pan. Once the mixture thickens, cook for another 2 minutes, stirring occasionally, then add the grated mozzarella and stir until the cheese is melted. Season to taste with salt and pepper.

Once the meatballs are chilled, heat the oil in a frying pan over a medium heat and brown the meatballs for 1–2 minutes on all sides. Once browned, transfer the meatballs to an ovenproof dish, arranging them in rows.

Preheat the oven to 180°C (360°F).

Pour the bechamel sauce over the meatballs in the ovenproof dish. Top with extra mozzarella, then bake for about 30 minutes until the cheese forms a golden-brown crust on the meatballs.

Serve with a garden salad.

- **Note**

Ajvar is easily found in most major grocers. You can also make it yourself, but an authentic version requires a fair investment of time and effort.

32
JAPAN

Everything Yukata 'Matsu' Matsuda turns his attention to is a felicitous delight, from the full-moon dinners he hosts for friends, the Tower of the Sun statues dotted around his Melbourne cafe (in homage to the iconic Osaka installation), and the 'MatsuDonald's' burgers he makes for his customers on Saturdays.

His chanko nabe with tori dango, which translates as 'sumo wrestler hot pot with meatballs', is in perfect keeping with his cosy ethos. Despite the hefty connotations that naturally attach themselves to such a dish, this is a light, nourishing variation, packed with vegetables. It's also flexible, able to take all manner of additions and subtractions. For a more sumo-weight dish, add seafood, chicken thighs and udon noodles.

Chanko nabe with tori dango
CHICKEN MEATBALL HOT POT

SERVES 4–6

- **Tori dango**

250 g (9 oz) minced (ground) chicken
1 egg
pinch of salt
¼ onion, grated
1–2 teaspoons grated fresh ginger (ideally grated on a Japanese grater to keep all the juice)
1 tablespoon soy sauce or ponzu sauce
1 teaspoon cooking sake
potato starch (katakuriko), for coating

- **Basic stock**

2 litres (68 fl oz/8 cups) chicken stock or dashi
2 tablespoons soy sauce
2 tablespoons mirin
2 tablespoons cooking sake

- **Hot pot**

2 carrots, cut into asymmetrical, triangular chunks (Rangiri style)
10 shiitake mushrooms, stems removed and scored in a star pattern across the top
1 bunch spring onions (scallions), chopped
100 g (3½ oz) enoki mushrooms
500 g (1 lb 2 oz) firm tofu, cubed
½ head of Chinese cabbage (wombok), shredded

- **To serve**

¼ teaspoon yuzu koshō
shichimi togarashi (optional)

Start by making the tori dango. In a bowl, combine all the ingredients, except the potato starch, and mix thoroughly. Shape the mixture into small meatballs about 3 cm (1¼ in) in diameter then roll them in the potato starch prior to adding to the hot pot. This is crucial as it makes the outside of the meatballs soft and allows them to absorb the flavours of the stock. If you prefer, you can refrigerate the meatballs to firm them up a bit before cooking as the mixture is quite wet.

For the stock, bring the basic stock ingredients to the boil, then reduce the heat to a low simmer. Add the carrots, shiitake mushrooms, spring onion and meatballs. Cook for about 5 minutes, then add the enoki mushrooms and tofu. Cook for another 7–10 minutes, or until the carrots are cooked through, then add the cabbage and remove from the heat (the cabbage will cook in the residual heat).

Serve the hot pot with ¼ teaspoon of yuzu koshō on the meatballs for a citrusy/salty flavour. Add shichimi togarashi to the broth if you prefer a touch of chilli.

- **Note**

The carrots can be parboiled first to speed things up. However, the shiitake must be thoroughly cooked through until the texture becomes somewhat slimy.

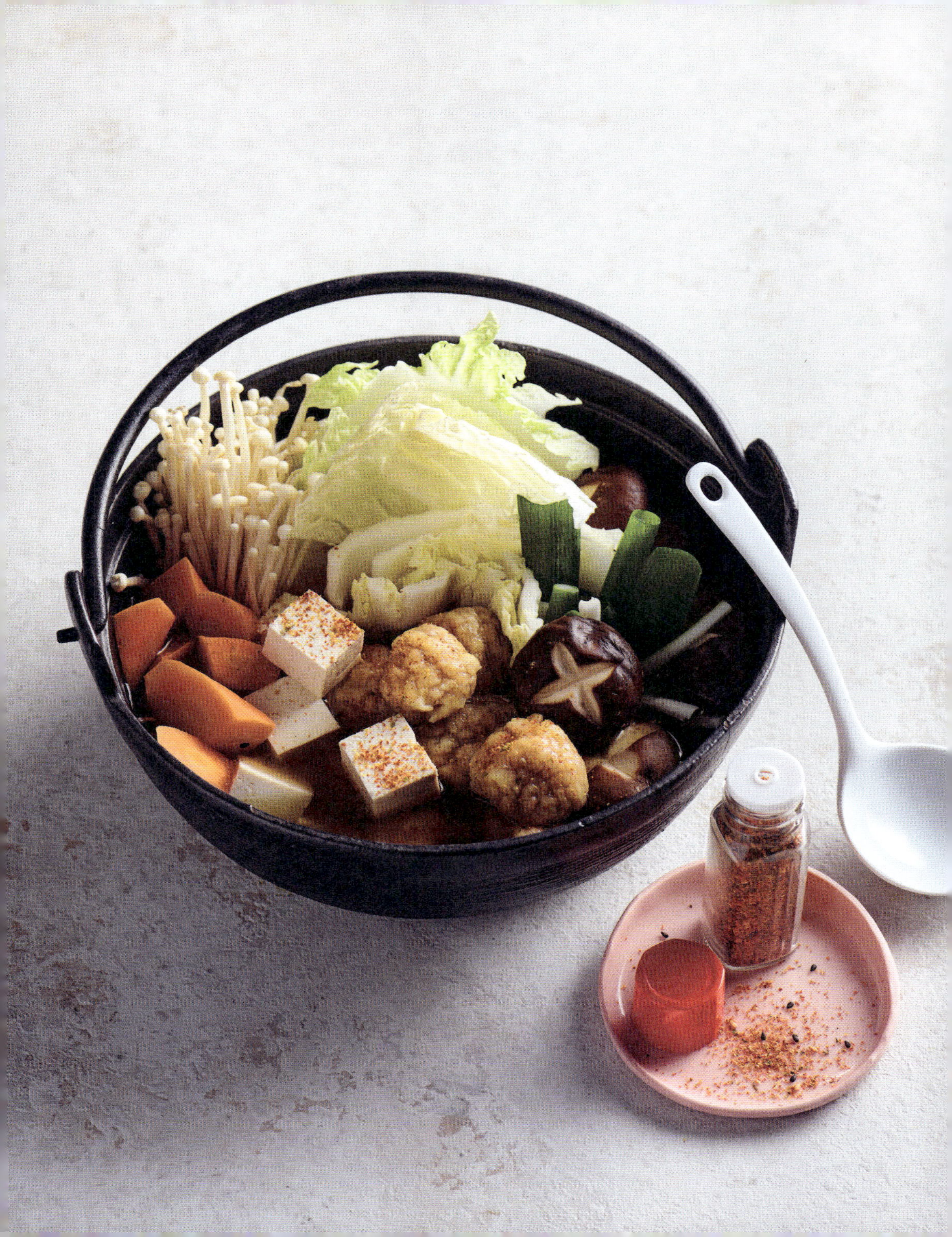

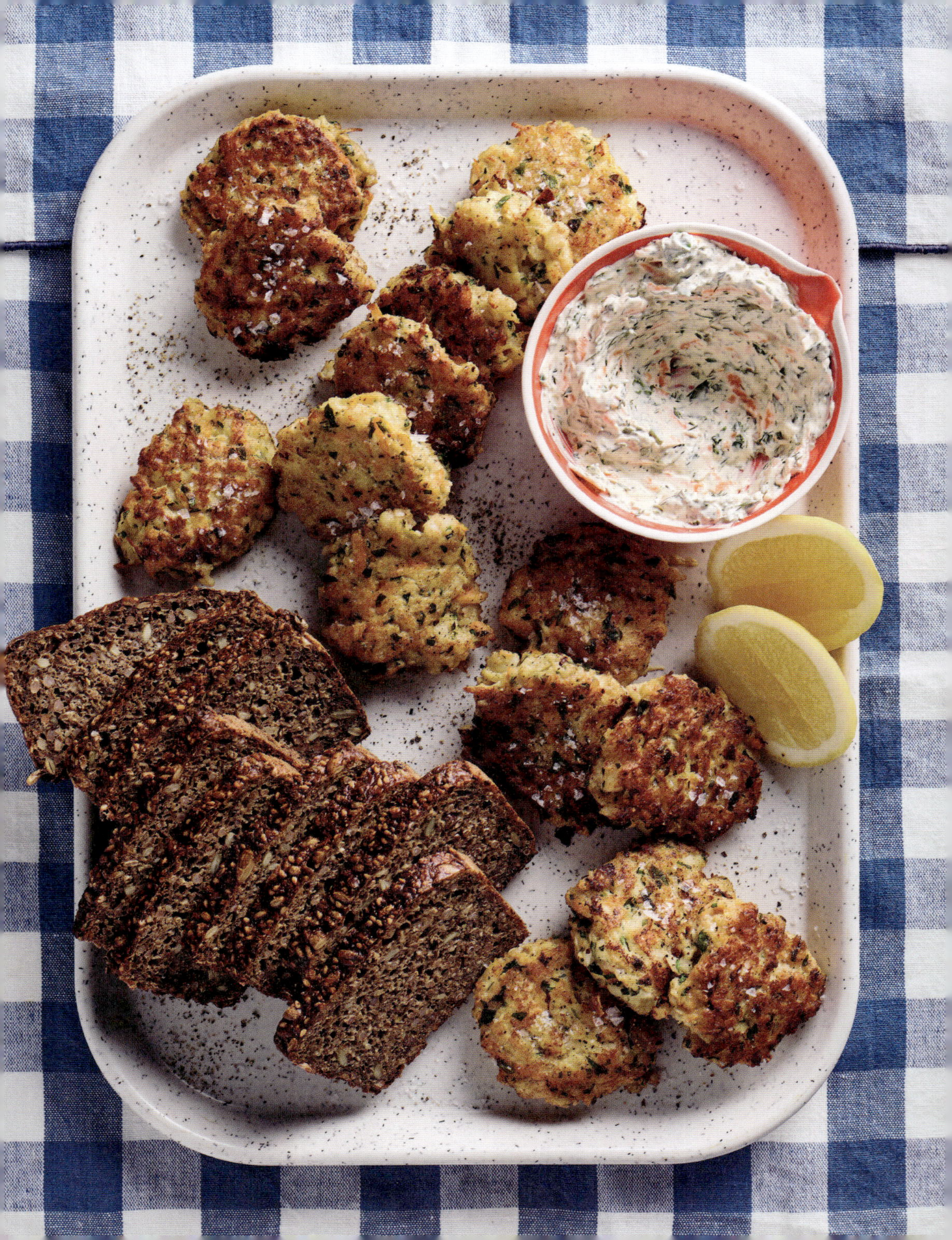

33
DENMARK

This interlude into the deep blue sea is brought to you by the Danes, who a) know a thing or two about what to do with fish, and b) know a thing or two about meatballs. Here, we have the perfect union of both in these light and lovely fish cakes and accompanying herb-loaded creamy sauce. They can be plated up with boiled potatoes or a fresh green salad, but for an off-the-rack Scandi experience, serve them with dark rye bread.

Fiskefrikadeller
DANISH FISH CAKES

SERVES 4–6

- **Meatballs**

600 g (1 lb 5 oz) firm white fish fillet of your choice, finely chopped
2 carrots, grated
1 onion, grated
7 g (¼ oz/¼ cup) parsley, finely chopped
2 tablespoons finely chopped tarragon
2 eggs, lightly beaten
100 ml (3½ fl oz) pouring (single/light) cream
70 g (2½ oz) rolled (porridge) oats
50 g (1¾ oz/⅓ cup) plain (all-purpose) flour
100 ml (3½ fl oz) soda water (club soda)
2 teaspoons sea salt flakes
freshly cracked black pepper
2 tablespoons salted butter
2–3 tablespoons olive oil
lemon slices, to serve

- **Sauce**

300 g (10½ oz) crème fraîche
3 carrots, coarsely grated
1 small bunch parsley, finely chopped
1 large bunch dill, finely chopped
zest of 1 small lemon
3 tablespoons lemon juice
salt and freshly cracked black pepper, to taste

- **To serve**

dark rye bread

Preheat the oven to 180°C (360°F). Combine the fish, carrot, onion, parsley, tarragon, eggs and cream in a large bowl and mix well. Add the rolled oats and plain flour and mix well again. Fold in the soda water (club soda) and season with the salt and some pepper.

Melt the butter with the olive oil in a large frying pan over a medium heat. Shape the mixture into fish patties about the size of golf balls, flatten slightly with your palm, and place them in the melted butter mixture. Fry for approximately 5 minutes on each side. Transfer the fried fish patties to an ovenproof dish and bake for about 10–15 minutes.

To make the sauce, combine the crème fraîche, carrot, parsley, dill and lemon zest in a bowl. Mix well and season with lemon juice, salt and pepper to taste.

Serve the fiskefrikadeller hot with the sauce, lemon slices and dark rye bread.

34
LEBANON

It is my strong contention that meatballs with any kind of yoghurt sauce on the side are one of the all-time greatest food pairings. This recipe goes one step further and unites them as one – 'on the side' be damned.

Kibbeh, an oval-shaped minced meat and burghul (bulgur wheat) ball, is a quintessential dish of the Levant; traditionally served on special occasions, its preparation is often a communal activity. The beauty of this dish is that it works wonderfully served cold or warm and lends itself particularly well to cold consumption on hot summer nights.

Kibbeh labanieh
MEATBALLS IN YOGHURT SAUCE

SERVES 4

- **Kibbeh casing**

500 g (1 lb 2 oz) burghul (bulgur wheat)
500 g (1 lb 2 oz) minced (ground) beef or lamb
1 onion, roughly chopped
½ teaspoon baharat or seven-spice
¾ tablespoon kamouneh spice mix (see Note)
¼ teaspoon freshly cracked black pepper
½ tablespoon salt
¾ tablespoon cornflour (cornstarch)
sunflower oil, for shaping

- **Kibbeh filling**

2 tablespoons olive oil
2 onions, chopped
125 g (4½ oz) minced (ground) lamb
125 g (4½ oz) minced (ground) beef
½ teaspoon baharat or seven-spice
¾ tablespoon kamouneh spice mix
¼ teaspoon freshly cracked black pepper
½ tablespoon salt
1 tablespoon sumac
80 g (2¾ oz/½ cup) pine nuts

Place the burghul in a bowl, cover with cold water and set aside.

To make the filling, heat the oil in a frying pan over a medium-low heat and sauté the onion until softened. Add the meat and cook over a medium-high heat for 6–8 minutes. Add the baharat, kamouneh spice, pepper and salt, breaking up the meat with the back of a wooden spoon. Once the meat is cooked, turn off the heat and add the sumac and pine nuts. Taste and adjust the seasoning if needed. Cover and set aside.

For the casing, drain the burghul and add it to a large bowl. Working in several batches, add the burghul to a food processor with equal amounts of meat and blend until it clumps together and starts to roll in the processor bowl. Remove and set aside in a large bowl.

Add the onion to the food processor with the baharat, kamouneh spice, pepper and salt. Blitz well. Add the blitzed onion spice mixture and cornflour to the burghul-meat mixture, then mix everything together with your hands. If the mix is too dry, add a bit of water. The mixture should hold together nicely, and not be too loose, sticky or crumbly. Adjust the salt if necessary.

Add some sunflower oil to a small bowl to dip your fingers into when shaping the kibbeh, to avoid sticking. Clean your workspace and arrange a workflow with a large, clean tray, the sunflower oil, the filling and the casing mixture. Shape the casing mixture into spheres the size of golf balls. Indent the middle of each sphere and hollow out the inside with your index finger until you have a half-shell. Add a spoon of the filling, closing up the casing around it. Compress well, and shape into a classic kibbeh shape.

- **Yoghurt sauce**

110 g (4 oz/½ cup) white short-grain rice (optional)
375 ml (12½ fl oz/1½ cups) boiling water
2 tablespoons cornflour (cornstarch)
1 teaspoon salt
1.5 kg (3 lb 5 oz) plain yoghurt
55 g (2 oz) salted butter
2–3 garlic cloves, finely chopped
1 handful coriander (cilantro) leaves, finely chopped
¼ teaspoon dried mint

Preheat the oven to 180°C (360°F).

If you're using rice in the yoghurt sauce, soak the rice in a bowl of water for 20 minutes, then drain and rinse under running water until the water runs clear. Add the rice and boiling water to a saucepan and simmer over a medium heat until cooked, about 20 minutes. Add the cornflour and salt to the yoghurt, stir well, then press through a fine-mesh sieve over the rice. Increase the heat to medium–high, stirring frequently to prevent burning. Bring to the boil, then lower the heat and simmer while you bake the kibbeh.

Put the kibbeh balls on a baking tray lined with baking paper and bake for 15 minutes, or until the outside turns slightly golden but not too brown. You only want to half-cook the kibbeh at this stage. Add the kibbeh to the yoghurt sauce and simmer for another 10 minutes.

Heat the butter in a small frying pan and sauté the garlic and coriander for a few minutes, then add this to the yoghurt sauce along with a pinch of dried mint. Stir well, adjust the salt if necessary, and turn off the heat.

Serve the kibbeh either hot or cold in small pasta bowls.

- **Note**

If you can't find kamouneh spice at the grocer, make your own by pulsing the following ingredients to a coarse texture in a blender or spice grinder: 2 tablespoons cumin seeds, 1 tablespoon dried rose petals, 1 tablespoon black peppercorns, 2 teaspoons dried marjoram, 2 teaspoons dried basil, 1 teaspoon dried mint, ½ teaspoon ground cinnamon, 1 tablespoon baharat or seven-spice and 1 teaspoon salt.

35
BRAZIL

Introduced to Brazilians by the Middle Eastern immigrants who arrived in the country in the late nineteenth century, you probably won't need Google to help you work out that 'kibe' is Portuguese for 'kibbeh'. A popular street food and bar snack in Brazil, these lend themselves to sunny afternoons and cold beers. Squeeze some lime over the top to finish.

Kibe
BURGHUL AND BEEF MEATBALLS

SERVES 4

- **Sauce**

1 tablespoon olive oil
18 truss tomatoes, peeled, seeded and roughly chopped, or 800 g (1 lb 12 oz) tinned chopped tomatoes
1 red chilli, seeded and finely chopped
2 tablespoons red-wine vinegar
2 teaspoons sugar
salt and freshly cracked black pepper, to taste

- **Kibe**

100 g (3½ oz) burghul (bulgur wheat)
boiling water, for soaking
500 g (1 lb 2 oz) minced (ground) beef
1 tablespoon vegetable oil, plus extra for pan-frying
½ small onion, finely chopped
2 garlic cloves, crushed
¼ teaspoon ground cinnamon
1 handful mint, finely chopped
1 handful parsley, finely chopped
½ teaspoon salt
½ teaspoon freshly cracked black pepper

- **To serve**

lime wedges

To make the sauce, heat the oil in a frying pan over a medium heat and cook the tomatoes and chilli for 2–3 minutes until they begin to soften. Stir in the red-wine vinegar and sugar and cook for another 5 minutes, crushing the tomato chunks as you go. Season to taste with salt and pepper. Leftover sauce will keep in an airtight container in the fridge for up to 5 days.

Put the burghul in a heatproof bowl and cover with boiling water. Cover the bowl with plastic wrap and leave to sit for 30 minutes, or until the burghul is completely tender.

Divide the beef into two portions, one weighing 100 g (3½ oz) and the other 400 g (14 oz). Set aside the larger portion. Heat the oil in a frying pan and cook the onion for a few minutes over a medium heat until softened, then stir in the smaller portion of meat and half the garlic. Cook until the beef is browned all over. Stir in the cinnamon, cook for 1 minute, then remove the pan from the heat and add half the mint, half the parsley, the salt and pepper. Allow to cool.

Drain the burghul, pressing it to remove as much excess water as possible. Add it to a large bowl with the remaining beef, garlic and herbs. Mix until well combined.

To make the kibe, shape the burghul mixture into spheres about the size of golf balls. Make a dent in the middle of each sphere and fill it with the cooked meat mixture, then press the burghul mixture over the top to seal it. Roll it into pointed oval shapes. Repeat with the rest of the mixture.

Add 1–2 cm (¾ in) of oil to a heavy-based frying pan over a medium heat. Cook the kibe in batches for 4–5 minutes on each side, or until they are cooked through, golden and crispy on the outside.

To serve, squeeze some lime wedges over the top of the kibe and serve with the sauce for dipping.

- **Note**

For instructions for how to peel tomatoes, see Notes on page 29.

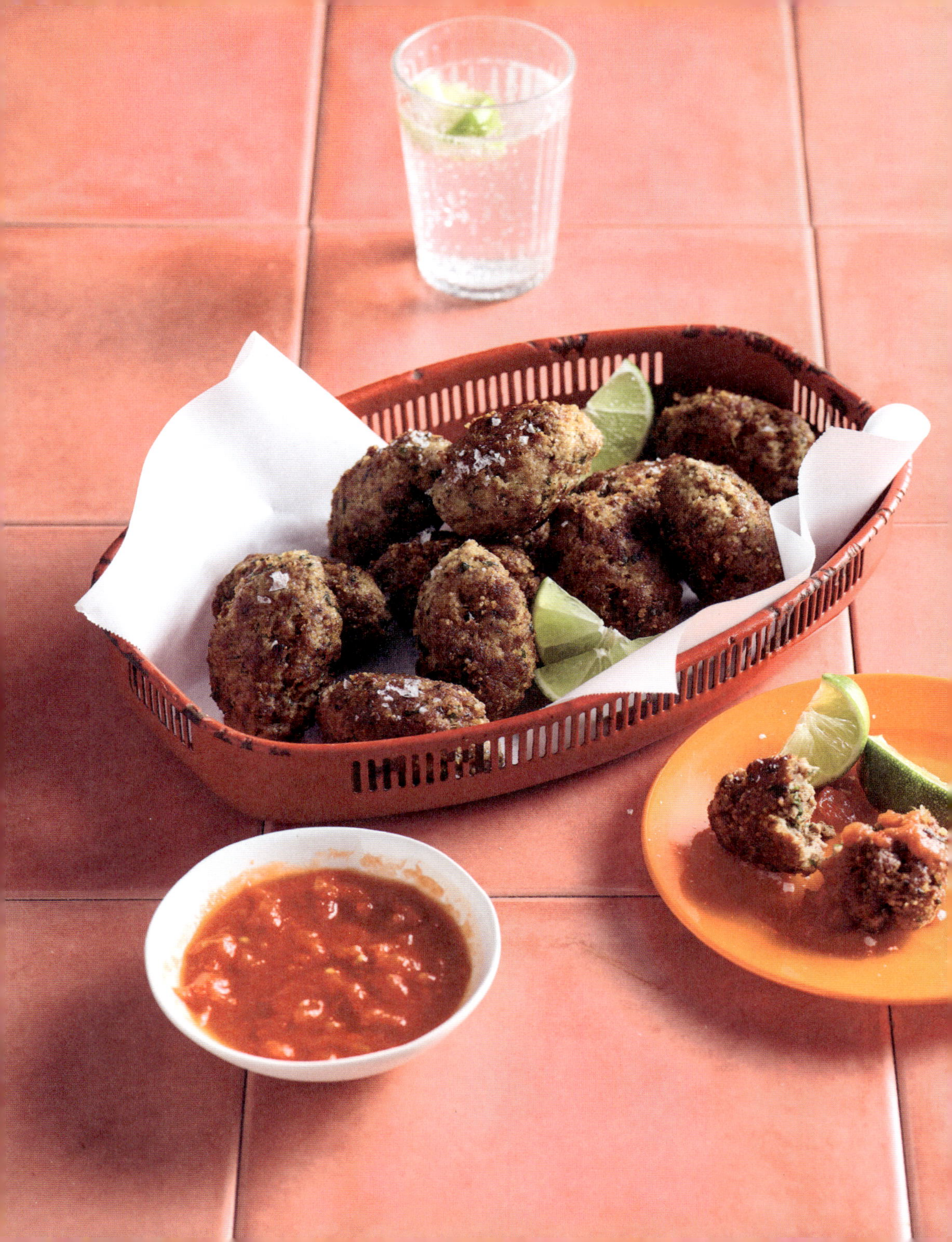

36 MOLDOVA

Moldova, a landlocked country hemmed in by Ukraine and Romania, combines all the best elements of the region in these parjoale, a beloved national staple. The stand-out feature here is the addition of the sautéed onions in the meatball mix, which gives the mixture a rich, umami depth.

Pair them with mujdei, a garlic dip common in both Moldova and Romania, for a nice sharp contrast. Given that Moldova is home to one of the world's largest underground wine cellars, Mileștii Mici, it would be improper not to enjoy a glass of red on the side, too.

Parjoale with mujdei
MEATBALLS WITH GARLIC DIPPING SAUCE

SERVES 6–8

● **Parjoale**
4–6 slices bread
150 ml (5 fl oz) full-cream (whole) milk
50 g (1¾ oz) salted butter
2 onions, finely chopped
2 garlic cloves, crushed
1 tablespoon mustard
1 teaspoon freshly cracked black pepper
60 g (2 oz) parsley, finely chopped
1 kg (2 lb 3 oz) minced (ground) beef and pork
1 egg
1 teaspoon salt
canola oil, for greasing and brushing

● **Mujdei**
6–8 garlic cloves
1 teaspoon salt
2 tablespoons vegetable oil
125 g (4½ oz/½ cup) sour cream

● **To serve**
mashed potato

Preheat the oven to 180°C (360°F). Grease a baking tray with oil and cover with baking paper.

For the parjoale, break the bread into small pieces and soak it in the milk until it becomes soft, then squeeze out any excess.

Melt the butter in a frying pan over a medium heat. Add the onion and sauté until golden and soft, then add the garlic and cook for another 1–2 minutes. Add the mustard, black pepper and parsley, then remove the pan from the heat and leave to cool slightly.

Combine the beef and pork, soaked and squeezed bread, sautéed onion and garlic mixture, egg and salt in a large bowl. Knead the mixture until well combined.

Shape the meat mixture into balls and place them on the tray. Brush with oil and bake for 25–30 minutes, or until cooked through.

To make the mujdei, use a mortar and pestle or food processor to grind the garlic and salt to a paste. Transfer to a bowl and add the vegetable oil, whisking until the mixture is fully combined and airy, then mix in the sour cream.

Serve the meatballs with mashed potato and mujdei on the side.

37

TUNISIA

Tunisian cuisine is a harmonious fusion of myriad culinary traditions, reflecting the multitudes of people who have inhabited, conquered and sought refuge within its borders; a list that includes Berbers, Romans, Greeks, Turks, Arabs, Italians, Spaniards and the French. Chebtiya are a brilliant example of this blend of Middle Eastern and European influences.

Chebtiya are often vegetarian, and these balls straddle the veggie/meat divide beautifully, loaded as they are with spinach (don't be alarmed by the large amount of spinach the recipe asks for – it shrinks dramatically when cooked). These are large but surprisingly light, and a genuinely off-the-beaten-track ball. For another meatball-adjacent Tunisian recipe, check out bantages: potato croquettes with a minced (ground) meat filling.

Chebtiya
HERBED GREEN MEATBALLS

SERVES 6

- **Meatballs**

2 small or 1 large onion, finely chopped
250–300 g (9–10½ oz) English spinach leaves, chopped
1 small bunch parsley, chopped
1 small bunch dill, chopped
½ teaspoon ground turmeric
1 teaspoon tabel karouia (Tunisian spice blend; see Notes)
1 egg
500 g (1 lb 2 oz) minced (ground) beef
1 tablespoon harissa
1 tablespoon tomato paste (concentrated puree)
40 g (1½ oz) couscous (see Notes)
salt and freshly cracked black pepper
olive oil, for pan-frying

- **Sauce**

1 large onion, chopped
4 carrots, peeled and sliced
125 ml (4 fl oz/½ cup) olive oil
3 tablespoons tomato paste (concentrated puree)
2 teaspoons harissa
1 teaspoon ground turmeric
1.5 litres (51 fl oz/6 cups) boiling water
salt and freshly cracked black pepper, to taste
160 g (5½ oz/1 cup) cooked chickpeas, rinsed and drained (tinned are fine)

- **To serve**

steamed couscous
fried hot green chillies (optional)

To prepare the meatballs, combine the onion, spinach, parsley, dill, turmeric, tabel karouia, egg, beef, harissa and tomato paste in a large bowl. Mix well and knead by hand for 5 minutes. Add the couscous, then mix again for about 10 minutes. Leave to rest for 10 minutes until the couscous is soaked, then mix again until firm.

Shape the mixture into large meatballs (about 9 or 10) and refrigerate for a few hours to allow the flavours to incorporate. After resting, add the salt and freshly cracked black pepper to taste.

While the meatballs are resting, prepare the sauce. In a large saucepan, fry the onion and carrot in the olive oil over a medium heat until soft. Add the tomato paste, harissa, turmeric, 185 ml (6 fl oz/¾ cup) boiling water and some salt and pepper. Cook over a high heat for 10 minutes, then add another 1.3 litres (44 fl oz) boiling water, reduce the heat to low and simmer gently for another 10–15 minutes while browning the meatballs.

Heat the olive oil in a frying pan and brown the meatballs for a few minutes on each side. Transfer the browned meatballs to the sauce and cook, turning after about 10 minutes, for a total of 15 minutes. Add the cooked chickpeas and allow to heat through for a few minutes. Taste and adjust the seasoning if needed.

Serve the meatballs with steamed couscous and, if desired, some fried hot green chillies.

- **Notes**

To make your own tabel karouia, dry-fry 3 tablespoons coriander seeds, 1 tablespoon caraway seeds and 1 tablespoon cumin seeds over a medium heat for about 2–3 minutes (see Note on page 97). Leave to cool completely, then grind to a fine powder with 1 teaspoon chilli flakes, using a mortar and pestle or spice grinder.

Use fine semolina couscous, not the larger pearl couscous, for this dish.

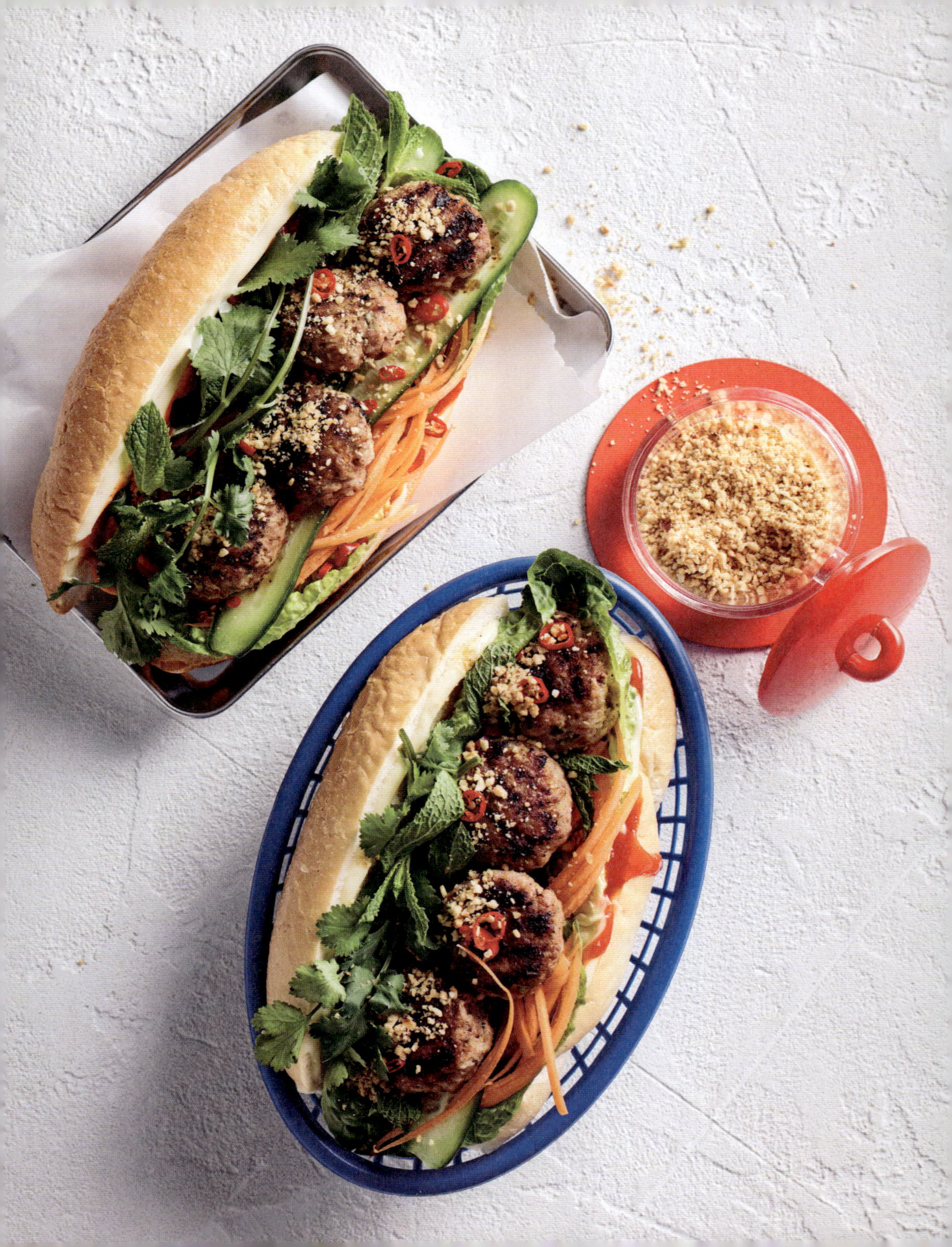

38
CAMBODIA

Num pang is a lot like Vietnamese banh mi, only cooler, because it's not as well known. Kroeung, a spice and herb paste starring lemongrass, galangal, garlic, and lime leaves, is the wonderfully forceful backbone of many Cambodian dishes. Here, it's mixed with minced pork to create a baguette bar none: think of it as anabolic banh mi. The two sandwiches may sing from a similar songbook, but it's the presence of kroeung that blasts num pang into a spicier stratosphere.

Num pang traditionally uses a denser baguette than banh mi, but no one is going to call the food police if you opt for a fluffier roll.

Num pang with pork meatballs

SERVES 4

- **Pickled carrots**

2 tablespoons sugar
120 ml (4 fl oz) rice vinegar
1 teaspoon fish sauce
⅛ teaspoon salt
3 carrots, peeled and cut into sticks

- **Kroeung paste**

1 × 3 cm (1¼ in) square shrimp paste, thinly sliced (see Notes)
2 tablespoons vegetable oil
3 lemongrass stems, hard outer layers removed, tender parts thinly sliced
2 shallots, peeled and finely chopped
50 g (1¾ oz) galangal, peeled and finely chopped
5 garlic cloves, finely chopped
8 makrut lime leaves, spines removed and finely shredded
1 tablespoon fish sauce

- **Meatballs**

500 g (1 lb 2 oz) minced (ground) pork

- **To serve**

3 tablespoons peanuts
4 baguettes
mayonnaise, to taste
sriracha sauce, to taste
coriander (cilantro) leaves, chopped, plus extra if desired
mint leaves, chopped, plus extra if desired
1 bird's eye chilli, finely sliced
6–8 cos (romaine) lettuce leaves
2 Lebanese (short) cucumbers, thinly sliced

To pickle the carrots, bring 125 ml (4 fl oz/½ cup) water and the sugar to a simmer in a small saucepan and cook until the sugar has dissolved. Remove from the heat and add the vinegar, fish sauce and salt. Place the carrot sticks in a heatproof bowl and pour the hot mixture over the top. Leave to cool, then cover the bowl with plastic wrap and refrigerate for 30 minutes.

Next, make the kroeung paste. Dry-fry the shrimp paste in a frying pan over a medium heat for approximately 15 minutes until dark on all sides (see Notes). Using a mortar and pestle, crush it to a powder-like consistency. Heat the oil in a frying pan over a medium heat, add the lemongrass, shallots, galangal, garlic and lime leaves. Cook for about 5 minutes, stirring until the mixture is just beginning to brown. Add the shrimp powder and cook for a further minute, then transfer the mixture to a blender with the fish sauce and blitz to a coarse paste.

Lightly toast the peanuts in a dry frying pan, taking care not to burn them. Allow to cool, then smash to a coarse powder in a mortar and pestle and set aside. Prepare the barbecue for direct cooking over a medium heat.

Combine the kroeung paste with the pork in a bowl and mix well. Divide the mixture evenly into 16 balls and flatten each one slightly into a patty. Grill the patties over direct heat on the barbecue for about 10 minutes, turning with tongs, until they've built up a caramelised crust on the outside and are cooked through.

To assemble the baguettes, spread each baguette with a little mayonnaise and sriracha. Add some of the meatballs, pickled carrots, herbs and chilli. Top with plenty of peanut powder. Serve with the lettuce leaves, cucumber and extra herbs, if desired.

- **Notes**

If measuring shrimp paste by weight, use approximately 10 g (¼ oz).

Dry-frying involves cooking food in a hot pan or wok with minimal oil or fat, using the fat already present in the food. This allows the food to dry out and develop a unique texture and flavour

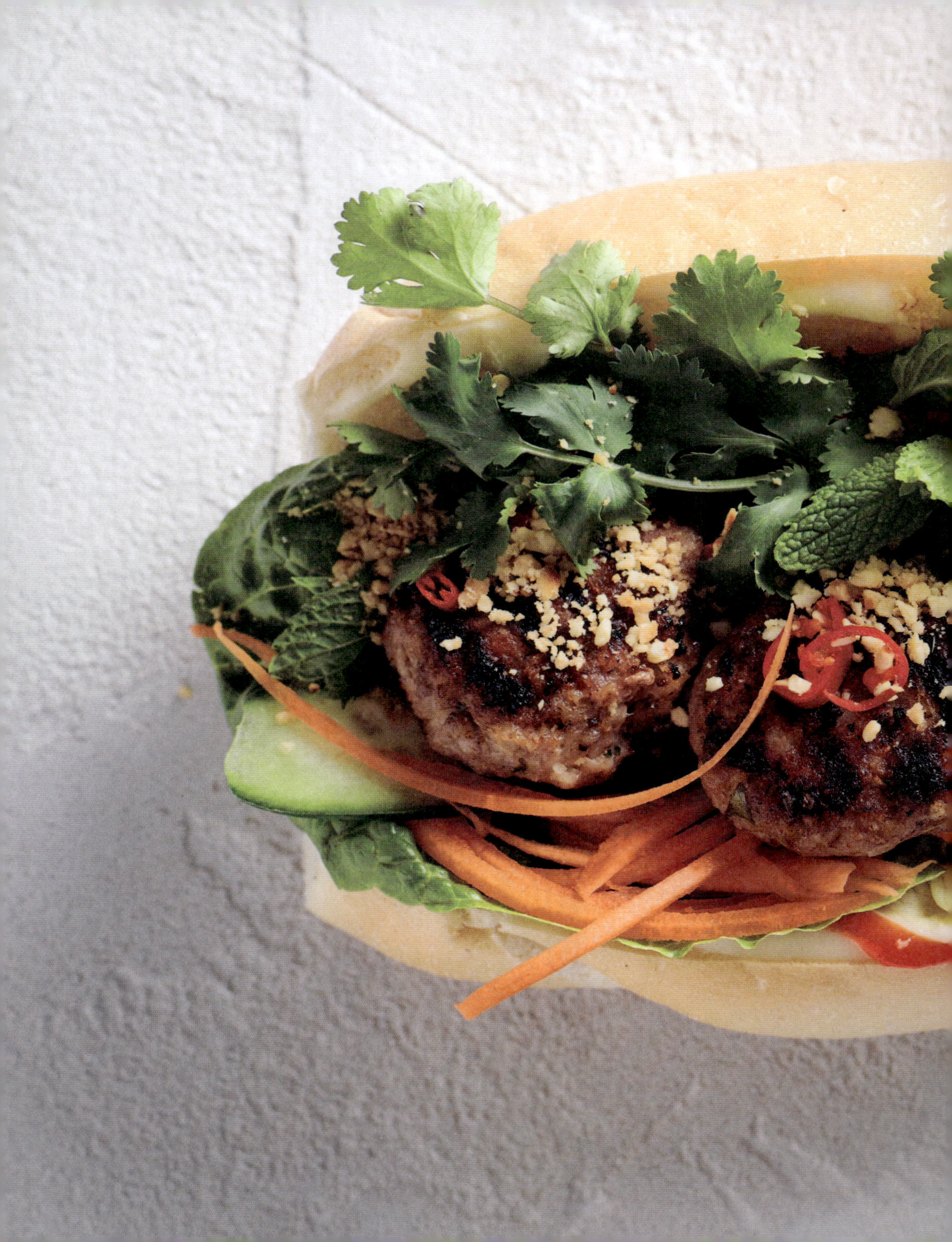

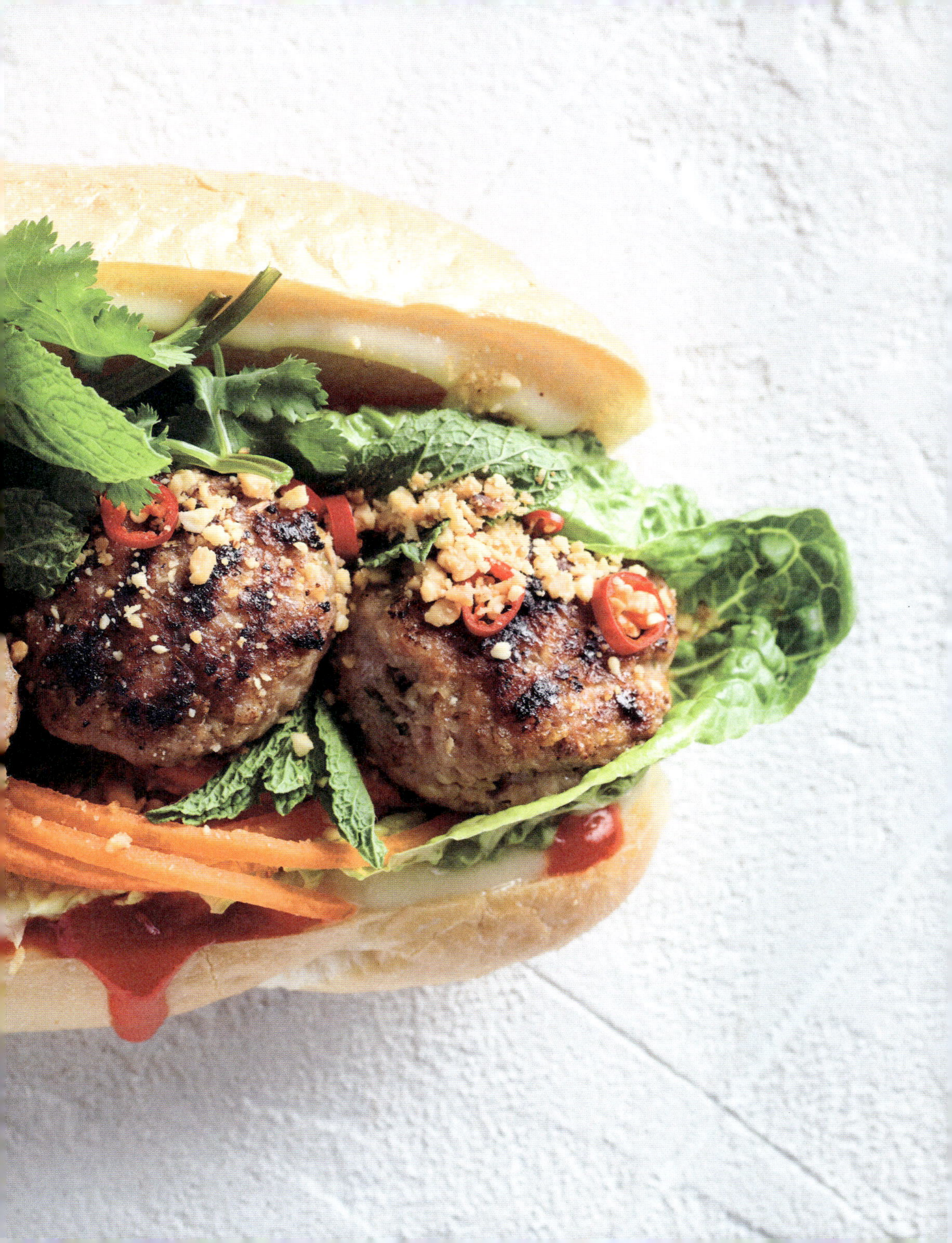

39
SERBIA

Translator Milica Stamenkovic was born in south Serbia, but for the last twenty-five years has called Belgrade home. She has zero tolerance for the snobbery and derision she so often hears directed at the people of south Serbia. 'We are ridiculed for our dialect, for being poor,' she says, and so this traditional south Serbian meatball dish represents for her not just the comfort of a beloved family recipe, but great pride in her place of birth, too.

According to Milica, the point of difference from other Balkan meatball recipes is all in the meat. 'The south of Serbia is well known for its barbecue, which is basically minced (ground) beef. Traditional preparation involves manually cutting the beef into very tiny pieces and preparing it on a wood grill, but you can also use a meat grinder. They use front parts – the neck, chuck, brisket, shank – mince it coarsely, season it with salt, then leave it to rest for 12–24 hours in temperatures under 4°C (39°F). They then mince it again finely until it becomes tender and elastic, like a dough. They add pepper and dried chilli flakes.'

If this sounds like a little more manual labour than time permits, rest assured that minced beef is an approved substitute – just ask your butcher to mince it on a finer grade.

Ćufte
SPICED BEEF MEATBALLS WITH TOMATO SAUCE

SERVES 4

● Meatballs
500 g (1 lb 2 oz) minced (ground) beef (see Notes)
1 egg
1 onion, very finely chopped
1 garlic clove, very finely chopped
2 tablespoons dry breadcrumbs
½ teaspoon sweet paprika
1 tablespoon vegetable oil
pinch of salt and freshly cracked black pepper

● Sauce
50 ml (1¾ fl oz) vegetable oil
3 teaspoons plain (all-purpose) flour
500 g (1 lb 2 oz/2 cups) passata (pureed tomatoes)
salt, to taste
1 tablespoon sugar
pinch of sweet paprika

● To serve
mashed potato (see Notes)

Mix all the meatball ingredients in a bowl and refrigerate for at least 30 minutes. Shape the mixture into small balls.

To make the sauce, warm the vegetable oil in a deep saucepan over a medium heat. Add the flour and stir continuously to prevent lumps, ensuring it does not brown. When the mixture turns slightly beige, add the passata and stir well. Gradually pour in 750 ml–1 litre (25½–34 fl oz/3–4 cups) water while stirring. Add salt to taste, followed by the sugar and paprika, then mix thoroughly.

Once the sauce starts boiling, add the meatballs one by one. Reduce the heat to low and simmer for about 40 minutes.

Serve the meatballs with mashed potato.

● Notes
If you do use coarsely minced (ground) meat that is elastic and homogenous, leave out the egg.

For a quicker option, make a thinner sauce by adding more water, then add potato wedges and simmer for 15 minutes, or until softened, then add the meatballs.

40
UNITED KINGDOM

You say tomato, I say tomato. You say meatball, I say faggot. There is no getting around it: this traditional British meatball dish certainly wasn't named with one eye on the social mores of the future. But we can safely assume that the name was not intended to be any sort of culinary slur; its name instead was taken from the old English word 'faggot' meaning 'bundle of sticks'. How the word came to be associated with this dish is not so clear, though it's most likely on account of the bundling together of the ingredients.

Enjoyed across the United Kingdom, but particularly in the English Midlands, and South and Mid Wales, it's a comfort food that attracts a variety of opinions. Also known by the much sweeter name of savoury ducks in Yorkshire, Lincolnshire and Lancashire, these hefty meatballs are traditionally made with offal and other discarded animal parts, but this recipe calls only for liver.

Faggots/savoury ducks with gravy

SERVES 6

- **Meatballs**

1 teaspoon vegetable oil, for greasing
170 g (6 oz) packet sage and onion stuffing mix
425 ml (14½ fl oz) boiling water
500 g (1 lb 2 oz) diced pork shoulder
300 g (10½ oz) pig liver
½ teaspoon ground mace
1 teaspoon salt
freshly cracked black pepper

- **Gravy**

1 tablespoon sunflower oil
2 onions, thinly sliced
2 teaspoons sugar
1 tablespoon red-wine vinegar
3 tablespoons plain (all-purpose) flour
850 ml (28½ fl oz) beef stock

- **To serve**

7 g (¼ oz/¼ cup) parsley, chopped
mashed potato
vegetables of your choice

Preheat the oven to 160°C (320°F). Lightly grease a large roasting tin with vegetable oil. Empty the stuffing mix into a large bowl, pour in the boiling water, stir, then set aside.

Pulse the diced pork shoulder in a food processor until finely chopped. Add the liver and pulse again until combined. Transfer to the bowl with the stuffing mix, then add the ground mace, salt and plenty of black pepper. Mix thoroughly. Shape the mixture into 24 large faggots and place them in the prepared tin.

For the gravy, heat the oil in a frying pan over a medium heat and fry the sliced onion until beginning to turn golden. Add the sugar and continue to cook, stirring frequently, until the onions are caramelised. Pour in the red-wine vinegar and allow it to sizzle. Mix the flour with 2 tablespoons of water to form a slurry. Pour the beef stock into the onion mix, then add the slurry, stirring constantly until the gravy is smooth and begins to thicken.

Once the gravy has thickened, pour it over the faggots in the roasting tin. Cover the tin with foil and bake for 1 hour until the faggots are fully cooked. Before serving, sprinkle with chopped parsley.

Serve with mashed potato and vegetables.

41

60

41. **PAKISTAN** Gola kabab with charred onions   106

42. **MEXICO** Sopa de albondigas   109

43. **LIBYA** M'battan   110

44. **FINLAND** Lihapullat   112

45. **THAILAND** Jok moo   113

46. **IRAN (PERSIA)** Koofteh berenji   115

47. **MYANMAR (BURMA)** A-thar-lohn-hin   116

48. **IRAN (PERSIA)** Fesenjoon   118

49. **IRAN (PERSIA)** Ash-e anar   119

50. **ITALY (CAMPANIA)** Polpette in sugo   121

51. **LATVIA** Kotlete in gravy   124

52. **INDONESIA** Bakso   127

53. **BOSNIA** Sogan dolma   128

54. **CHINA (UYGHUR)** Vermicelli meatball soup   130

55. **AUSTRIA** Faschierte laibchen   131

56. **LEBANON** Kafta with tarator sauce and tabbouleh   133

57. **CANADA** Ragoût de boulettes   134

58. **ITALY** Minestra maritata   139

59. **ALGERIA** Kefta b'zeitoun   140

60. **AFGHANISTAN** Korme kofta   141

41
PAKISTAN

Pakistan is teeming with A+ meatball offerings, and these smoky spheres are among the very best I've ever had.

Gola kabab are not 'kebabs' as you might know them. 'Gola' means 'spherical', so it's a skewer-free situation, but you will be making a hole in the middle of each ball with whatever's at hand – the end of a fork, a wooden spoon handle – which helps them to cook quickly and evenly and infuses them with smoke from the charcoal. Don't panic if you can't get your hands on a lump of coal; these meatballs are so boldly flavourful, very little is lost if that step is skipped.

These meatballs are commonly served at weddings in Pakistan, but I would not want to wait for a set of nuptials to enjoy these smoky gems again.

Gola kabab with charred onions

SERVES 4

- 500 g (1 lb 2 oz) minced (ground) beef
- ¾ tablespoon ginger paste
- ¾ tablespoon garlic paste
- 3–6 green chillies, blended to a paste
- 1¼ tablespoons papaya paste (optional; see Notes)
- 2 tablespoons chopped coriander (cilantro) leaves
- 25 g (1 oz/⅓ cup) fried onion
- 1 tablespoon ghee, plus extra if needed
- 1 teaspoon salt
- 1 teaspoon garam masala
- 1 teaspoon red chilli powder
- 1 teaspoon ground coriander
- ½ teaspoon ground ginger
- ¼ teaspoon ground turmeric
- small pinch of ground mace
- small pinch of freshly grated nutmeg
- ½ teaspoon ground allspice
- 1–2 tablespoons besan (chickpea flour), if needed
- 1 piece of coal, for smoking (optional; see Notes)
- vegetable oil, for pan-frying

● **To serve**
- charred onions and chillies
- paratha (flatbreads)
- green chutney (optional)

Combine all the ingredients in a food processor and process until combined. Check if you can easily shape the mixture into a kabab. If the mix is too soft, add 1–2 tablespoons besan (chickpea flour). If it is too dry, add an extra 1 tablespoon of ghee or yoghurt. Fry a small piece of the meat mixture in a little oil, then taste and adjust the flavours and seasoning as needed.

Transfer the mixture to a heatproof bowl with a lid or cover it with a plate. Take a piece of coal and heat it on the stovetop – directly over the flame for a gas stove, or on a rack for a ceramic cooktop.

Place an onion peel or a piece of foil on top of the meat mix in the bowl. Once the coal is hot, place it on top of the peel and drizzle a little oil on it. It will immediately smoke up. Cover the bowl and leave to sit for 15 minutes to let the smoke fully infuse the meat.

Grease your hands and whatever you are using for shaping (a skewer, the end of a spoon, a straw, or even your finger) with a little oil. Shape the mixture into 5 cm (2 in) long kababs and use the shaping tool to create a hole in the middle. Once firm and shaped, carefully slide the kabab off. Repeat with the remaining mixture.

Heat a large frying pan over a medium heat and add enough oil to cover the base. Once hot, add the meatballs, ensuring they do not touch. Let the bottom brown for about 6 minutes, then flip the meatballs over and brown the other side. Cover the pan and cook for another 3–6 minutes, or until the meatballs are cooked through. If they are browning too quickly, reduce the heat.

Serve the kababs on a bed of charred onions and chillies, with paratha (flatbreads) and green chutney, if desired.

● **Notes**

Papaya paste is available in Asian and Middle Eastern grocers, but if you can't access this ingredient, just leave it out – the end result will still be delicious.

If charcoal is not available, you can omit the smoking step and proceed with shaping and cooking the kababs directly. Be careful not to overcook them.

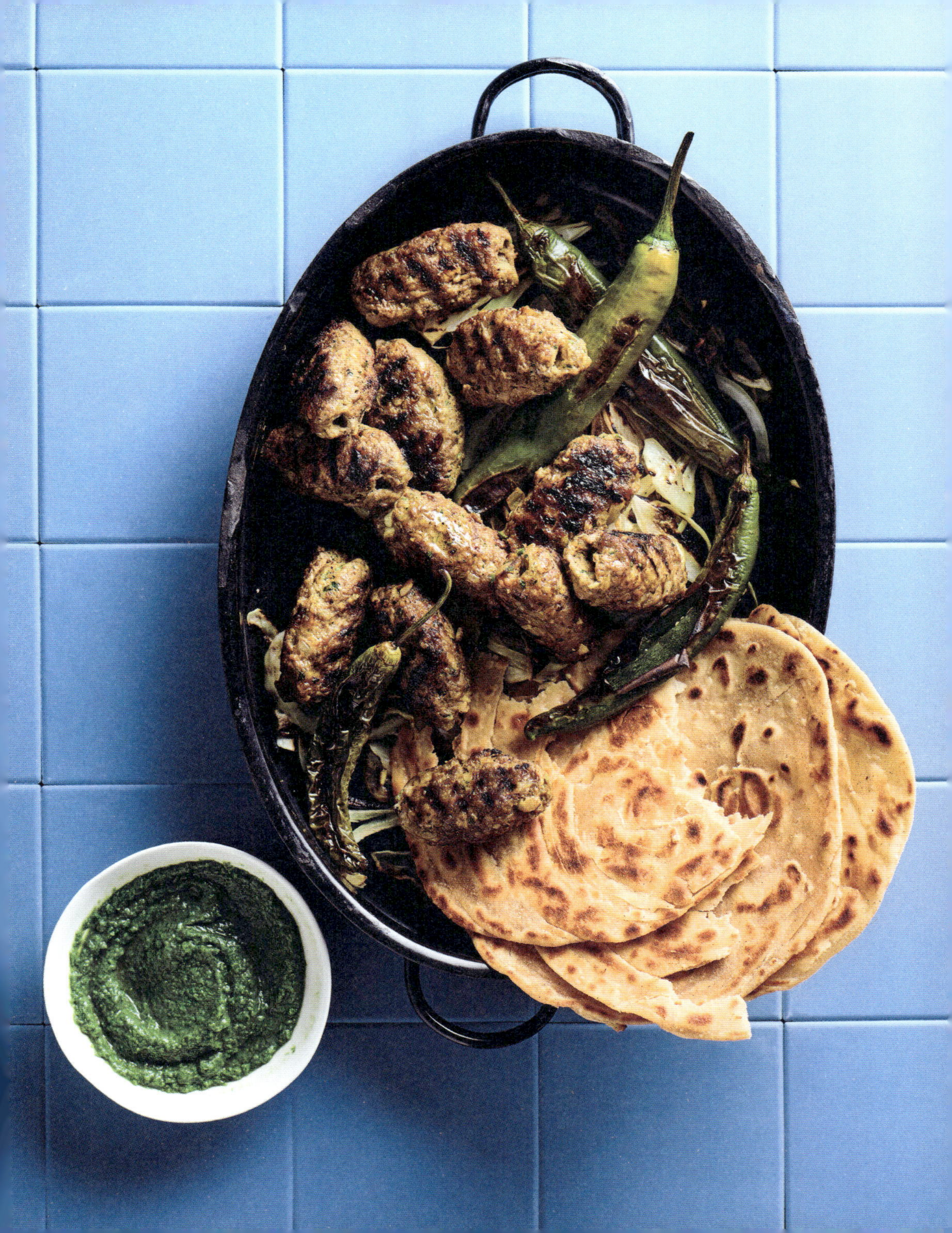

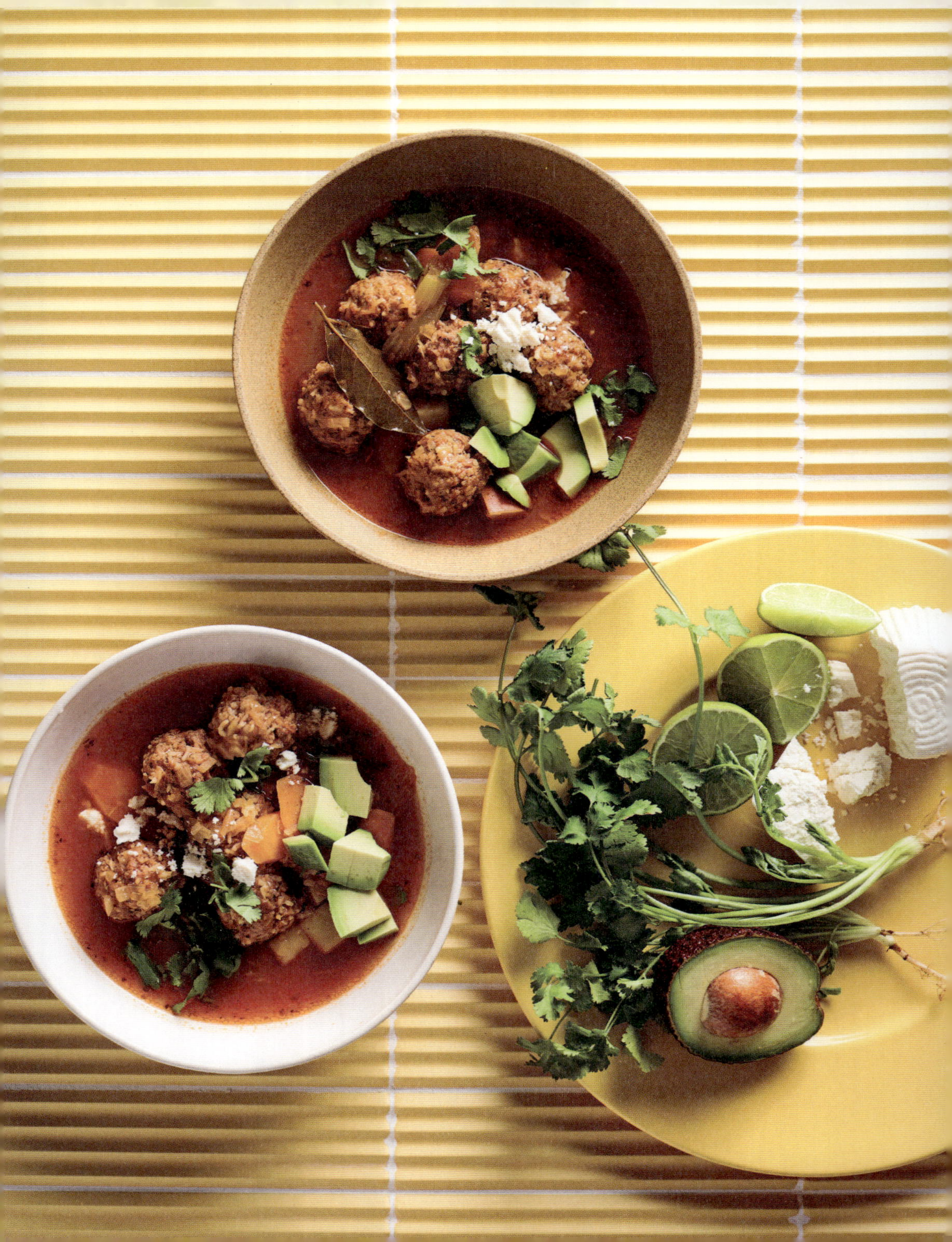

42
MEXICO

There are approximately eight billion people in the world, and 7.9 billion of them, it would seem, have pretty strong opinions on what constitutes an authentic sopa de albondigas, a traditional Mexican meatball soup; some argue strenuously that potato has no place, others insist it does (I will always err on the side of the potato).

This version includes easily accessible ingredients; choko (chayote), a type of squash common in Mexico but harder to access in other regions (hello, Australia), is often a component of authentic sopa de albondigas, as is Mexican oregano.

Sopa de albondigas

SERVES 6–8

- **Meatballs**

900 g (2 lb) minced (ground) beef
450 g (1 lb) minced (ground) pork
90 g (3 oz) white long-grain rice
20 g (¾ oz/⅓ cup) mint, chopped
3 garlic cloves, minced
1 tablespoon salt
1 teaspoon freshly cracked black pepper

- **Soup**

2 tablespoons olive or vegetable oil
1 onion, diced
4 carrots, peeled and cut into 1 cm (½ in) diagonal slices
3 celery stalks, peeled and cut into 1 cm (½ in) diagonal slices
1 large red potato, cut into 2.5 cm (1 in) cubes
3 tablespoons tomato paste (concentrated puree)
3 garlic cloves, minced
2 bay leaves
2 teaspoons dried oregano
2 teaspoons ground cumin
2 litres (68 fl oz/8 cups) chicken or vegetable stock
227 g (8 oz) passata (pureed tomato)
salt and freshly cracked black pepper, to taste

- **To garnish**

crumbled queso fresco, queso panela or queso cotija
2 avocados, halved and thinly sliced
habanero chillies, very thinly sliced
fresh coriander (cilantro) leaves, roughly chopped
lime wedges, for squeezing

Start by making the meatballs. Combine all the ingredients in a large bowl and mix gently until well combined. Shape the mixture into meatballs about the size of a golf balls, then transfer them to a large rectangular baking tray.

For the soup, heat the olive oil in a large saucepan over a medium–high heat. Add the onion, carrot, celery and potato, and season with salt and pepper. Cook for 5 minutes, stirring occasionally until the vegetables have softened slightly, then add the tomato paste, garlic, bay leaves, oregano and cumin. Cook, stirring frequently, until the tomato paste starts to caramelise, about 3 minutes. Add the chicken stock and passata and bring to a simmer over a high heat.

Once the sauce begins to bubble, reduce the heat to medium-low. Carefully add the meatballs, one by one, distributing them evenly in the pot. If necessary, reduce the heat to maintain a low simmer until the meatballs and rice are cooked through, about 40 minutes. Avoid stirring for the first 20 minutes so the meatballs don't break apart before they've firmed up. Season to taste with salt.

Divide the soup between serving bowls, with 4–5 meatballs per portion, and set out bowls of optional garnishes, such as crumbled cheese, sliced avocado, sliced chilli, coriander and lime wedges.

43

LIBYA

This is another meatball-in-fancy-dress inclusion; not strictly spherical, it's helpful to think of it as a meatball slider, with the 'slider' made not of bread, but potato. Do I have your attention now? Commonly prepared for Ramadan, this Libyan comfort treat requires a little practice to correctly cut the potatoes, but the rewards make it well worth the fiddle. Make sure you have a good sharp knife to work with and some extra potatoes to allow for a few botched attempts. They should be sliced thickly, then slit down the middle, but not all the way through; just enough to fill them with the meat mixture. Once you get the hang of this, the rest of the prep is a breeze.

M'battan
FRIED POTATO SANDWICHES WITH MEATBALL FILLING

SERVES 6

- **Potato pouches**

6–8 large floury potatoes
vegetable oil, for deep-frying

- **Meat stuffing**

500 g (1 lb 2 oz) minced (ground) beef or lamb
1 bunch spring onions (scallions), finely chopped
20 g (¾ oz) parsley, finely chopped, plus extra to serve
30 g (1 oz) coriander (cilantro) leaves, finely chopped, plus extra to serve
1 garlic clove, finely grated
1 teaspoon grated fresh ginger
1 teaspoon freshly cracked black pepper
1 teaspoon ground cinnamon
1 tablespoon salt
1 chilli, finely chopped (optional)
1 egg, beaten
15 g (½ oz) fresh breadcrumbs, soaked in water or milk
1 tablespoon tomato paste (concentrated puree)

- **Coating**

55 g (2 oz/⅔ cup) fine dry breadcrumbs
60 g (2 oz) plain (all-purpose) flour
4 eggs, beaten

For the potato pouches, soak the potatoes in a bowl of hot water to soften them.

While the potatoes are soaking, combine all the ingredients for the meat stuffing in a large bowl until evenly incorporated.

Peel the softened potatoes, cut in half lengthways and then cut thick slices out of them, down the middle of the flat side, without cutting all the way through. Carefully fill each potato pouch with the meat stuffing.

Make the coating by mixing the breadcrumbs and flour together. Dip the meat-stuffed potatoes into the beaten egg, then coat them in the breadcrumb–flour mixture, ensuring they are well covered.

Preheat the oven to 175°C (345°F).

Heat enough vegetable oil for deep-frying in a saucepan until it reaches approximately 165°C (330°F) on a cooking thermometer. Deep-fry the stuffed potato slices until golden, about 5 minutes each. Remove and set aside on paper towels to drain the excess oil. Transfer the fried potatoes on a baking tray lined with baking paper and bake for 5–10 minutes.

Serve the potato pouches on a platter garnished with parsley or coriander.

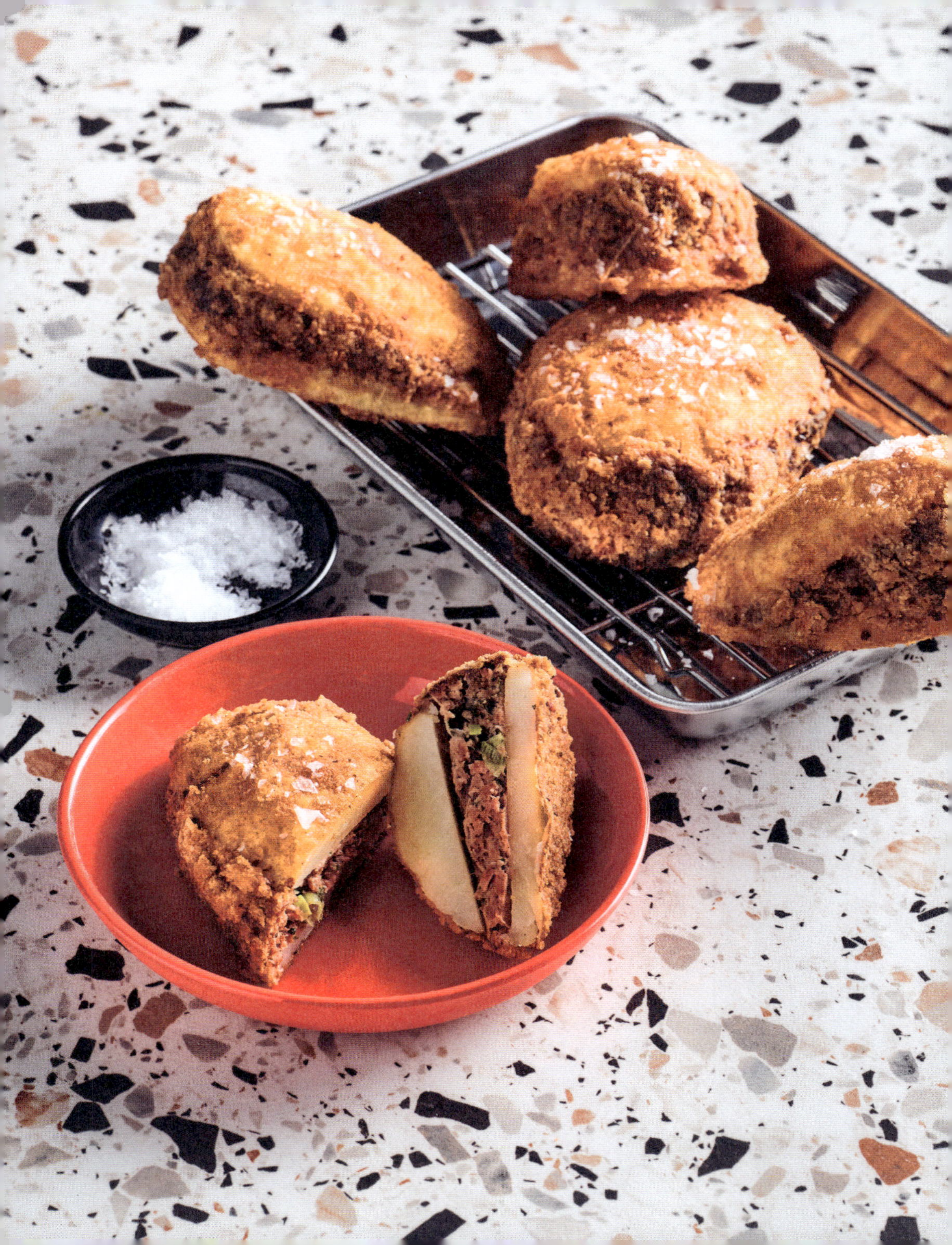

44

FINLAND

Closely related to their Swedish cousins, Kottbullar (page 175), I love these meatballs for a few reasons: the name, which makes me think of an architecturally impressive doll's house, and the lighter quality that comes with being both baked and gravy-free. If your doctor has told you to cut down on cholesterol and you cannot face a life without Scandi balls, these lihapullat might be a good alternative. (Just don't tell the doc about the cream component; what's a few tablespoons between friends, anyway?)

Lihapullat
NORDIC BAKED MEATBALLS

SERVES 4–6

3 tablespoons vegetable oil
1 small onion, finely chopped
500 g (1 lb 2 oz) minced (ground) beef
70 g (2½ oz) dry breadcrumbs, soaked in water or milk to soften
1 egg
80 ml (2½ fl oz/⅓ cup) thick (double/heavy) cream
1 teaspoon minced garlic
¼ teaspoon ground allspice
1½ teaspoon salt
¼ teaspoon freshly cracked black pepper

● **To serve**
rye bread or mashed potato
lingonberry jam

Preheat the oven to 200°C (390°F). Line a large baking tray with baking paper.

Heat 1 tablespoon of the oil in a frying pan over a medium heat and pan-fry the onion until soft and translucent but not overly browned.

Combine the fried onion, beef, breadcrumbs, egg, cream, minced garlic, allspice, salt and pepper in a large bowl and mix well. A fork works well to break up the beef in the process.

Shape the mixture into meatballs about the size of golf balls, then place them on the baking tray, leaving a little space between each. Add the remaining 2 tablespoons of oil to a small bowl. Using a pastry brush, brush the top and sides of each meatball with the oil. Bake for 25 minutes, or until the meatballs are cooked through and golden brown.

Serve warm with rye bread or mashed potato and lingonberry jam.

45
THAILAND

How early is too early in the day for balls? Thailand has an agreeable answer to this question: never. Jok moo, aka rice congee with pork meatballs, is traditionally eaten for breakfast, but there's nothing stopping you from having it for lunch, or as a premium iteration of 'breakfast for dinner'. After trying this recipe, you'll never again eat a bowl of cornflakes at 7pm*.

If you want to supercharge the protein content, try cracking a raw egg into your jok while it's piping hot; it will cook as you stir it in.

*You might.

Jok moo
RICE CONGEE WITH PORK MEATBALLS

SERVES 4

- **Meatballs**

225 g (8 oz) minced (ground) pork
1 teaspoon fish sauce
1 teaspoon light soy sauce
½ teaspoon sugar
generous pinch of ground white pepper

- **Rice porridge**

1.5 litres (51 fl oz/6 cups) chicken stock
600 g (1 lb 5 oz) cooked jasmine rice
1 tablespoon fish sauce
2 tablespoons Thai soy sauce (see Notes)
¼ teaspoon ground white pepper

- **To garnish**

3 spring onions (scallions), chopped
½ bunch coriander (cilantro) leaves, chopped
1 tablespoon finely julienned ginger
fried garlic (store-bought is fine; see Notes)

To make the pork meatballs, combine all the ingredients in a large bowl and mix well. Shape into small meatballs then set aside.

To make the rice porridge, bring the chicken stock to the boil in a saucepan. Drop the pork balls into the stock and cook for about 5 minutes, or until firm to the touch and cooked through. Set aside until ready to serve.

Reduce the stock to a medium heat, add the cooked rice and bring back to a simmer. Cover and cook for 10–15 minutes, until the mixture resembles a loose porridge with the grains of rice soft but still intact. Season with the fish sauce, soy sauce and white pepper. You can add salt to taste, but the mixture will already be quite salty.

To serve, ladle the rice porridge into bowls, top with the meatballs and garnish with the spring onion, coriander, ginger and fried garlic.

- **Notes**

Thai soy sauce is available from Asian supermarkets and can be substituted with kecap manis (sweet soy sauce).

Ready-fried garlic is available from Asian supermarkets. If unavailable, you can fry thin slices of fresh garlic in oil until lightly browned then drain on paper towel.

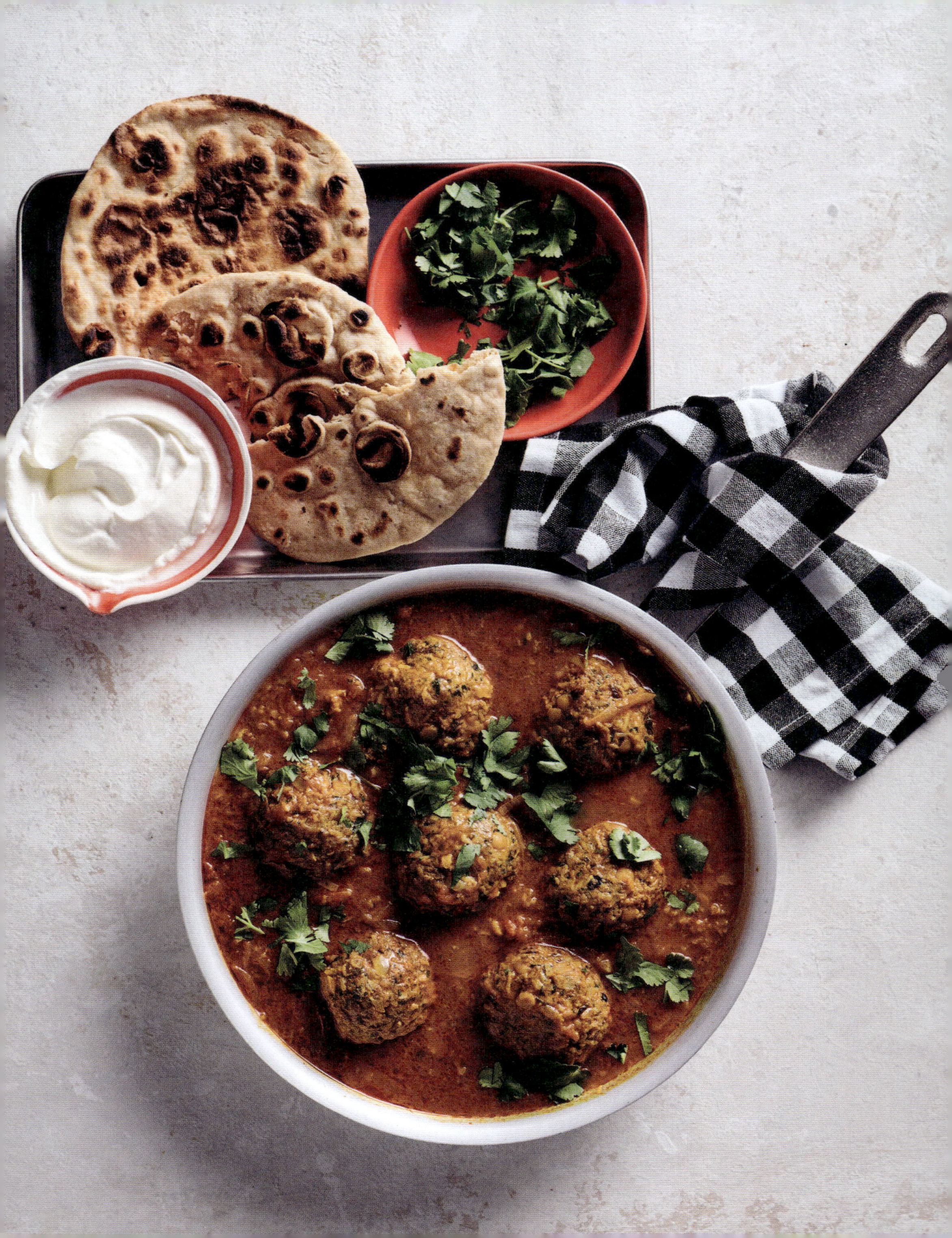

46
IRAN (PERSIA)

Persia is one of only a handful of regions, along with Ancient Rome and Greece, that can legitimately claim to have midwifed the meatball into the world – so when they say 'put berries into your koftas', you best listen. That being said, I have to confess: I do not usually appreciate the combination of fruit and meat, but I relax my stance where koofteh are concerned. Barberries are readily available at Middle Eastern and independent grocers, but cranberries will do in a pinch.

Koofteh berenji
RICE MEATBALLS IN SPICED TOMATO SAUCE

SERVES 4

- **Koofteh**

2.75 litres (93 fl oz/11 cups) boiling water
150 g (5½ oz/¾ cup) basmati rice
100 g (3½ oz) yellow split peas
500 g (1 lb 2 oz) minced (ground) lamb
1 small bunch parsley, finely chopped
1 small bunch dill, finely chopped
1 small bunch fresh chives, destemmed and finely snipped
1 small bunch coriander (cilantro) leaves, finely chopped
3 tablespoons plain (all-purpose) flour
1 teaspoon ground turmeric
1 large onion, finely chopped
2 handfuls barberries, finely chopped
3 eggs
salt and freshly cracked black pepper

- **Sauce**

olive oil, for pan-frying
1 large onion, thinly sliced into half-moons
1 teaspoon ground turmeric
3 garlic cloves, crushed
2 tablespoons passata (pureed tomatoes)
400 g (14 oz) tinned chopped tomatoes

- **To serve**

extra fresh herbs, roughly chopped
plain yoghurt
flatbreads

Pour 1 litre (34 fl oz/4 cups) boiling water into a large saucepan over a medium–high heat. Season with salt, then add the rice and boil for 7 minutes. Drain, then set aside to cool. Repeat the process, cooking the yellow split peas in 1.7 litres (57 fl oz) boiling water in the same pan. Season with salt, bring to the boil, then reduce the heat to medium and cook for 25 minutes. Drain, then set aside to cool.

Combine the cooled rice and split peas, the meat, herbs, flour, turmeric, onion, barberries, eggs and salt and pepper in a large bowl. Mix well, then shape the mixture into large, oval-shaped meatballs.

To make the sauce, add enough oil to coat the base of a flameproof casserole dish and fry the sliced onion over a medium–low heat for 6–8 minutes, or until it begins to brown. Add the turmeric and garlic and fry for another 2–3 minutes. Add the passata and salt and pepper to taste and stir well.

Pour 1 litre (34 fl oz/4 cups) water into the pot, add the chopped tomatoes and bring to the boil. Lower each meatball carefully into the pot, partially cover the pot with the lid and cook gently over a medium–low heat for 1¼–1½ hours.

To serve, bring the pot to the table, scatter the fresh herbs over the meatballs and serve with yoghurt and flatbreads.

47

MYANMAR (BURMA)

This dish is popular all over Burma, but particularly in the upper regions, and the higher through the country you travel, the more likely it is that A-thar-lohn-hin will feature pork. Also often made with goat, this is a go-with-the-flow kind of dish, easily permitting you to make your own call on the question of lamb, beef or pork. Lamb is particularly well suited to the dish, albeit uncommonly used in Burma for a simple reason: the Burmese word for 'lamb' sounds perilously similar to the Burmese word for 'rotten', a word devoid of positive connotations, particularly in the dining arena.

Traditionally served with steamed rice, it's also great with naan. Burmese cuisine makes concessions to multiple surrounding regions, such as China, India, Thailand and Bangladesh, and this recipe incorporates all the best of them, well deserving of a star on the meatball walk of fame.

A-thar-lohn-hin
BURMESE MEATBALL CURRY

SERVES 4

- **Sauce**

80 ml (2½ fl oz/⅓ cup) canola or vegetable oil
4 onions, very finely diced
2 garlic cloves, finely chopped
1 teaspoon ground turmeric
400 g (14 oz) tinned chopped tomatoes
3 red chillies, finely chopped (see Notes)
1 tablespoon sweet paprika
2 tablespoons fish sauce

- **Meatballs**

500 g (1 lb 2 oz) minced (ground) lamb, beef or pork
1 onion, minced
1 bunch coriander (cilantro), stalks minced, leaves to garnish
1 heaped tablespoon tapioca flour
1 egg white
1 teaspoon salt
1 vegetable stock (bouillon) cube

- **To serve**

steamed rice or naan bread

To make the sauce, heat the oil in a large frying pan over a medium heat and fry the onion (see Notes), garlic and turmeric for about 5 minutes, then add the tomatoes. Fry for another 10 minutes, then add 825 ml (28 fl oz/3¼ cups) of water. Bring to the boil, then reduce the heat to medium–low. Add the chillies, paprika and fish sauce, and simmer for 45 minutes.

Meanwhile, combine all the meatball ingredients in a large bowl with 2 tablespoons water and mix well. Shape the mixture into meatballs about the size of ping-pong balls.

Pour water into a large frying pan to a depth of 1 cm (½ in) over a high heat and bring to the boil. Add the meatballs in a single layer, then reduce the heat to medium and cook for about 5 minutes on each side.

Continue cooking the meatballs over a medium heat until the water has evaporated, the meatballs are browned all over and the fat begins to seep out. Discard this fat, then combine the meatballs with the tomato sauce and heat through for a couple of minutes.

Serve with steamed rice or naan bread, and garnish with fresh coriander leaves.

- **Notes**

Ensure the onion is cooked until soft to bring out its sweetness.
Adjust the number of chillies to suit your preferred spice level.

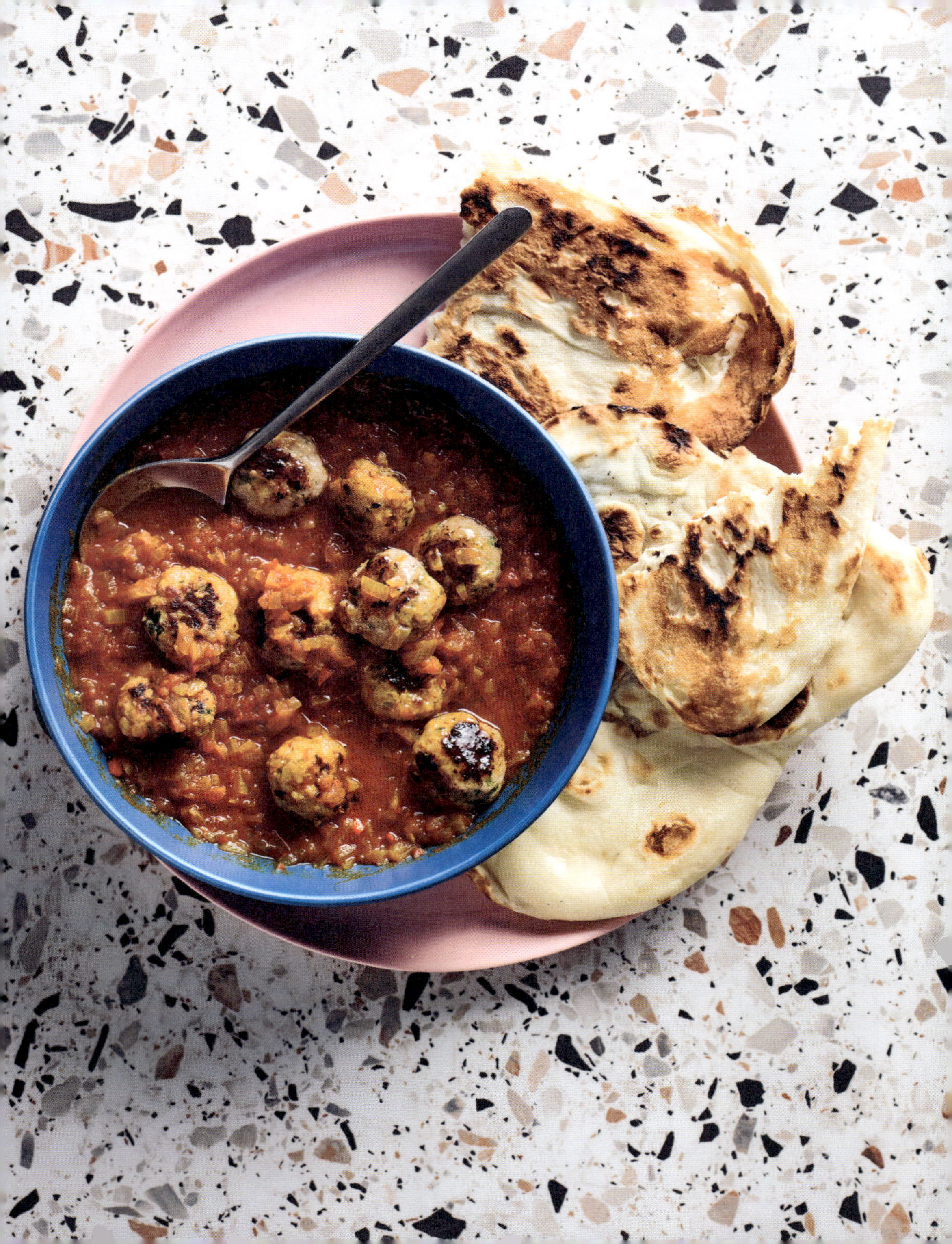

48
IRAN (PERSIA)

Eating the main meal at dinner has never made sense to me; why fill the tank when the only journey will be from table to sofa, sofa to bed? Iranians have long understood this, and treat lunch rather than dinner as the main event. Helie Kholosi, who migrated to Australia in the seventies with her husband, Fredy, was raised on regular lunches of fesenjoon, or Persian meatball stew, and she notes, 'It was always everyone's favourite meal.'

However, Helie didn't fully appreciate the unique flavours of traditional Persian cuisine until arriving in Australia, where a 'hot lunch' consisted of a Vegemite sandwich left in the sun too long. She began preparing fesenjoon for her own children, and says, 'When I cook this now, I try to put the same attention and love into it that my own mother did. Sometimes, I feel in my mind that I'm consulting with her, to make it perfect.'

Fesenjoon's origins are contested, with some believing it can be traced all the way back to the Sassanid Dynasty of the seventh century, while others are convinced its roots are Zoroastrian. Originally popular in the region of Gilan in the north of Iran, it gradually spread across the country, in the process becoming something of a national icon. The walnuts give this stew a luxurious, exuberant richness.

Fesenjoon
MEATBALL STEW WITH POMEGRANATE AND WALNUTS

SERVES 4

500 g (1 lb 2 oz) minced (ground) lamb
1 onion, grated
3 tablespoons vegetable oil
375 ml (12½ fl oz/1½ cups) hot water
3 tablespoons pomegranate molasses (see Notes)
1 large onion, chopped and fried
½ tablespoon sugar, plus extra if desired
115 g (4 oz/1 cup) coarsely ground walnuts
salt and freshly cracked black pepper
basmati rice, to serve
saffron threads, soaked in 2 tablespoons of boiling water, to garnish (optional)

Mix the lamb and grated onion in a bowl with some salt and pepper. Shape the mixture into small meatballs.

Heat the oil in a frying pan over a medium heat and fry the meatballs for about 4 minutes on each side, in batches to avoid overcrowding the pan if necessary. Set aside.

In a saucepan, mix the hot water, pomegranate molasses, fried onion and sugar.

In a separate frying pan, dry-toast the ground walnuts over a medium–low heat, stirring continually until they gradually change colour to beige or light brown.

Tip the toasted walnuts into the sauce. Bring to the boil, stirring continuously, then boil gently for 5 minutes.

Add the meatballs to the pan and bring it back to the boil over a medium heat. Cook for 1 hour to develop the sauce's sweet-and-sour flavour. If the mixture is too sour, add more sugar gradually. As the stew cooks, it will thicken and darken to a dark brown colour. The walnuts will release a lot of oil, enhancing the flavour. Stir the dish occasionally to prevent it from forming a crust on the bottom of the pan and burning.

Serve with basmati rice. Saffron is also a traditional, but optional, garnish.

• **Notes**

Fesenjoon can also be made with chicken instead of lamb; Helie's mum always made it with minced (ground) lamb. Helie also notes that this dish is ideal for people required to restrict their salt intake, as its rich flavours don't necessitate the addition of salt unless desired.

Pomegranate molasses is available from Persian or Afghan supermarkets.

49
IRAN (PERSIA)

Don't be alarmed by the presence of the word 'ash' here; this recipe does not require the addition of any fiery by-products. In Persian cooking, 'ash' simply refers to slow-cooked, hearty soups.

Yet another exceptional example of what can be created using meatballs as your foundation, this soup is perfect for making on a weekend, as it does require a bit of time to prep and cook. Don't let that deter you, as this dish is guaranteed to win the hearts and stomachs of all who encounter it. Smokin', indeed.

Ash-e anar
POMEGRANATE AND HERB SOUP WITH MEATBALLS

SERVES 4

• Soup
1 tablespoon olive oil
3 large onions, diced
4 garlic cloves, peeled and crushed
85 g (3 oz) yellow split peas
1 teaspoon salt
1 teaspoon freshly cracked black pepper
1 teaspoon ground turmeric
1 large bunch parsley, chopped
1 bunch coriander (cilantro) leaves, chopped
1 small bunch mint, stalks removed, chopped
1 bunch chives, snipped
85 g (3 oz) basmati rice
400 ml (13½ fl oz) pomegranate juice
3 tablespoons pomegranate molasses
120 g (4½ oz) caster (superfine) sugar

• Meatballs
400 g (14 oz) minced (ground) beef
1 large onion, grated (including juices)
1 teaspoon salt
1 teaspoon freshly cracked black pepper

• To garnish
½ tablespoon dried mint
1 small onion, finely sliced and caramelised

To make the soup, heat the oil in a stockpot over a medium–low heat. Add the diced onion and cook for 10–15 minutes, or until nicely caramelised. Add the garlic and lightly brown with the onion. Add the yellow split peas with 2 litres (68 fl oz/8 cups) water and bring to the boil. Reduce the heat to medium, partially cover the pan and simmer for 30 minutes.

Add the salt, pepper, turmeric, parsley, coriander, mint and chives. Simmer for 20 minutes over a low heat, stirring regularly to prevent the peas from sticking to the bottom of the pan.

To make the meatballs, combine the beef, grated onion, salt and pepper in a bowl and mix well. Shape the mixture into small meatballs and add them to the soup. Add the rice, cover and simmer for 30 minutes over a medium–low heat.

Add the pomegranate juice and molasses, and the sugar to the soup. Stir the mixture thoroughly. Partially cover the pot with the lid and simmer for another 30 minutes over a low heat.

To serve, garnish the soup with dried mint and caramelised onion.

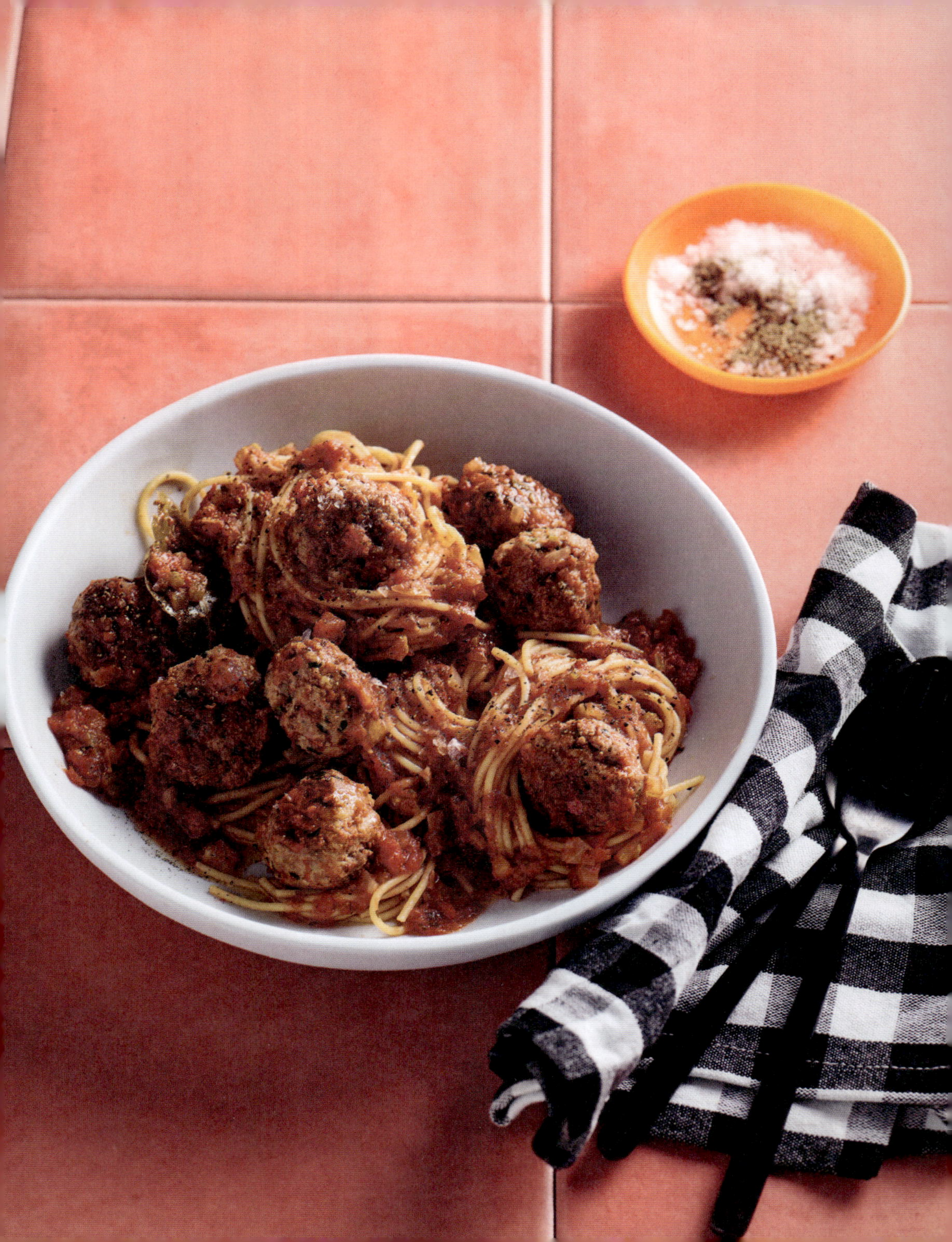

50
ITALY (CAMPANIA)

Italians show remarkably good grace about the many ways in which their seductive, exuberant cuisine has been defiled by Anglo cooks (barbecue chicken pizza, I am looking at you). That said, Angela Costanzo, a first generation Australian whose family hail from the Campania region, would like to correct the record on just one count.

'In our parts, the meatballs are never served with pasta! They're cooked in the sauce, which is then used to dress the pasta as a first course. The meatballs are then served with salad or vegetables as a second course. It's a great way of getting two courses of saucy goodness for very little effort!'

Angela cooks her nonna Libera's polpette recipe as a means of keeping her memory alive. 'She didn't have much of a legacy to leave – she didn't have heirlooms or treasures to speak of – so I feel I am honouring her, and my heritage, when I make polpette.'

With the greatest respect to Angela, her polpette are pictured here atop a bed of spaghetti, as I know that's how most of you will choose to eat them anyway. Oof, Madone! Old habits die hard.

Polpette in sugo
ITALIAN MEATBALLS IN TOMATO SAUCE

SERVES 4

- **Meatballs**

40 g (1½ oz/½ cup) fresh white breadcrumbs
500 g (1 lb 2 oz) minced (ground) pork and beef or veal
7 g (¼ oz/¼ cup) parsley, chopped
2 garlic cloves, minced
1 egg
salt and freshly cracked black pepper
plain (all-purpose) flour, for rolling
3 tablespoons vegetable oil

- **Sugo**

60 ml (2 fl oz/¼ cup) olive oil
1 small onion, finely chopped
3 garlic cloves, minced
2 celery stalks, finely chopped
1 small carrot, finely chopped
1 bay leaf
3–4 parsley sprigs
1–1.5 kg (2 lb 3 oz–3 lb 5 oz) fresh tomatoes, peeled, or chopped tinned tomatoes
1 teaspoon tomato paste (concentrated puree)
2–3 sprigs basil
2–3 sprigs oregano
salt and freshly cracked black pepper

- **To serve**

crusty bread

To make the meatballs, moisten the breadcrumbs with a little bit of water. Combine the breadcrumbs with the meat, parsley, garlic, egg, salt and pepper in a bowl and knead until well mixed. Shape the mixture into walnut-sized meatballs, then roll the balls in the flour. At this stage you can refrigerate the meatballs for up to 24 hours, until ready to cook.

Heat the oil in a frying pan over a medium heat and pan-fry the meatballs for 5–7 minutes, or until golden brown. Set aside on paper towels to drain the excess oil.

Heat the oil for the sugo in a separate saucepan and sauté the onion, garlic, celery, carrot, bay leaf and parsley until the onion is translucent. Add the tomatoes and stir over a high heat for 5 minutes. Add the tomato paste, basil, oregano and salt and pepper to taste, then cover the pan and simmer for 40 minutes over a low heat.

After 40 minutes, add the cooked meatballs to the sauce and simmer gently for about 10 minutes.

Serve the meatballs with some of the sauce and some crusty bread.

- **Notes**

The meatball recipe itself is very basic but allows for endless variations. Add 100 g (3½ oz/1 cup) grated parmesan, or some pine nuts and currants for a more Sicilian-style take on this dish.

Angela's favourite way to enjoy these meatballs as a child was layered in lasagne. Her nonna would scatter small ones through the layers, along with sliced, hard-boiled eggs, as is quite common in Campania.

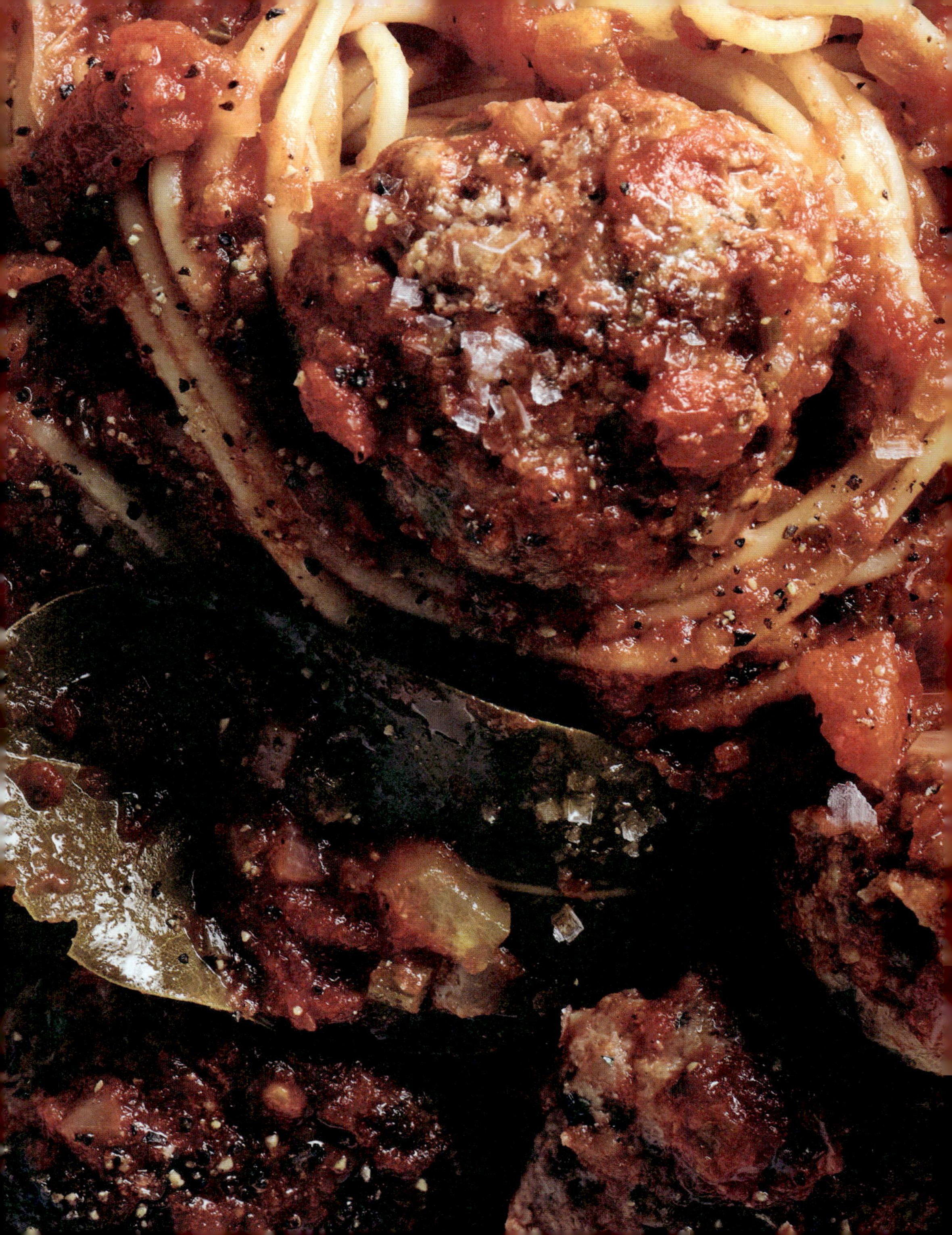

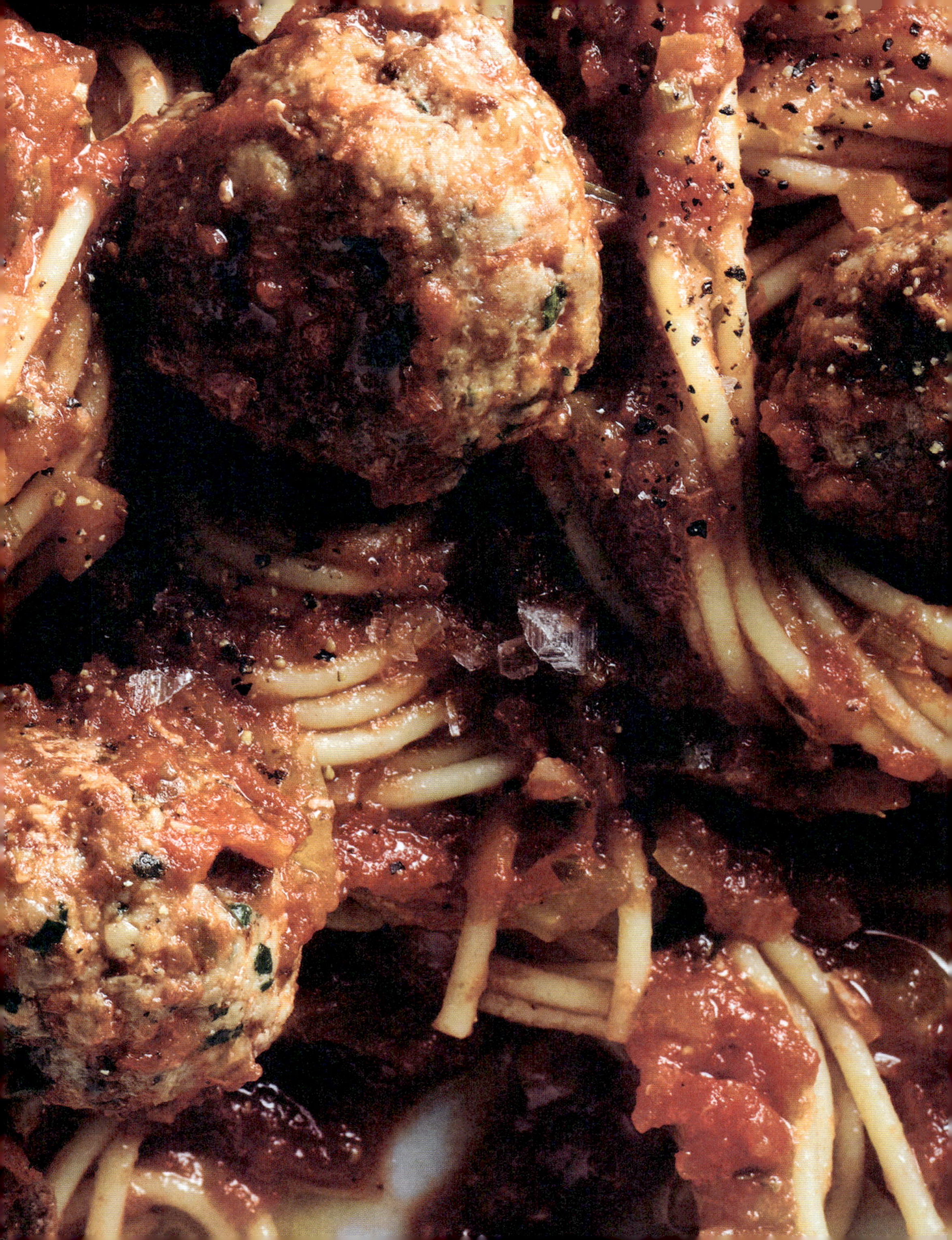

51
LATVIA

Occupying the blissful space between Polish pulpety (see page 26) and Swedish kottbullar (see page 175) sit these Latvian kotlete. Cooked in a sauce that could be described as either a thick broth or a featherweight gravy, it's perfect for those who can't stomach heavier sauces, and still delivers a hefty wallop in the flavour department.

This is a slightly modified version of a Latvian friend's beloved family recipe and is typically served atop a throne of pillowy mashed potato. If you'd prefer a baked version, parboil the rice before adding it to the meatball mixture, whack it in the oven for 30 minutes, then immerse the meatballs in the broth before serving.

Kotlete in gravy

SERVES 6

- **Meatballs**

750 g (1 lb 11 oz) minced (ground) chicken
100 g (3½ oz/½ cup) white rice
1 large egg
1 tablespoon thick (double/heavy) cream
1 tablespoon finely chopped dill or parsley
2 garlic cloves, minced
salt and freshly cracked black pepper

- **Gravy**

2 tablespoons olive oil
1 large onion, finely chopped
1 large carrot, grated
1 tablespoon plain (all-purpose) flour
1 litre (34 fl oz/4 cups) chicken, beef or vegetable stock or broth
1½ teaspoons tomato paste (concentrated puree)
1 teaspoon ground cumin
⅛ teaspoon freshly grated nutmeg
1½ teaspoons sweet paprika
1–2 bay leaves
salt and freshly ground black pepper, to taste

- **To serve**

1 tablespoon finely chopped parsley
mashed potato or crusty bread

Start by making the meatballs. Combine the chicken, rice, egg, heavy cream, dill and garlic in a large bowl. Season with salt and pepper and mix until the ingredients are well combined.

Wet your hands and shape the mixture into meatballs about the size of golf balls, then set aside.

To make the gravy, heat the oil in a large saucepan over a medium heat. Add the onion and carrot and sauté for 3–4 minutes. Add the flour, mix well with the vegetables, and cook for another minute.

Slowly add the stock to the pan, stirring until smooth and thickened.

In a small bowl, whisk together the tomato paste with 250 ml (8½ fl oz/1 cup) cold water. Stir this mixture into the gravy along with the cumin, nutmeg, paprika and bay leaves. Season with salt and pepper to taste. When the gravy has thickened and become smooth, add the meatballs to the pan. Bring the sauce to the boil, then reduce the heat to low, cover and cook for 25 minutes.

Sprinkle with fresh parsley before serving with mashed potato or fresh crusty bread.

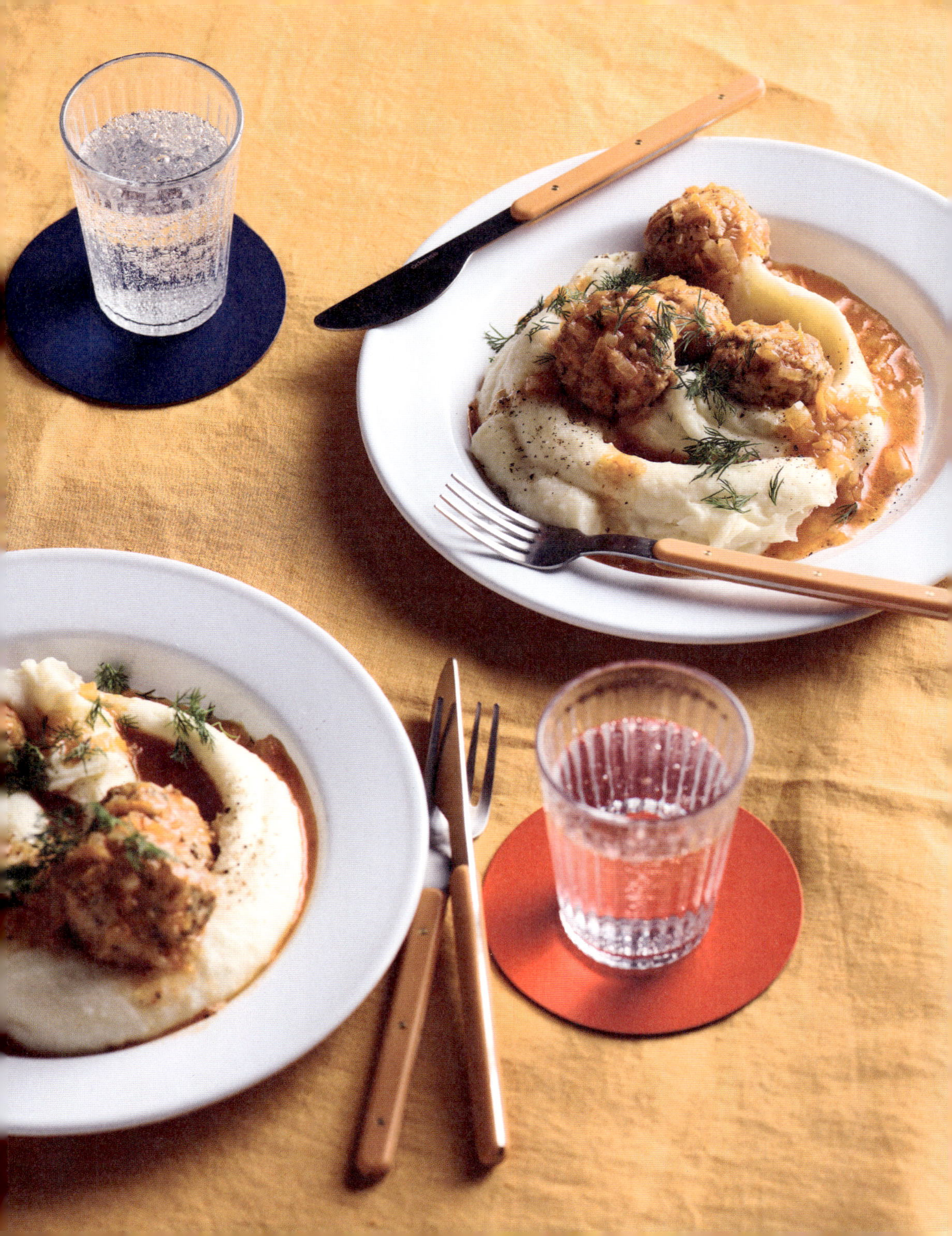

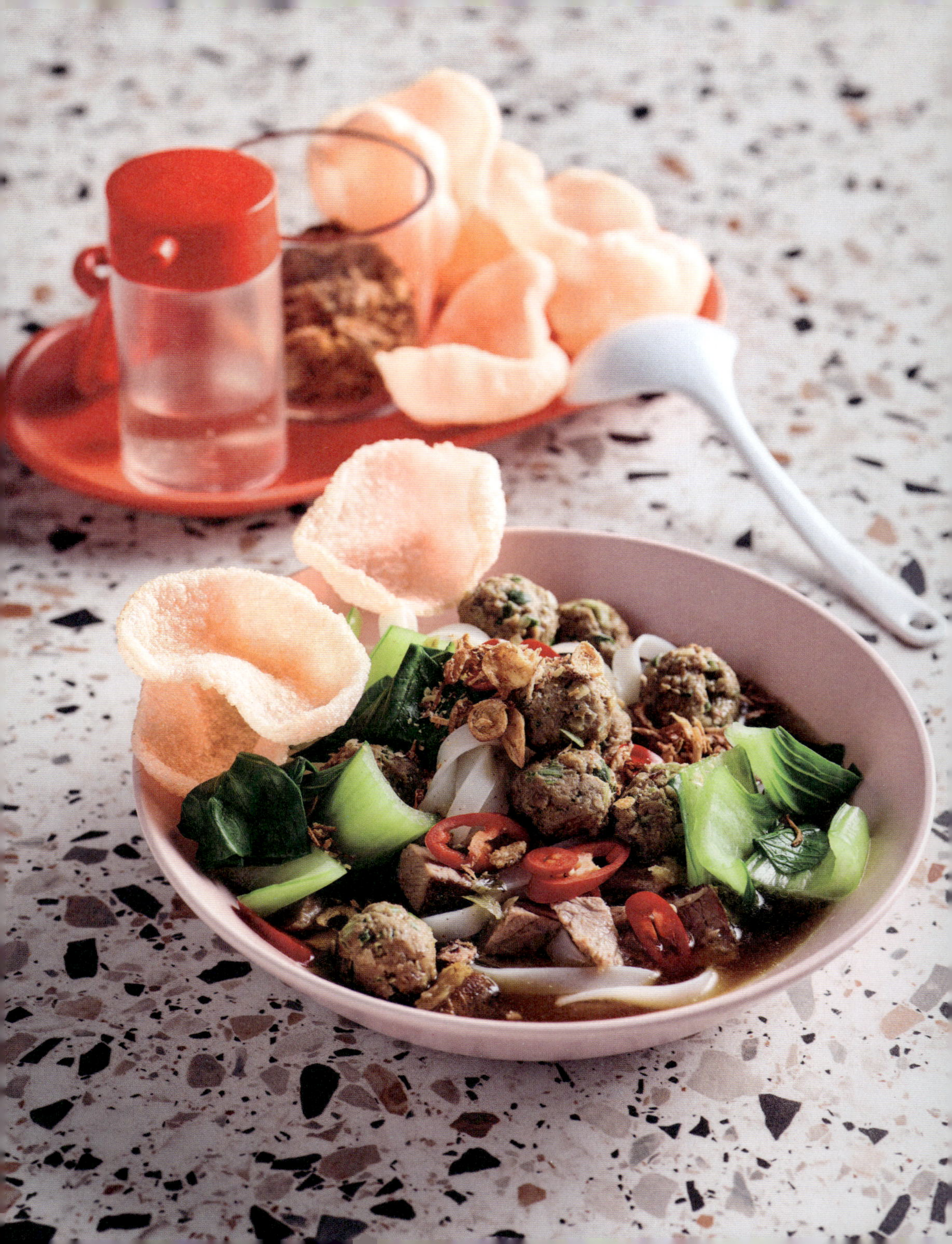

52

INDONESIA

For all their myriad virtues, few of the meatballs in this book can claim to have a presidential seal of approval. This bakso – aka spiced meatball soup – is a notable exception, having won the heart and stomach of a young Barack Obama, who spent four years of his childhood in Jakarta.

Obama's boyhood favourite dish is a winning combination of rice noodles, broth, and flavourful meatballs that practically bounce in your mouth. An Indonesian national treasure, the word 'bakso' is derived from the Hokkien 'bak-so', which translates into the beautifully evocative 'fluffy meat'. You'll be floating on your own fluffy meat cloud after a bowl of bakso. Slurping is mandatory.

Bakso
INDONESIAN MEATBALL SOUP

SERVES 4–6

- **Broth**

600 g (1 lb 5 oz) beef brisket, fat trimmed, cut into 3 cm (1¼ in) cubes
15 garlic cloves, peeled and lightly crushed
8 shallots, peeled, roots removed, halved lengthways
800 ml (27 fl oz) beef stock
1.5 litres (51 fl oz/6 cups) chicken stock
2 bok choy (pak choy), cut into rough chunks
240 g (8½ oz) flat rice noodles, cooked, drained and rinsed in cold water
3 spring onions (scallions), thinly sliced diagonally

- **Meatballs**

2 tablespoons sunflower oil, for pan-frying
3 garlic cloves, peeled and crushed
4 small shallots, peeled and finely chopped
500 g (1 lb 2 oz) minced (ground) beef
2 spring onions (scallions), thinly sliced diagonally
½ teaspoon salt
¼ teaspoon ground white pepper
2 tablespoons ground coriander
1 teaspoon ground cumin
2 teaspoons cornflour (cornstarch)

- **To garnish**

1 long red chilli, thinly sliced
2 tablespoons fried shallots (store-bought is fine)
kecap manis, to taste
prawn crackers, to taste
rice vinegar, to taste

To make the broth, place the beef brisket in a large, deep saucepan along with the garlic and shallots. Pour both stocks into the pan and bring to the boil over a high heat. Reduce the heat to low and simmer uncovered for 2 hours, or until the stock has reduced by around half.

To make the meatballs, heat the oil in a frying pan over a medium heat. Add the garlic and shallots and cook for 2–3 minutes to soften, then allow to cool. Add the beef, cooled shallots and garlic, and the remaining meatball ingredients to a food processor and pulse until a fine paste forms. Take tablespoons of the mixture and roll into tight balls to make 24–30 meatballs.

When the broth has reduced, add the meatballs to the pan and bring to the boil, then lower the heat and simmer for 5 minutes, or until the meatballs are cooked all the way through. Add the bok choy, noodles and spring onions and warm through for 1–2 minutes.

To serve, ladle the broth with meatballs into serving bowls with some bok choy and noodles. Garnish with thinly sliced red chilli, fried shallots, kecap manis, prawn crackers and a splash of rice vinegar.

53
BOSNIA

There are many foods as beautiful to the eye as they are to the mouth. Sogan dolma is not one of them. Of course, meatballs are not generally known for their looks, but sogan dolma takes this a step further; they could easily do double duty as Halloween decorations, on account of their resemblance to large, meaty eyeballs.

But to swipe left on account of their ghoulish appearance would be to do yourself a grave disservice. For reasons beyond my understanding, when you wrap meatballs in boiled onion bodices, the result is pure gustative pleasure. As you may have guessed from the 'dolma' bit, an Ottoman influence is at play – the Empire ruled Bosnia from the fifteenth to the nineteenth centuries – but the flavours are pure Balkan. Separating the onion layers takes a little practice, so be sure to cook a few extra onions until you get the hang of it.

Sogan dolma
MEATBALL-STUFFED BAKED ONIONS

SERVES 8

- 8 onions (see Note)
- 120 ml (4 fl oz) white vinegar
- 1 kg (2 lb 3 oz) minced (ground) beef
- 120 g (4½ oz) white long-grain rice, partially cooked until just tender, cooled
- 2 eggs, lightly beaten
- 4 garlic cloves, minced
- 2 tablespoons tomato paste (concentrated puree)
- 1½ teaspoons sweet paprika
- 2 tablespoons finely chopped parsley
- 1 tablespoon salt
- 1 tablespoon freshly cracked black pepper
- 2 tablespoons olive oil, for greasing
- 1 litre (34 fl oz/4 cups) beef stock

• **To serve**
- lemon juice
- sour cream

Cut the ends off the onions and peel off the papery skin. Place them in a large saucepan, cover with cold water, and add the vinegar. Bring to the boil then simmer until just soft, about 15 minutes. Remove the onions from the pot and allow to cool for easy handling.

Carefully separate the onion layers by gently squeezing them out one at a time, taking care not to tear them. This is easier if you push out the centre first, then separate the layers by sliding your finger in between. Rub or peel off any fine membranes from each layer. Set aside the larger rings most suitable for stuffing, then chop up the centres, small rings and any badly damaged rings.

Prepare the stuffing by combining the beef, rice, egg, garlic, tomato paste, paprika, parsley, salt and pepper in a bowl. Mix with clean hands, then fill the onion rings with the mixture.

Preheat the oven to 190°C (375°F) and grease a large ovenproof dish with the oil. Spread the chopped onions over the bottom of the dish and then arrange the stuffed onions on top, packing them in tightly. Pour in enough beef stock to come about three-quarters of the way up the onions. Cover with foil and bake for 30–40 minutes, or until the onions are soft and the rice is cooked through, turning the onions over halfway through.

Serve drizzled with the cooking juices, a squeeze of lemon juice and a dollop of sour cream.

• **Note**
Using onions of the same size and shape helps to ensure even cooking time.

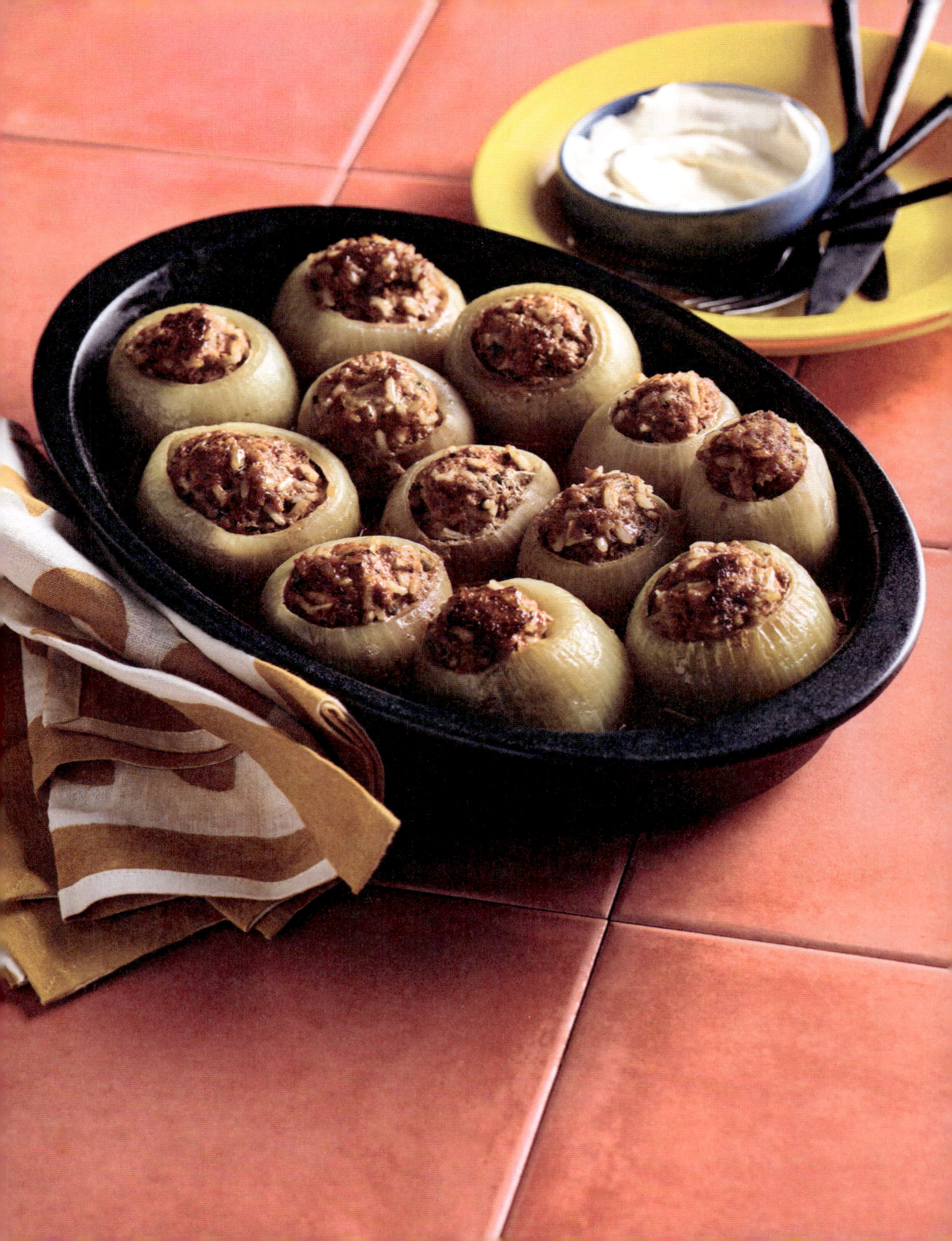

54
CHINA (UYGHUR)

The Uyghurs are the Chinese-Turkic people living primarily in the Chinese region of Xinjiang, which borders Russia, India, Mongolia and all the 'stans. This unique geography results in a cuisine with both Asian and Turkic elements, but this dish leans towards the Chinese side of things, with sichuan peppercorns, ginger and tofu firmly in the mix. Uyghur cuisine tends to fly under the radar, but this bold soup should put it firmly on yours; it's spicy, refreshing and deeply fortifying, a happy riot of textures and flavours best suited to depths-of-winter dining.

Vermicelli meatball soup

SERVES 4

- **Meatballs**
1 heaped tablespoon sichuan peppercorns
500 g (1 lb 2 oz) minced (ground) beef
1 onion, finely chopped
1½ teaspoons salt
1 teaspoon ground white pepper
1 teaspoon ground ginger
3 teaspoons potato starch
2½ teaspoons wheat starch
1 egg
2 tablespoons olive oil

- **Soup**
100 g (3½ oz) sweet potato vermicelli (see Note)
3 tomatoes, peeled and chopped
1 hot red chilli, finely sliced
250 g (9 oz) oyster mushrooms
2 large garlic cloves, finely chopped
250–300 g (9–10½ oz) silken tofu, cubed
60 g (2 oz) fresh English spinach leaves
Chinese black vinegar, to season (optional)

Discard any hard black seeds you find in the sichuan peppercorns, then grind the husks in a mortar and pestle. Sift to remove any remaining hard yellow bits.

To make the meatballs, combine the ground sichuan peppercorns, beef, onion, salt, pepper, ginger, potato starch, wheat starch and egg in a large bowl. Mix well with your hands. Shape the mixture into meatballs about the size of walnuts and set aside for 15–20 minutes. You should have about 15–18 balls.

Cook the sweet potato vermicelli according to the packet instructions, then rinse under cold water and drain. Set aside.

Heat the oil in a frying pan over a medium heat and fry until golden brown, about 8–10 minutes. Remove the meatballs from the pan and allow to cool a little, then cut them in half.

Bring 1.5 litres (51 fl oz/5 cups) water to the boil in a large saucepan, add the meatballs and reduce the heat to a simmer. Add the tomatoes and cook for about 5 minutes, then add the cooked vermicelli and chilli. Gently tear the oyster mushrooms into strips and add them to the soup with the garlic and tofu. Cook for another 2 minutes, then remove from the heat.

To serve, ladle the soup into bowls and tear a handful of fresh spinach leaves into each bowl. Season with a little Chinese black vinegar, if desired.

- **Note**
If preferred, you can substitute the sweet potato vermicelli with rice vermicelli.

55
AUSTRIA

Is it a burger, is it a patty, is it a ball? The traditional Austrian faschierte laibchen is more patty-like than spherical in shape; think of them as naughty meatballs who've had a recent run-in with the palm of a stern hand. A transeasonal winner, they're as good on a cold night with mashed potato or peas as they are on a warm afternoon with gherkins, mustard and tomato sauce (ketchup). Caramelised onions are also de rigueur.

Faschierte laibchen
AUSTRIAN MEAT PATTIES

SERVES 4

- **Meatballs**

250 g (9 oz) minced (ground) pork
250 g (9 oz) minced (ground) beef
2 teaspoons salt
¼ teaspoon freshly cracked black pepper
2 white bread rolls
1 onion, finely chopped
2 garlic cloves, minced
2 teaspoons dried marjoram (see Notes)
2 tablespoons finely chopped parsley
1 tablespoon dry breadcrumbs (optional, to firm up the mixture)
vegetable or other neutral oil, for pan-frying (see Notes)

- **Breading**

150–300 g (5½–10½ oz/1–2 cups) plain (all-purpose) flour
2–3 eggs
190 g (6½ oz/2 cups) dry breadcrumbs

- **To serve**

mashed potato or parsnip
gherkins (pickles)
caramelised onions

To make the meatballs, season the meat with the salt and pepper.

Cut the bread into slices and soak in a bowl of water for about 10 minutes, then squeeze firmly to remove the excess water.

Combine all the meatball ingredients, except the breadcrumbs and oil, in a large bowl and mix well with your hands. If the mixture is too loose to form patties, gradually add breadcrumbs until it firms up.

Shape the mixture into small patties. To bread the patties, roll them first in the flour, then the egg and, finally, the breadcrumbs. Ensure the patty is well covered on all sides.

Heat about 1 cm (½ in) oil in a large frying pan and fry the patties until brown and cooked through, about 5–7 minutes on each side.

Serve with mashed potato or parsnip, gherkins and caramelised onions.

- **Notes**

Make sure the oil is hot enough before frying the patties to ensure a crispy crust, and use a neutral oil with a high smoking point.

You can also add thyme, caraway and nutmeg for additional flavour.

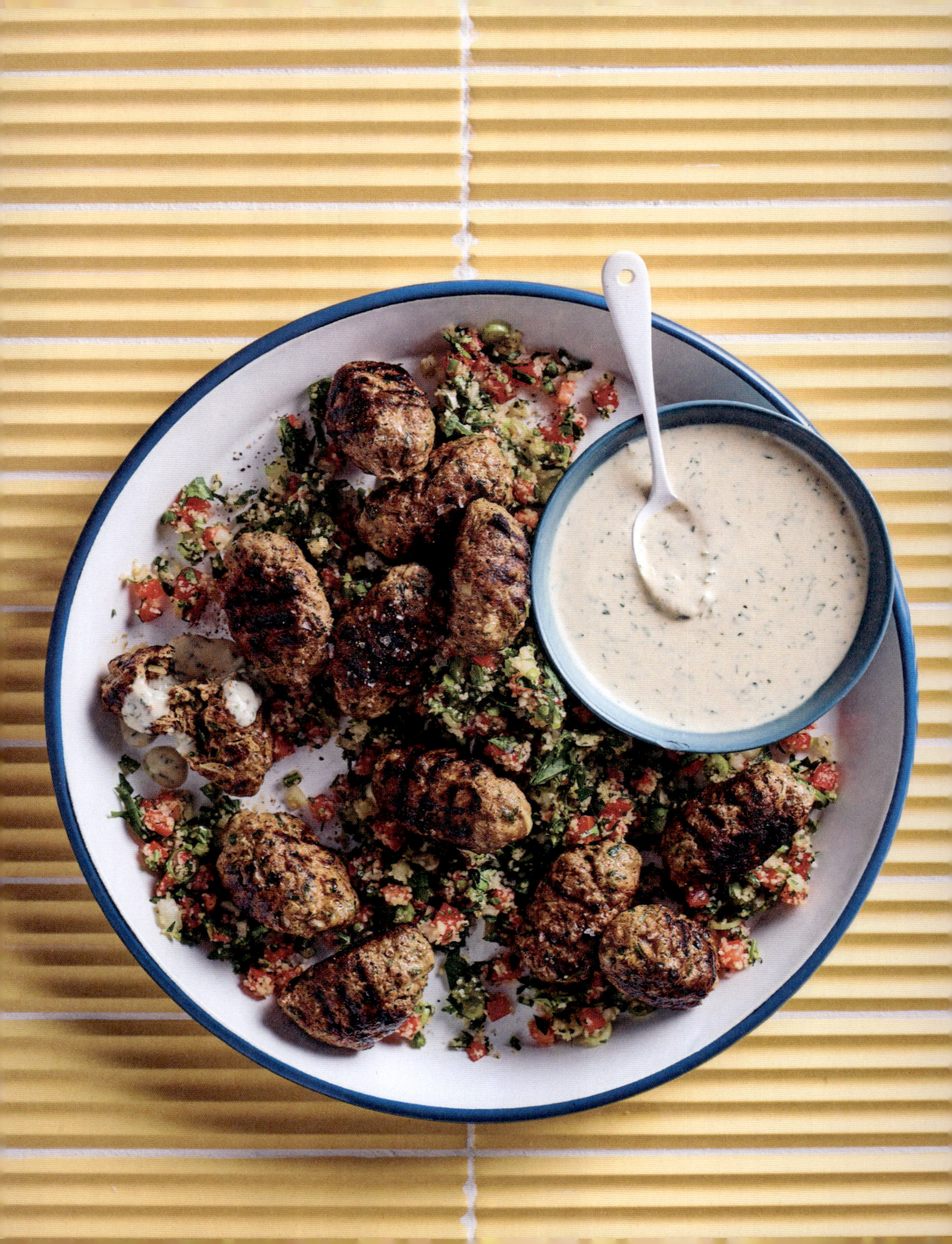

56
LEBANON

Lebanon contributes much of value to the meatball melting pot of the Middle East. This kafta (in Lebanon, they are known as kafta rather than kofta) recipe is a simple one, and no less delicious for it. The rug that ties the room together, so to speak, is the tarator sauce – a creamy tahini concoction with a sit-up-in-your-chair tang courtesy of strong lashings of lemon juice and garlic.

To my mind, these are the perfect summer kafta. Served with a traditional tabbouleh salad, they're light, quick and easy to prepare and don't require any great commitment to the oven or stovetop. Sub out the burghul for quinoa if you're looking for a gluten-free option.

Kafta with tarator sauce and tabbouleh

SERVES 4

- **Kafta**

15 g (½ oz/½ cup) parsley, chopped
1 small onion, chopped
550 g (1 lb 3 oz) minced (ground) beef
2 teaspoons baharat or seven-spice
½ teaspoon ground cumin
½ teaspoon ground cinnamon
½ teaspoon ground coriander
⅛ teaspoon cayenne pepper
1 teaspoon salt
¼ teaspoon freshly cracked black pepper
vegetable or sunflower oil, for greasing

- **Tarator sauce**

135 g (5 oz/½ cup) hulled tahini
80 ml (2½ fl oz/⅓ cup) lemon juice
3 garlic cloves, minced
1 teaspoon ground cumin
½ teaspoon salt
7 g (¼ oz/¼ cup) parsley, finely chopped

- **Tabbouleh**

1 bunch parsley
2 tablespoons fine burghul (bulgur wheat)
80 ml (2½ fl oz/⅓ cup) lemon juice
2 roma (plum) tomatoes, finely diced
2 spring onions (scallions), finely diced
40 g (1½ oz/¼ cup) onion, finely diced
2–3 mint sprigs, finely chopped
60 ml (2 fl oz/¼ cup) olive oil
1 teaspoon salt
freshly cracked black pepper, to taste

To prepare the kafta, pulse the parsley in a food processor until finely chopped, then remove and set aside. Pulse the onion until finely chopped, then drain to release any excess moisture. Add the parsley back to the food processor along with the onion, beef, baharat, cumin, cinnamon, coriander, cayenne pepper, salt and black pepper. Pulse until all the ingredients are well combined, then transfer to a large bowl and form the mixture into oblong shapes, or kafta, approximately 2.5 cm (1 in) thick.

Preheat a chargrill pan or plate and grease it with a little oil. Transfer the kafta to the grill and cook for about 5 minutes per side, taking care not to overcook them.

To prepare the tarator sauce, combine the tahini, lemon juice, minced garlic, cumin and salt in a bowl. Gradually add 80 ml (2½ fl oz/⅓ cup) water, mixing constantly until you get a creamy consistency. Add more water if the mixture is too thick. Add the chopped parsley and mix well.

To prepare the tabbouleh, wash the parsley and let it dry completely before chopping finely. To a small bowl, add the burghul and lemon juice and leave to soak until the burghul is soft and plumped, about 15–20 minutes. Place the tomatoes in a fine-mesh sieve and drain any excess liquid to prevent the burghul from becoming too bloated. Put the chopped vegetables in a large bowl. Add the soaked burghul, salt, pepper and olive oil, and gently toss to combine.

Serve the kafta with the tarator sauce and tabbouleh.

57
CANADA

This traditional French-Canadian meatball stew is not dissimilar to Swedish meatballs, but with a triple-threat combo of beef, pork and salted pork, it's got a bit of extra heft: jacked kottbullar (see page 175), if you will.

A Québécois speciality (try saying that after knocking back a pre-dinner glass of cab sav), this is a great recipe for Christmas in July (if you're south of the equator) and Christmas-at-Christmas (if you're north of the equator).

Ragoût de boulettes
FRENCH-CANADIAN MEATBALL STEW

SERVES 4–6

450 g (1 lb) minced (ground) beef
250 g (9 oz) minced (ground) pork
120 g (4½ oz) salted pork, or bacon or lightly fried pancetta
1 onion, minced
2 tablespoons finely chopped parsley
¼ teaspoon ground ginger
¼ teaspoon ground cinnamon
¼ teaspoon ground cloves
½ teaspoon freshly cracked black pepper
¼ teaspoon mustard powder
2 slices white bread, cut into cubes
125 ml (4 fl oz/½ cup) full-cream (whole) milk
3 tablespoons vegetable oil
500 ml (17 fl oz/2 cups) lukewarm water
55 g (2 oz) browned flour (see Notes)
250 ml (8½ fl oz/1 cup) lukewarm chicken stock

Put all the meat in a food processor and pulse until just combined. Transfer to a large bowl and add the onion, parsley, spices and mustard to the meat mixture. Mix well.

In a small bowl, combine the bread and milk. Once the bread has softened, mix well then add to the meat mixture and mix it by hand until thoroughly combined. Roll the mixture into meatballs.

Heat 2 tablespoons of the vegetable oil in a large frying pan over a low heat. Add the meatballs and cook for 12–15 minutes, or until they are cooked through. Tip off any fat from the pan, then add the warm water, cover and cook over a low heat for 30 minutes, stirring occasionally.

In a jar or bowl, combine the flour and chicken stock and mix until smooth, then pour this slurry into the stew. Stir regularly until the gravy thickens, about 15–30 minutes. If the gravy is not thick enough, add a bit more browned flour mixed with warm water as needed.

● **Notes**

To brown the flour, add it to a dry frying pan set over a low heat and stir until the flour is evenly browned. Remove the flour from the pan as soon as it reaches a sandy colour.

The traditional way of making this gravy uses water instead of stock, but stock is used here for additional flavour.

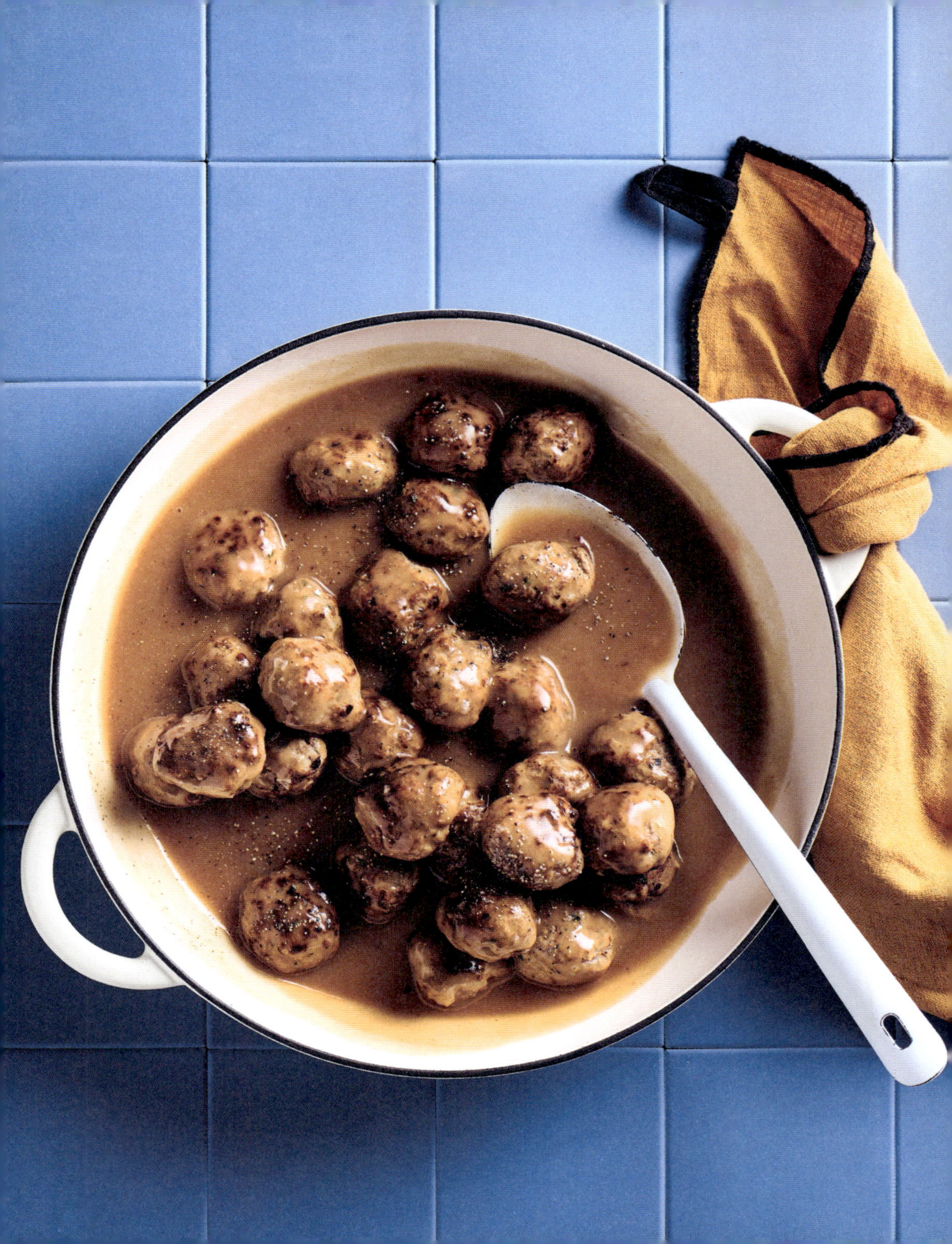

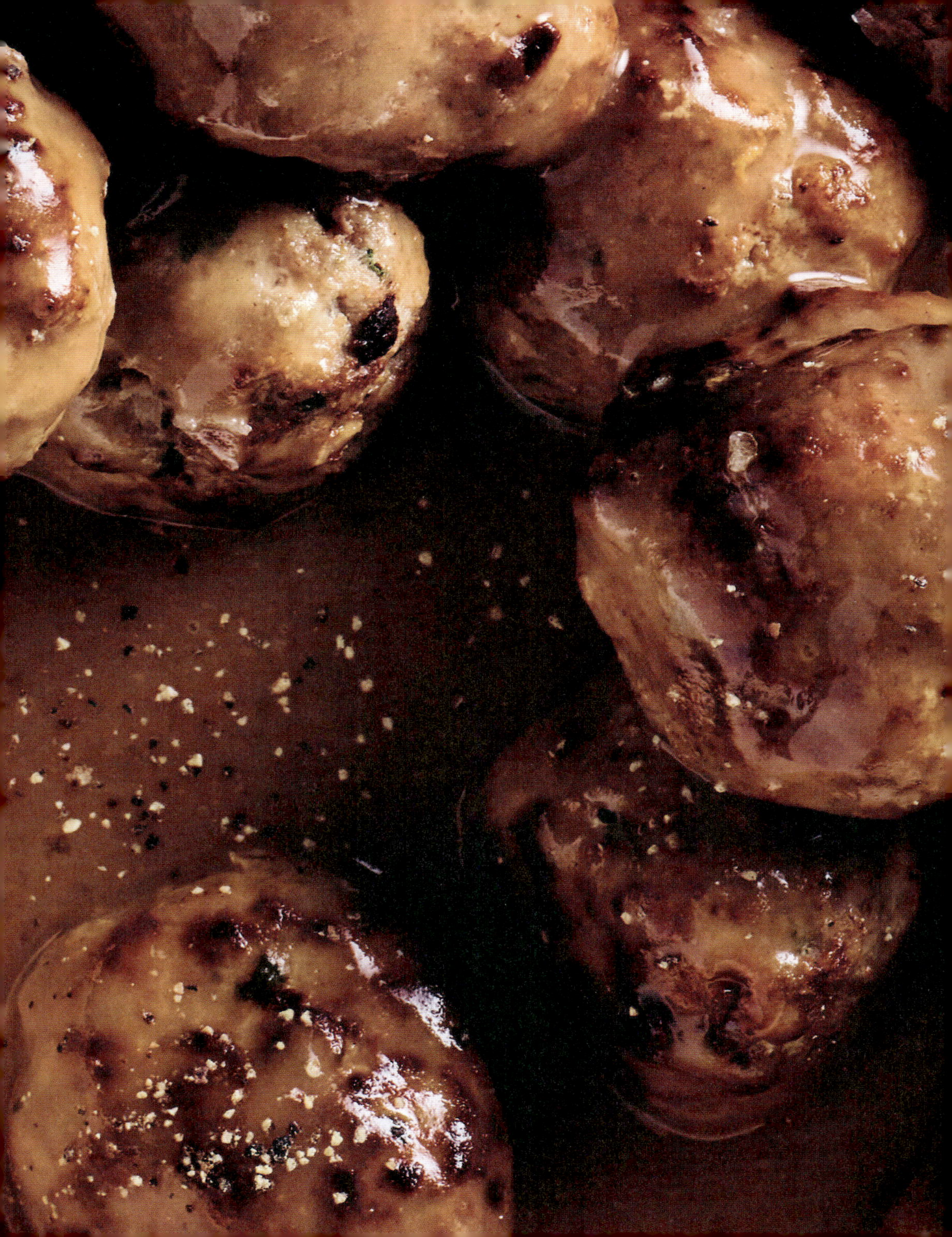

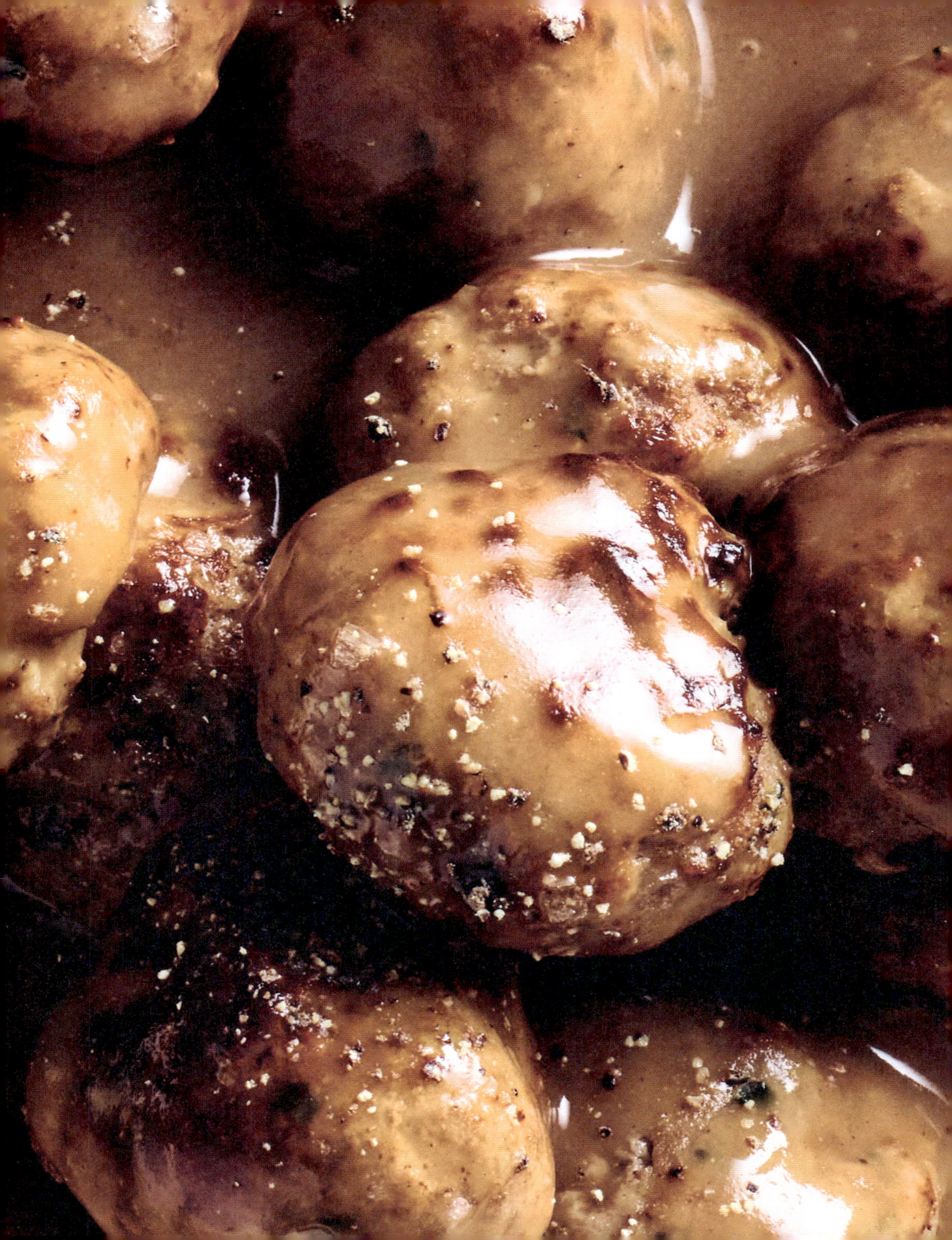

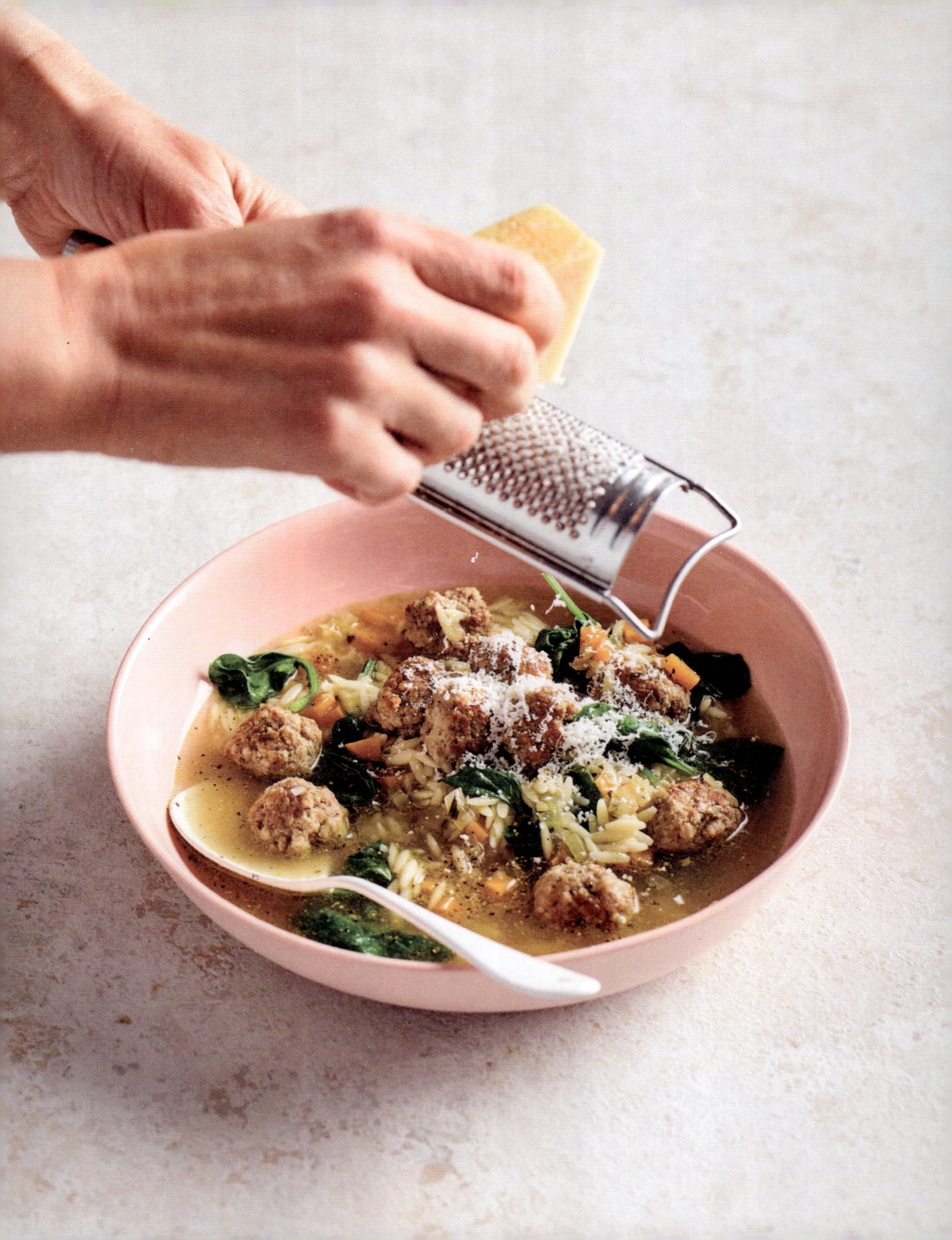

58
ITALY

While I quite like the idea of a special soup served exclusively at weddings, the name of this dish, with roots all the way back to ancient Italy, refers not to any sacred wedding tradition, but rather to the harmonious combining, or 'marriage', of ingredients. All of Italy's biggest culinary swingers make an appearance here, including oregano, garlic and parmesan, making it a must-try soup for chilly Italophiles. Go ahead, fall in love.

Minestra maritata
ITALIAN WEDDING SOUP

SERVES 4

- **Meatballs**

250 g (9 oz) minced (ground) pork
250 g (9 oz) minced (ground) beef or veal
1 egg
35 g (1¼ oz/⅓ cup) grated parmesan cheese, plus extra to serve
1 teaspoon dried oregano
½ teaspoons fine salt
2 garlic cloves, grated
50 g (1¾ oz/½ cup) dry breadcrumbs
freshly cracked black pepper
2 tablespoons olive oil, for pan-frying

- **Soup**

1 onion, diced
2 celery stalks, finely diced
2 large carrots, finely diced
4 garlic cloves, finely chopped
pinch of salt
¼ teaspoon fresh or dried rosemary, finely chopped
1.5 litres (51 fl oz/6 cups) chicken stock
1 parmesan rind
85 g (3 oz/½ cup) orzo
280 g (10 oz) baby English spinach
salt and freshly cracked black pepper, to taste

Combine all the meatball ingredients, except for the oil, in a large bowl and mix well. Shape the mixture into small meatballs of about 1 heaped teaspoon per ball. Set aside on a plate.

Heat the oil in a stockpot over a medium–high heat and brown the meatballs on all sides. Work in batches if you need to avoid overcrowding the pan. Remove and set aside.

To make the soup, add the onion, celery, carrot and garlic to the pot with a pinch of salt and cook over a medium heat until the vegetables have softened and the onion is translucent, about 10–15 minutes. Add the rosemary and cook for another minute. Add the stock and parmesan rind and bring to a simmer, then return the meatballs to the pot and simmer for 10–15 minutes.

Add the orzo and cook until al dente (usually 1–2 minutes less than what the packet instructions recommend). When the pasta is al dente, add the spinach, remove the pot from the heat and leave it to sit for a couple of minutes until the spinach has wilted. Remove the parmesan rind.

Ladle the soup into bowls and serve with extra grated parmesan on top.

59 ALGERIA

What is it you plan to do with your one wild and precious life? If, like me, your answer to this question is 'eat as many olives as possible', this is the recipe for you. Like many traditional Algerian dishes, kefta b'zeitoun is flavoured with olives, alongside tart preserved lemon, and then served with yet more olives.

Traditionally served with fresh bread, this dish also works beautifully with couscous, quinoa or rice.

Kefta b'zeitoun
MEATBALLS WITH OLIVES

SERVES 4

● **Meatballs**

90 g (3 oz) pitted green olives, finely chopped (see Note)
80 g (2¾ oz/1 cup) cubed day-old bread
250 ml (8½ fl oz/1 cup) full-cream (whole) milk
3 tablespoons olive oil
1 small onion, minced
2 garlic cloves, minced
½ teaspoon ground cumin
1 teaspoon salt
¼ teaspoon freshly cracked black pepper
500 g (1 lb 2 oz) lean minced (ground) beef
1–2 teaspoons harissa (depending on your preference for heat)
½ preserved lemon, cut into small pieces
1 egg
7 g (¼ oz/¼ cup) parsley, finely chopped, plus extra to serve
7 g (¼ oz/¼ cup) coriander (cilantro) leaves, finely chopped, plus extra to serve
plain (all-purpose) flour, for dusting

● **Sauce**

1 onion, chopped
2 garlic cloves, minced
1 teaspoon paprika
2 teaspoons tomato paste (concentrated puree)
½ preserved lemon, cut into small pieces
2 ripe tomatoes, grated
180 g (6½ oz) pitted green olives, plus extra olives to garnish
1¼ teaspoons salt, to taste
¼ teaspoon freshly cracked black pepper, to taste

Bring a small saucepan of water to the boil and blanch the olives twice to remove bitterness and excess salt.

Soak the bread in the milk until softened, about 5 minutes, then squeeze it dry.

Heat 1 tablespoon of the olive oil in a tagine or shallow flameproof casserole dish over a medium heat and fry half the pitted green olives for the meatballs, the onion and the garlic for 4 minutes. Add the cumin, salt and pepper, and cook until fragrant, about 1 minute. Transfer the mixture to a large bowl and leave to cool.

Once the onion mixture has cooled, add the beef, harissa, preserved lemon, remaining chopped olives for the meatballs, bread, egg and herbs. Mix with your hands until thoroughly combined, then roll into meatballs about the size of walnuts. Dust each meatball in flour and set aside on a large plate.

Heat the remaining olive oil in a frying pan over a medium heat and lightly brown the meatballs for about 2 minutes. Set aside on paper towel to drain.

To make the sauce, add the onion and garlic to the same pan and sauté over a medium heat until softened, about 5 minutes. Add 125 ml (4 fl oz/½ cup) water to deglaze the pan, then add the paprika, tomato paste, preserved lemon, grated tomatoes, green olives, salt and pepper.

Return the meatballs to the pan and add enough water to cover them. Lower the heat, cover the pan with a lid and simmer for about 20 minutes, or until the meatballs are tenders. The sauce should be reduced and fragrant.

Transfer to a serving platter and garnish with chopped parsley, coriander and extra olives. Serve with fresh bread, rice, couscous or quinoa.

● **Note**

Adjust the amount of olives in this dish to suit your preferences (presumably, you're an olive fan if you've come this far with the recipe). Small whole mushrooms are also often added to the sauce.

60
AFGHANISTAN

Often served on festive occasions such as New Year, or Nowruz, this spiced stew is earthy, cosy and nourishing in the most palpable sense; you can almost feel your cells regenerating with each mouthful.

Korme kofta is commonly served with a simple Afghan rice dish called challow, of which there are myriad variations, usually cooked in oil or ghee. Here, it's presented with plain basmati rice, also an authentic accompaniment.

Korme kofta

SERVES 4

- **Sauce**
220 g (8 oz/1 cup) yellow split peas
125 ml (4 fl oz/½ cup) vegetable oil
1 onion, finely chopped
2 garlic cloves, finely chopped
1 tablespoon paprika
1 tablespoon ground turmeric
2 teaspoons tomato paste (concentrated puree)
½ teaspoon cayenne pepper
1 teaspoon dried mint
1 teaspoon salt flakes
½ teaspoon ground coriander
3 dried sour plums (optional)

- **Meatballs**
1 onion, roughly chopped
3 large garlic cloves, roughly chopped
1½ cups coriander (cilantro) leaves, chopped
500 g (1 lb 2 oz) minced (ground) lamb
1 tablespoon ground coriander
2 teaspoons ground turmeric
1 teaspoon ground cumin
½ teaspoon sea salt flakes
½ teaspoon freshly cracked black pepper
¼ teaspoon cayenne pepper

- **To serve**
steamed basmati rice

To make the sauce, bring 1 litre (34 fl oz/4 cups) water to the boil in a saucepan over a medium–high heat. Add the split peas and cook for about 20 minutes, or until they are just beginning to soften. Strain, discarding the cooking liquid, then set aside.

Heat the oil in a large saucepan over a medium heat. Add the onion and cook, stirring occasionally, until golden brown, about 12–14 minutes. Add the garlic and cook until fragrant, about 1 minute. Add the paprika, turmeric, tomato paste, cayenne pepper, mint, salt and ground coriander, and cook while stirring until the spices are lightly toasted and aromatic, about 30 seconds. Stir in 500–750 ml (17–25½ fl oz/2–3 cups) cool water, bring to a simmer and cook, stirring occasionally, until the liquid reduces slightly and begins to thicken, approximately 15–20 minutes.

To make the meatballs, combine the onion, garlic and coriander leaves in a food processor and blend until finely minced. Transfer to a bowl, then add the lamb, ground coriander, turmeric, cumin, salt, black pepper and cayenne pepper. Mix well, then shape the mixture into ten small meatballs.

Carefully add the meatballs and the dried sour plums, if using, to the sauce and cook, stirring occasionally, until the meatballs begin to firm up, about 15 minutes. Stir in the split peas and cook for another 15 minutes, or until the peas are soft, but not mushy. Remove the pan from the heat.

Serve the korme kofta ladled over steamed basmati rice.

61

86

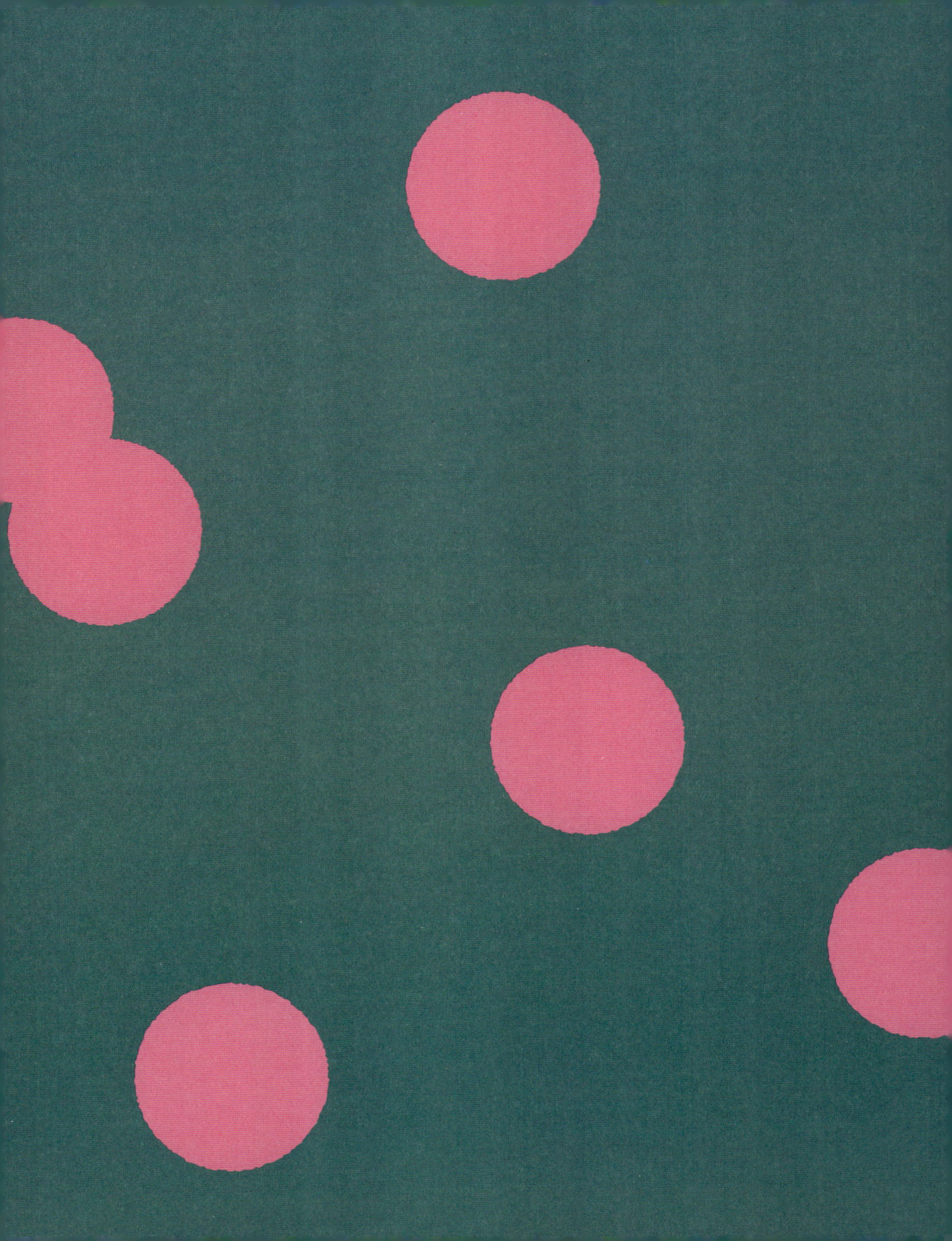

61.	**ITALY (SARDINIA)** Polpette with melanzane alla sassarese	**146**
62.	**TÜRKIYE** Fistkili kebab	**149**
63.	**CHINA** Lion's head meatballs with cabbage	**150**
64.	**CHINA** Lion's head meatballs with thick sauce	**152**
65.	**CHINA** Zhou rou wan	**153**
66.	**MALTA** Pulpetti tal-laham and brodu tal-laham	**155**
67.	**LEBANON** Shorba hamra	**156**
68.	**ITALY (SICILY)** Polpettine al limone	**157**
69.	**POLAND** Klopsiki with cwikla z chrzanem	**158**
70.	**HUNGARY** Fasirozott with nokedli	**161**
71.	**CHINA** Gongwan	**162**
72.	**MALAYSIA** Begedil	**163**
73.	**AUSTRALIA** Porcupine meatballs	**164**
74.	**IRAN (PERSIA)** Kal leh gonjishki	**167**
75.	**RUSSIA** Grechanyky with mushroom sauce	**168**
76.	**KOREA** Goji-wanja-jeon	**171**
77.	**SPAIN** Albondigas Mama Pepa in white wine sauce	**172**
78.	**PALESTINE** Kafta and tahini bake with Palestinian salad	**173**
79.	**SWEDEN** Kottbullar	**175**
80.	**TIBET** Tibetan meatball soup	**178**

61
ITALY (SARDINIA)

Ever wondered just what it takes to fill the belly of a miner? (Hint: a lot more than what is required to fill the belly of a desk-bound writer.) Sardinian-born Carmen Curreli's polpette recipe came to her via her mother, who learned to make the dish while working as a cook's assistant for the miners of the Canaglia region of Sardinia.

Those meatballs were originally called 'bombas', and contained pecorino, rather than parmesan, as well as chopped dried tomatoes – ingredients typical of the island. The addition of potato makes these little polpette both soft and crunchy, rich in all the things one needs to believe in the goodness of life: parmesan, milk, garlic, salt, bread.

Carmen and her husband like to serve them with roasted eggplants (aubergines; melanzane alla sassarese), another common Sardinian recipe. Her son prefers them with ketchup and a green salad.

Polpette with melanzane alla sassarese
MEATBALLS WITH BAKED EGGPLANT

SERVES 4

- **Polpette**
- 500 g (1 lb 2 oz) minced (ground) beef, 5–10% fat, or a mix of 150 g (5½ oz) pork and 350 g (12½ oz) beef
- 180–200 g (6½–7 oz) potato, peeled, boiled and mashed
- 1 small garlic clove, minced
- 1 tablespoon finely chopped parsley
- 50 g (1¾ oz) fresh breadcrumbs, soaked in water or milk
- 1 egg
- 80 g (2¾ oz) grated parmesan cheese
- salt
- full-cream (whole) milk, if needed
- salted butter, for cooking

- **Melanzane**
- 1 large eggplant (aubergine; see Note)
- 1 large garlic clove, finely chopped
- ½ teaspoon finely chopped parsley
- 2–3 tablespoons olive oil
- ½–1 teaspoon salt
- 1 small chilli, or ¼ teaspoon chilli flakes (optional)

Preheat the oven to 180°C (360°F).

To prepare the polpette, combine all the ingredients, except the milk and butter, in a large bowl and mix until evenly incorporated. If the mixture feels too dry, add a little milk to achieve the desired consistency.

Using your hands, shape the mixture into meatballs approximately 4–5 cm (1½–2 in) in diameter.

Place the meatballs in an ovenproof dish and add a small knob of butter on top of each one. Bake for 30–40 minutes, or until the meatballs are nicely browned and cooked through. Leave the oven on.

To prepare the melanzane, wash and dry the eggplant with paper towel. Trim the top and cut the eggplant into 2–3 cm (¾–1¼ in) discs. Score the flesh with a knife, making deep cuts both horizontally and vertically to create a grid pattern without cutting all the way through.

Combine the garlic and parsley with the oil, salt and chilli, if using. Mix well. Drizzle the flavoured oil over the eggplant, ensuring each piece is well seasoned, including inside the cuts.

Transfer the eggplant on a baking tray lined with baking paper and bake for 20–30 minutes, or until the surface of the eggplant is well browned and it is cooked all the way through.

Serve the polpette hot with the baked melanzane on the side.

- **Note**

If you like, you can cut the eggplant, salt it and place in a colander to remove the bitterness. After a couple of hours, rinse well then proceed with the recipe.

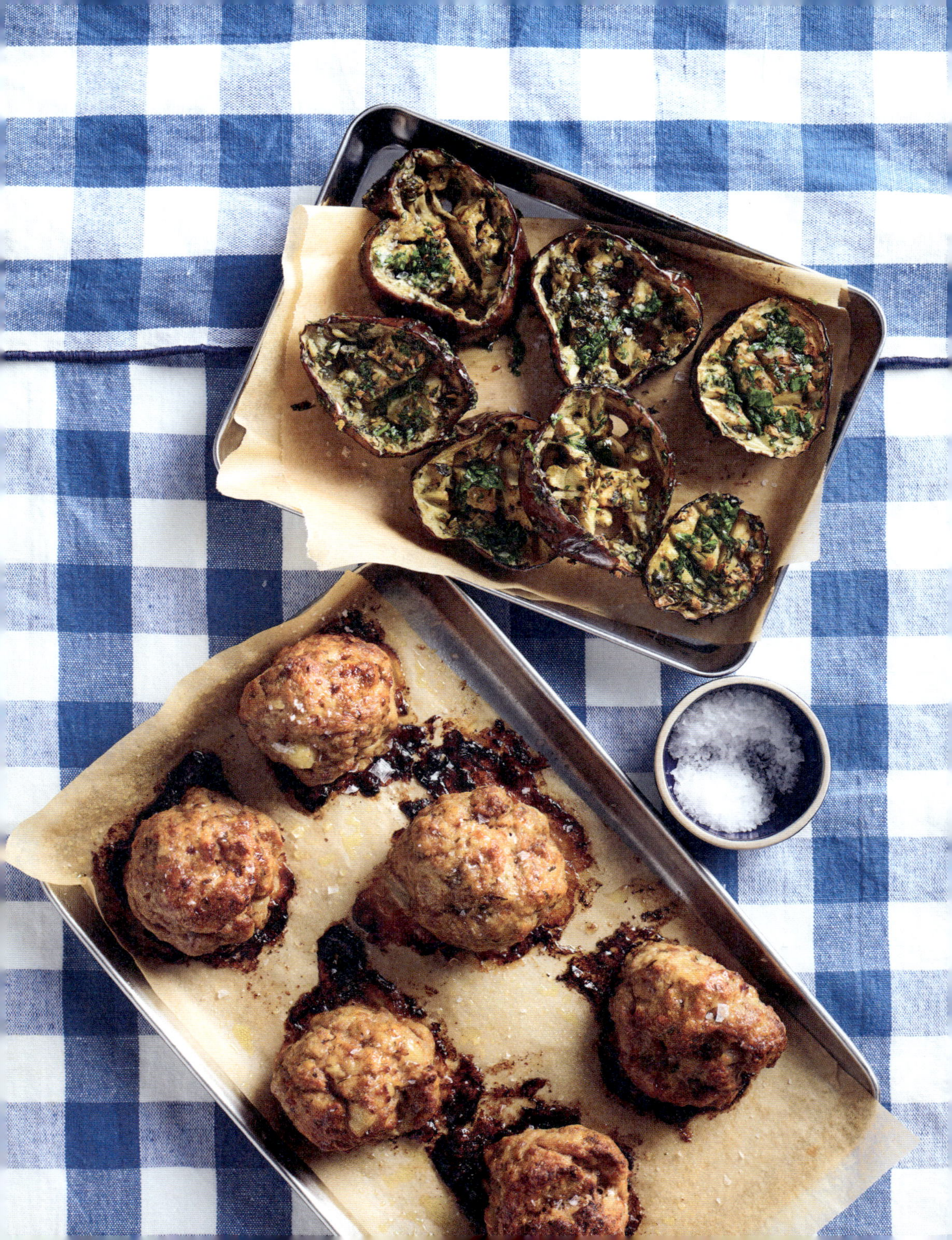

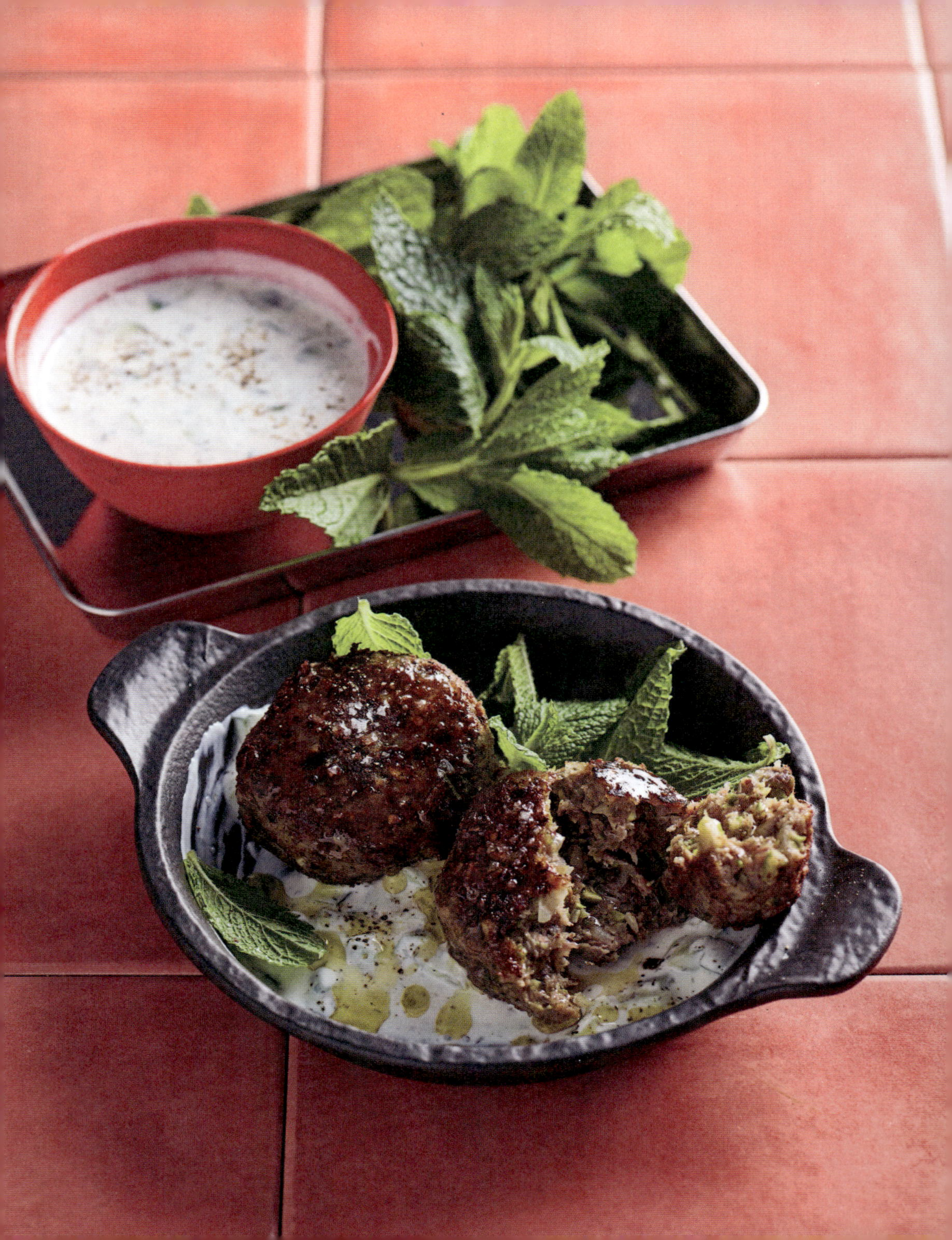

62
TÜRKIYE

Of the more than two hundred varieties of köfte Türkiye has bestowed upon us, fistkili kebab, or pistachio kebab, surely ranks as one of the finest. Simplified here into a ball rather than a kebab, it's popular in the south-eastern region of Türkiye and an essential string in the bow of any true mince afficionado.

Super juicy and satisfyingly plump, they're served here with cacik, aka Turkish tzatziki. Unlike Greek tzatziki, the cucumber in cacik is often chopped rather than grated; it's also heavier on the herbs and, with its thinner consistency, often served as a cooling soup in summer.

Fistkili kebab
PISTACHIO LAMB PATTIES

SERVES 4

● **Pistachio lamb patties**
150 g (5½ oz/1 cup) pistachio nuts
550–600 g (1 lb 3 oz–1 lb 5 oz) minced (ground) lamb
1 onion, finely chopped
2 teaspoons sumac
1 teaspoon ground coriander
1 teaspoon dried oregano
zest of 1 lime
1 tablespoon salt
1 teaspoon freshly cracked black pepper
2 large eggs
olive oil, for pan-frying

● **Cacik**
300 g (10½ oz) cucumbers, partly peeled and finely chopped
1 garlic clove, crushed to a paste with a little salt
500 g (1 lb 2 oz/2 cups) Greek-style yoghurt
2 teaspoons dried mint
salt, to taste

● **To serve**
2 tablespoons olive oil
chopped fresh mint

To make the patties, pulse 100 g (3½ oz) of the pistachios in a food processor until very finely ground. Lightly pulse the remaining pistachios, then roughly chop them and put them into a large bowl with the finely ground nuts. Add the lamb, onion, sumac, coriander, oregano, lime zest, salt, pepper and eggs. Mix well using your hands until the texture has broken down and the egg and pistachio are evenly distributed.

Place a large, non-stick frying pan over a medium heat and preheat the oven to 50–70°C (122–158°F), or as low as your oven will go.

Divide the meat mixture into approximately ten balls and flatten them into patties. Drizzle enough olive oil to coat the base of the frying pan and fry several patties at a time without overcrowding the pan. Cook for about 6 minutes, or until a nice brown crust forms, then flip and cook for another 6 minutes on the other side. Transfer the cooked patties to an ovenproof dish and keep warm in the oven while frying the remaining patties.

To make the cacik, put the cucumber in a bowl and season well with salt. Leave for 5 minutes. In another bowl, mix together the garlic, yoghurt and dried mint. Gently incorporate the cucumber.

Serve immediately with the pistachio lamb patties drizzled with olive oil and garnished with fresh mint.

● **Note**
Add ice-cold water to the cacik to turn it into a summer soup.

63
CHINA

There are countless variations on lion's head meatballs throughout the many regions of China, and given their history with the meatball is approximately as ancient as the Persians' (first century BC), it seems reasonable – nay, essential – to share more than one version.

It's worth mentioning that lion's head balls contain no lion's heads. (The same cannot be said for horse meatballs. Each to their own, but growing up next to a pony club rules out ye olde horse ball for moi.) The name is inspired by the oversized shape of these balls, which, when laid out with the cabbage they're customarily served with, are said to resemble a lion's head and mane.

Lion's head meatballs with cabbage

SERVES 4–6

- **Meatballs**

500 g (1 lb 2 oz) minced (ground) pork
60 ml (2 fl oz/¼ cup) Chinese rice wine or dry sherry
40 ml (1½ fl oz) light soy sauce or soy sauce
1 teaspoon dark soy sauce
1½ teaspoons salt
2 teaspoons sugar
2 teaspoons grated fresh ginger
1 tablespoon cornflour (cornstarch)
4 spring onions (scallions), minced
227 g (8 oz) tinned water chestnuts, drained and finely chopped
3 eggs
100 g (3½ oz) panko (Japanese) breadcrumbs, plus extra if needed
1 tablespoon sesame oil
3 teaspoons vegetable oil

- **Sauce**

500 ml (17 fl oz/2 cups) chicken stock, plus extra for the cornflour slurry
4 cm (1½ in) piece fresh ginger
1 spring onion (scallion), cut into thirds
1 garlic clove, peeled
1 tablespoon soy sauce
1 teaspoon dark soy sauce
1½ tablespoons cornflour (cornstarch) mixed with 125 ml (4 fl oz/½ cup) cold chicken stock

- **To serve**

braised cabbage garnished with soy sauce and a pinch of sugar, to serve

Combine the pork with 80 ml (2½ fl oz/⅓ cup) water in a large bowl and mix well with a spatula until the water is fully incorporated. Add the Chinese rice wine, light soy sauce, dark soy sauce, salt, sugar, grated ginger, cornflour and spring onion and mix thoroughly. Add the water chestnut, eggs and breadcrumbs and continue mixing until well combined. Finally, stir in the sesame oil until the mixture forms a soft paste.

Heat the vegetable oil in a frying pan over a medium–high heat until hot, then reduce the heat to medium. Scoop about ⅓ cup of the meat mixture and shape it into a large meatball. The meatball will be quite soft. If needed, add some more breadcrumbs to help it hold together. Repeat with the remaining mixture to make three large meatballs.

Carefully place the meatballs in the pan and brown them on all sides by rolling the meatballs gently with a spatula (see Note). Transfer them to a deep plate or a bowl that fits into your steamer basket. If you don't have a steamer, you can use the double-boiler method. Place one saucepan with holes in the base inside another saucepan filled halfway with gently simmering water. Place the meatballs in the top pot, cover with a lid and steam them in batches. If you're using a steamer, place the plate of meatballs on the steaming rack. If you're using a double-boiler, you can line the pot with a piece of baking paper and place the meatballs on top. Cover and steam for about 30 minutes, or until fully cooked. Repeat with the remaining meatballs, topping up the water as necessary.

While the meatballs are steaming, prepare the sauce. Combine all the ingredients, except the cornflour, in a small saucepan and bring to a gentle boil over a medium heat, then reduce the heat to low and simmer for 10 minutes.

Add the cornflour slurry to the sauce, stirring well to avoid lumps, and cook for another 5 minutes over a low heat until the sauce has thickened slightly.

Add the meatballs to the sauce and cook over a medium–low heat for another 10 minutes.

Serve the meatballs hot in the sauce with braised cabbage on the side.

- **Note**

Handle the meatballs gently to keep them round. Cook the top and bottom first, then cook the sides by holding the meatballs in place with two spatulas.

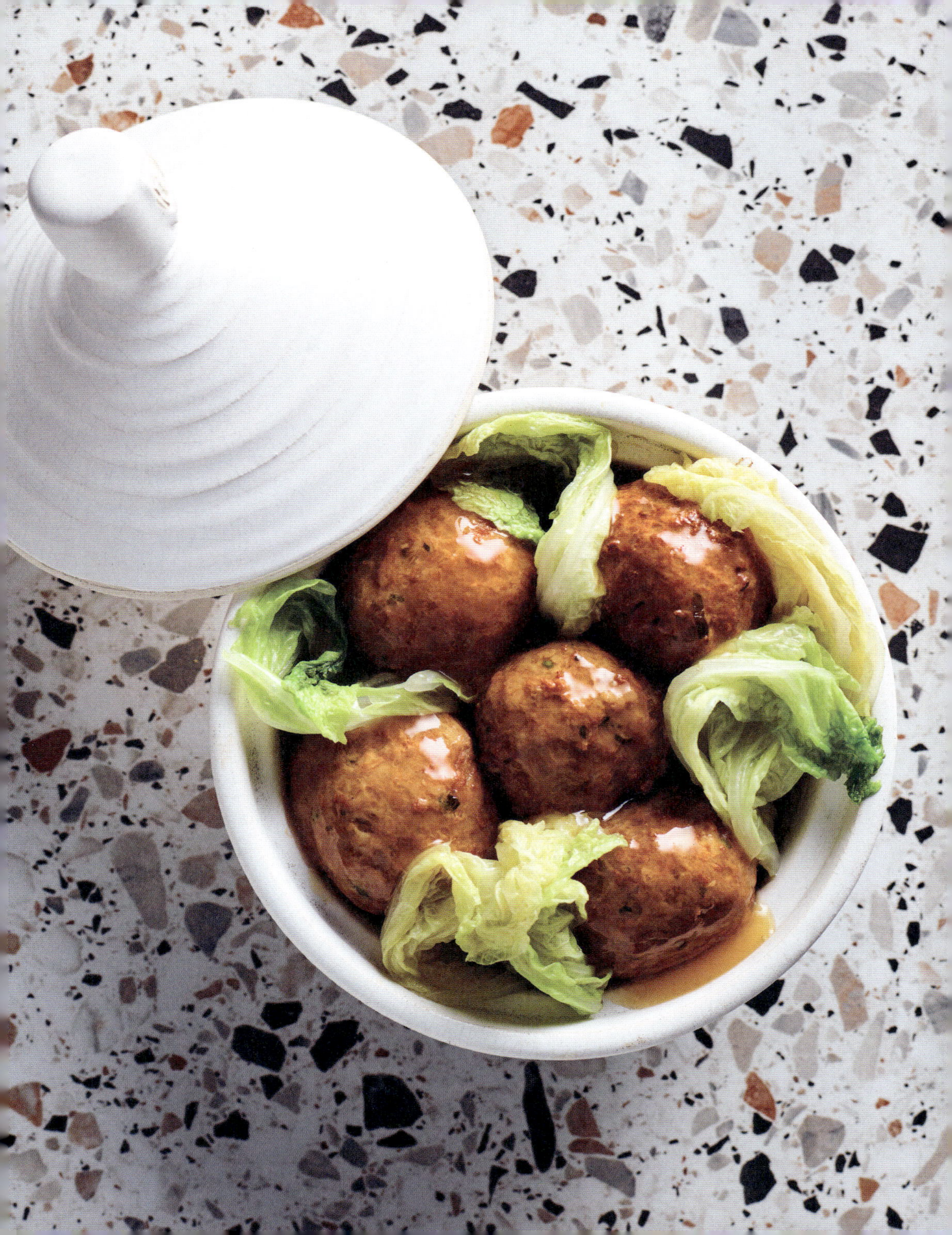

64
CHINA

This variation is topped with a lovely thick soy sauce and is commonly served during spring festivals.

Lion's head meatballs with thick sauce

SERVES 3–4

- **Meatballs**

320 g (11½ oz) minced (ground) pork
1 tablespoon light soy sauce
⅛ teaspoon salt
1 tablespoon oyster sauce
¼ teaspoon ground white pepper
70 g (2½ oz/½ cup) lotus root, chopped
1 tablespoon cornflour (cornstarch)

- **Braise**

2 tablespoons vegetable oil
2 spring onions (scallions), chopped
1 tablespoon grated fresh ginger
1 star anise
2 tablespoons light soy sauce
2 teaspoons dark soy sauce
1 tablespoon oyster sauce
2 dashes of ground white pepper
20 g (¾ oz) palm sugar (jaggery)
¼ teaspoon salt (optional)
2 bunches bok choy (pak choy) or choy sum
½ tablespoon cornflour (cornstarch)

For the meatballs, combine the pork, soy sauce, salt, oyster sauce, white pepper and lotus root in a bowl. Mix the ingredients together in one direction until the mixture becomes paste-like. Add the cornflour and continue mixing until the mixture is sticky and light in colour. Use a tablespoon to scoop the mixture into meatballs about 5 cm (2 in) in diameter.

Bring a saucepan of water to the boil, then carefully lower the meatballs into the boiling water, being sure not to overcrowd the pan. Simmer gently for 10 minutes over a low heat to firm them up. Do not let the water boil. When fully cooked, remove the meatballs from the pot and set them aside, reserving the cooking water.

For the braise, heat the vegetable oil in a separate pan and sauté the spring onion, ginger and star anise until fragrant. Add 600 ml (20½ fl oz) of the reserved cooking water, light soy sauce, dark soy sauce, oyster sauce, white pepper, palm sugar and salt, if using. Stir to combine and bring to the boil.

Return the meatballs to the pan and simmer for 20 minutes, or until most of the braising liquid has evaporated.

While the meatballs are simmering, blanch the bok choy in the remaining meatball cooking water in the pan with 1 teaspoon of vegetable oil and a pinch of salt. In a small bowl, whisk together the cornflour and 1 tablespoon cold water to make a slurry. Add this to the pan with the meatballs and stir. Continue to simmer until the sauce reaches your desired consistency.

Transfer the cooked meatballs to a serving dish. Remove the ginger, spring onion and star anise from the sauce.

Serve the meatballs with the thickened sauce and blanched bok choy on the side.

65
CHINA

Shady Chen, who was born and raised in Guangdong before immigrating to Melbourne in 2006, created this recipe based on happy childhood memories of her father's cooking. 'My Dad, Liner, was always the one who cooked for the family, and me and my siblings loved his pork meatballs.'

Shady now regularly prepares zhou rou wan for her meatball-obsessed son, making continual adaptations and adjustments to keep the recipe evolving and improving; she recommends adding 1 teaspoon each of oyster and soy sauce if you want to supersize the flavours. Shady takes a loose approach to side dishes: 'noodles or rice, some steamed bok choy on the side and plenty of chopped up spring onion/scallion always work well'.

With life-affirming hits of ginger, sichuan peppercorns and spring onion, these balls are both bold and nurturing; the intergenerational appeal is easy to understand. These meatballs also give you plenty of leeway to add your own touches, so if you're looking for a recipe to build on and make your own, you have Shady's blessing.

Zhou rou wan
MEATBALLS IN BROTH

SERVES 4

- 3 cm (1¼ in) piece fresh ginger, sliced into thin strips
- 2 spring onions (scallions), chopped, plus extra to serve
- 10 sichuan peppercorns (optional)
- 150 ml (5½ fl oz) warm water
- 500 g (1 lb 2 oz) minced (ground) pork
- 1 teaspoon salt
- 1 teaspoon chicken seasoning
- 1 egg white
- 1 tablespoon potato starch or flour
- 1 teaspoon soy sauce, or to taste (optional)
- 1 teaspoon oyster sauce, or to taste (optional)
- freshly cracked black pepper

● **To serve**
- steamed rice or noodles
- Asian greens of your choice

Add the ginger, spring onion and sichuan peppercorns to a bowl. Add the warm water and squeeze the ginger and spring onion in the water to release their flavours. Let the mixture sit for 10 minutes.

In a large bowl, combine the pork, salt, chicken seasoning and some pepper. Strain half of the warm water mixture (discarding the solids) into the bowl with the pork. Add the egg white and mix into the meat mixture with your hand. Add the remaining warm water mixture, straining out the solids. Continue to mix until well combined.

Add the potato starch to the meat mixture, and the soy sauce and oyster sauce, if using. Mix thoroughly until you have a sticky consistency, about 3 minutes.

Shape the mixture into meatballs. Bring a pot of water or light broth to the boil, then reduce to a simmer and carefully drop the meatballs in one by one. Cook until they float to the surface and are cooked through or transfer the meatballs to a steamer and steam for 20–25 minutes until fully cooked.

Serve with steamed rice or noodles and Asian greens of your choice. Sprinkle with plenty of chopped spring onion.

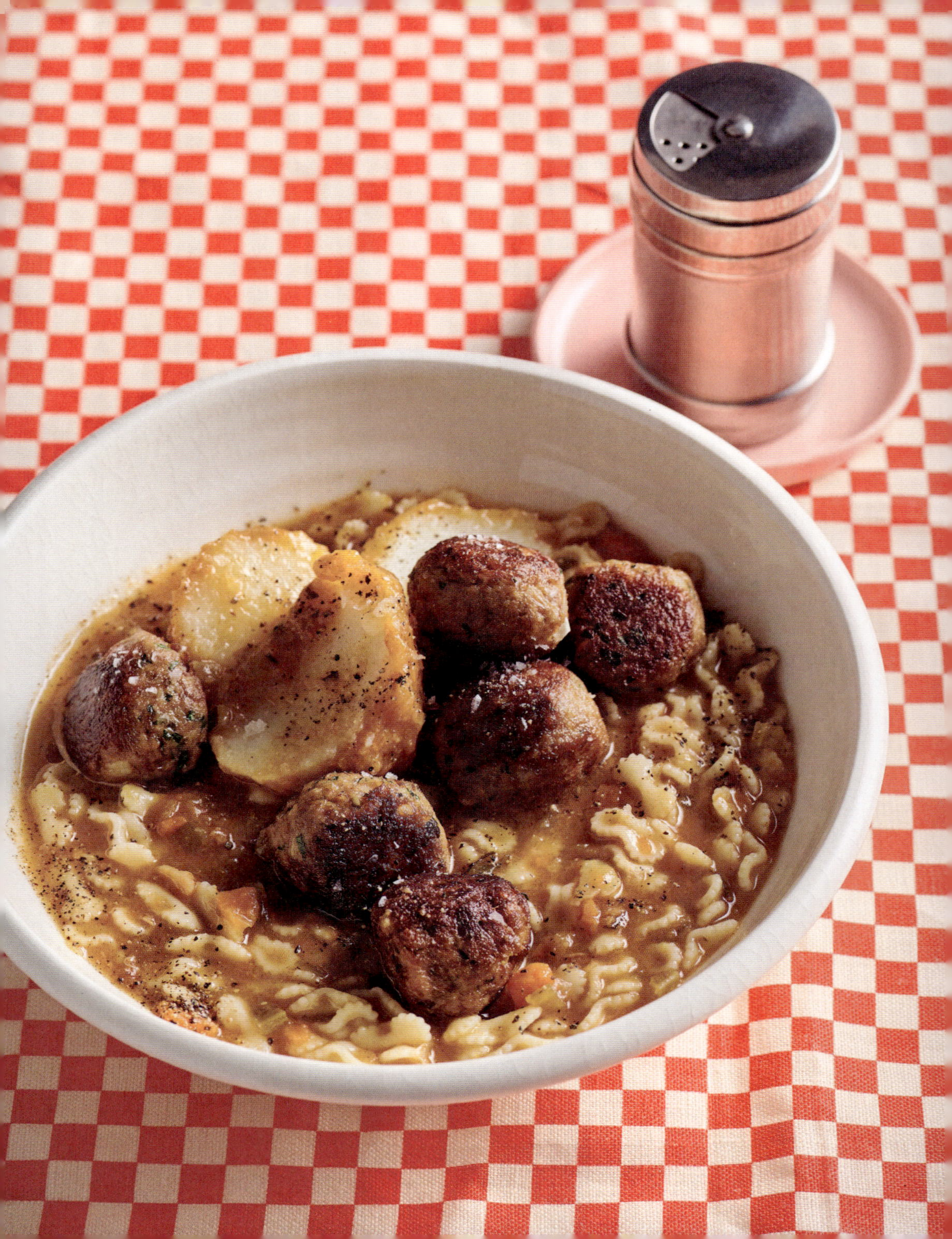

MALTA

> First-generation Australians share a few common traits no matter which corner of the globe their elders arrived from. Chief among these is acute embarrassment at the contents of their lunchbox. For me, it was sandwiches containing liverwurst, Polish sausage and la vache qui rit, aka Laughing Cow cheese. For Leanne Parnis, the daughter of Maltese immigrants, it was all Maltese food – with one notable exception. She says, 'I was a chicken-and-chips girl all the way, and I never ate Mum's soups, but when I would spy a little plate of pulpetti on the cooktop, behind the soup, the genetic stirrings were just too strong to fight.'

A delicious meat broth serves as the base for Leanne's pulpetti tal-laham, a traditional Maltese meatball dish.

Pulpetti tal-laham and brodu tal-laham
MALTESE MEATBALLS AND MEAT BROTH

SERVES 4–6

- **Meat broth**

2 tablespoons olive oil
1 kg (2 lb 3 oz) gravy beef
1 onion, finely chopped
2 carrots, diced
1 zucchini (courgette), diced
3 celery stalks, diced
4 potatoes, peeled and left whole
1 tablespoon tomato paste (concentrated puree)
1 packet chicken noodle soup mix
2 bay leaves
45 g (1½ oz/⅓ cup) small pasta
1 bunch parsley
salt and freshly cracked black pepper

- **Pulpetti**

cooked gravy beef from the broth (see above)
2 slow-cooked potatoes (from the broth; see above), mashed with a fork
¼ bunch continental parsley, finely chopped
20 g (¾ oz/⅓ cup) panko (Japanese) breadcrumbs
25 g (1 oz/¼ cup) grated parmesan cheese, plus extra to serve
3 eggs, lightly beaten, plus extra if needed
salt and freshly cracked black pepper
1–2 tablespoons olive oil

To prepare the meat broth, heat the oil in a stockpot over a medium–high heat and brown the meat on all sides. Remove the meat to a plate. To the same pot, add the onion and sweat for 10 minutes, or until translucent. Add the carrot and cook for 2 minutes, then add the zucchini and cook for another 2 minutes. Add the celery and cook for a further 2 minutes. Add the whole potatoes, season with salt and pepper, and stir to combine.

Add the tomato paste to the pot, stirring for about 1 minute to caramelise the sugars. Return the browned meat to the pot with 2 litres (68 fl oz/8 cups) water, chicken noodle soup mix and bay leaves. Bring to the boil, then reduce the heat to low, cover and simmer for about 3–3½ hours.

Add the small pasta with 15 minutes of cooking time remaining. Remove the potatoes, mash 2 for the pulpetti mixture and reserve 2 for mashed potato to serve. Remove the meat, dice it and return some to the soup, if desired. Reserve the rest for the pulpetti. Add the parsley to the soup and check and adjust the seasoning if necessary.

To prepare the pulpetti, mix the diced gravy beef, 2 mashed potatoes, parsley, breadcrumbs, grated parmesan, some salt and pepper in a large bowl until well combined. Add the beaten egg to the mixture, ensuring it is wet enough to hold together. If needed, add another egg.

Heat the oil in a frying pan over a medium heat. Using a tablespoon, scoop the mixture and shape it into balls. Fry the meatballs in the hot oil for 5 minutes, or until browned on one side. Flip the meatballs and cook for another 3 minutes, or until golden brown. Remove the meatballs to a plate lined with paper towel to drain the excess oil.

Serve the pulpetti hot in the meat broth with mashed potato on the side. Garnish the meatballs with some extra grated parmesan.

67
LEBANON

Nothing provides a more tangible connection with history than an intergenerational recipe. Nada Berjaoui's stepmother, Intisar, inherited this earthy tomato meatball soup recipe from her own mother, and it has ably stood the test of time.

For Nada's own children, one of the most happily anticipated traditions when visiting their beloved teta's is a bowl of her famous meatball soup. With pint-sized meatballs, a simple tomato broth and fried egg noodles coming to the party, the kid-friendly factor is obvious, but it's a tart, lemony treat for slurpers of all ages.

Shorba hamra
MEATBALLS IN TOMATO SOUP

SERVES 4

- **Meatballs**

500 g (1 lb 2 oz) minced (ground) beef
1 teaspoon baharat or seven-spice (see Notes)
1½ teaspoons onion powder
1 teaspoon salt
1 teaspoon paprika
15 g (½ oz/½ cup) parsley, finely chopped
1–2 tablespoons olive oil, plus extra as needed

- **Soup**

100 g (3½ oz/1½ cups) crushed egg noodles
750 ml (25½ fl oz/3 cups) chicken stock
2 tablespoons tomato paste (concentrated puree)
½–1 tablespoon sugar, or to taste
salt and freshly cracked black pepper, to taste

- **To serve**

juice of 1 small lemon
green salad (optional)

To make the meatballs, combine the beef, baharat, onion powder, salt, paprika and parsley in a bowl. Mix well and roll into balls about 2 cm (¾ in) in diameter.

Heat the oil in a frying pan over a medium heat and cook the meatballs until golden brown, about 4 minutes on each side.

Heat a little olive oil in a separate saucepan over a medium heat and cook the crushed noodles for 1–1½ minutes until golden brown. Remove from the heat and set aside.

Bring the chicken stock to the boil in a saucepan. Add the tomato paste and stir well, then add the meatballs and fried egg noodles. Add the sugar, and salt and pepper to taste. Cover with the lid and simmer for 20 minutes over a low heat.

Serve the meatball soup hot with a squeeze of lemon juice and a simple green salad if desired.

- **Notes**

Baharat is sometimes sold as 'Middle Eastern spice blend'.

Adjust the salt and paprika according to your taste. The meatballs can also be fried, if you prefer. Simply add to an oiled pan and fry until golden brown on both sides and cooked all the way through.

68
ITALY (SICILY)

In the eighties, Madonna famously wore a T-shirt emblazoned with the bold claim that 'Italians do it better'. I would go one step further and say Sicilians do it better still. Show me someone who's not been seduced by the food of Sicily and I'll show you an idiot. Case in point, these lemon polpettine – light, tangy babies that will quickly disabuse you of the notion that all Italian meatballs come submerged in a pool of tomato sugo.

Polpettine al limone
LITTLE LEMONY MEATBALLS

SERVES 4

- 80 g (2¾ oz/1 cup) fine fresh breadcrumbs
- 60 ml (2 fl oz/¼ cup) full-cream (whole) milk
- 250 g (9 oz) minced (ground) pork (see Notes)
- 250 g (9 oz) minced (ground) veal or beef
- 60 g (2 oz/⅔ cup) grated pecorino
- 1 egg
- 2 tablespoons finely chopped parsley
- 2 tablespoons finely grated lemon zest
- 1 teaspoon fennel seeds, roughly ground
- 1 garlic clove, finely chopped
- 2 teaspoons salt
- freshly cracked black pepper
- 24 lemon leaves (see Notes)
- 50 ml (1¾ fl oz) olive oil
- lemon wedges, to serve

Combine the breadcrumbs and milk in a large bowl, then squeeze with your hands to form a smooth paste.

Add the pork, veal, pecorino, egg, parsley, lemon zest, fennel seeds, garlic, salt and some pepper, and combine well with your hands.

Take a small amount of mixture and form a 3 cm (1¼ in) meatball, then wrap it in a lemon leaf, securing the leaf in place with a toothpick, and place it on a baking tray.

Continue with the remaining mixture and lemon leaves until everything has been used. Refrigerate the meatballs for at least 30 minutes before cooking; this helps the bread soak into the meat and keep the meatballs together. It also allows the lemon leaves to impart their flavour.

Heat the olive oil in a large frying pan or on a flat barbecue plate over a medium–high heat. Remove the leaves and toothpicks from the meatballs and fry the meatballs for 3 minutes on each side, or until browned and cooked through.

Serve hot with a squeeze of lemon.

● **Notes**

You can use minced (ground) pork only if preferred.

If no lemon leaves are available, you can substitute them with bay leaves or orange leaves.

69
POLAND

Inga, from Przemyśl in south-eastern Poland, doesn't mince words (so to speak) when discussing her feelings about cooking: 'I do not like it,' she says. Inga does, however, hold begrudging space in her heart for her grandmother's klopsiki recipe, passed down the generations and on high rotation in Inga's kitchen when her kids were little, and cooking was a mandatory chore.

Inga emphasises the flexible nature of the recipe: 'In Poland, my grandmother wasted no food. She would improvise the side dishes based on whatever was at hand. Different regions of Poland serve their klopsiki with different side dishes based on their proximity to other countries. We would always have mashed potato, often with a side of cooked beetroot (beets) and horseradish, or sliced dill cucumbers.' While Inga may not regard the kitchen with any great fondness, her klopsiki feel a lot like love.

Klopsiki with cwikla z chrzanem
MEATBALLS WITH HORSERADISH BEETROOT

SERVES 4–6

- **Horseradish beetroot**

5 beetroot (beets)
salt, to taste
3 tablespoons lemon juice
60 g (1 oz/½ cup) horseradish or 1 horseradish root, grated

- **Klopsiki**

125 ml (4 fl oz/½ cup) full-cream (whole) milk
1 day-old white bread roll
1 kg (2 lb 3 oz) minced (ground) beef, pork or chicken, or 500 g (1 lb 2 oz) beef and 500 g (1 lb 2 oz) pork
2 garlic cloves, minced, plus 1 whole clove
2 small eggs
salt and freshly cracked black pepper
1 heaped tablespoon plain (all-purpose) flour, for rolling
1 tablespoon olive oil (see Notes)
1 tablespoon salted butter (see Notes)

- **To serve**

mashed potato

Preheat the oven to 180°C (360°F).

To make the horseradish beetroot, clean the beetroot and wrap each one in aluminium foil, place on a baking tray and bake for 1 hour. Remove from the oven and leave to cool. Once cooled, peel and grate the beetroot, then season with salt and add the lemon juice. Add the horseradish to the beetroot gradually, tasting as you go ensure it's not too hot.

For the klopsiki, mix the milk with 125 ml (4 fl oz/½ cup) water in a bowl. Soak the bread roll in the milk and water mixture until soft, then squeeze out the excess liquid. Combine the soaked bread, meat, minced garlic and eggs in a large bowl. Mix thoroughly, then season with salt and pepper. Shape the mixture into meatballs or small logs, then roll in the flour to coat.

Heat the oil and butter in a deep, large frying pan over a medium heat and fry the meatballs until they are nicely browned on all sides.

Reduce the heat to low and add the whole garlic clove to the pan. When the garlic starts to turn yellow, add a little water to the pan. Let the meatballs simmer for a few minutes to finish cooking and to develop the sauce.

Serve the meatballs hot, accompanied by mashed potato and the horseradish beetroot.

- **Notes**

Inga's mother used to fry the meatballs in pork fat, but Inga prefers to use oil and butter. Adjust the amount of oil and butter based on your frying pan size and personal preference.

The horseradish beetroot will keep in a jar in the fridge for up to 1 week.

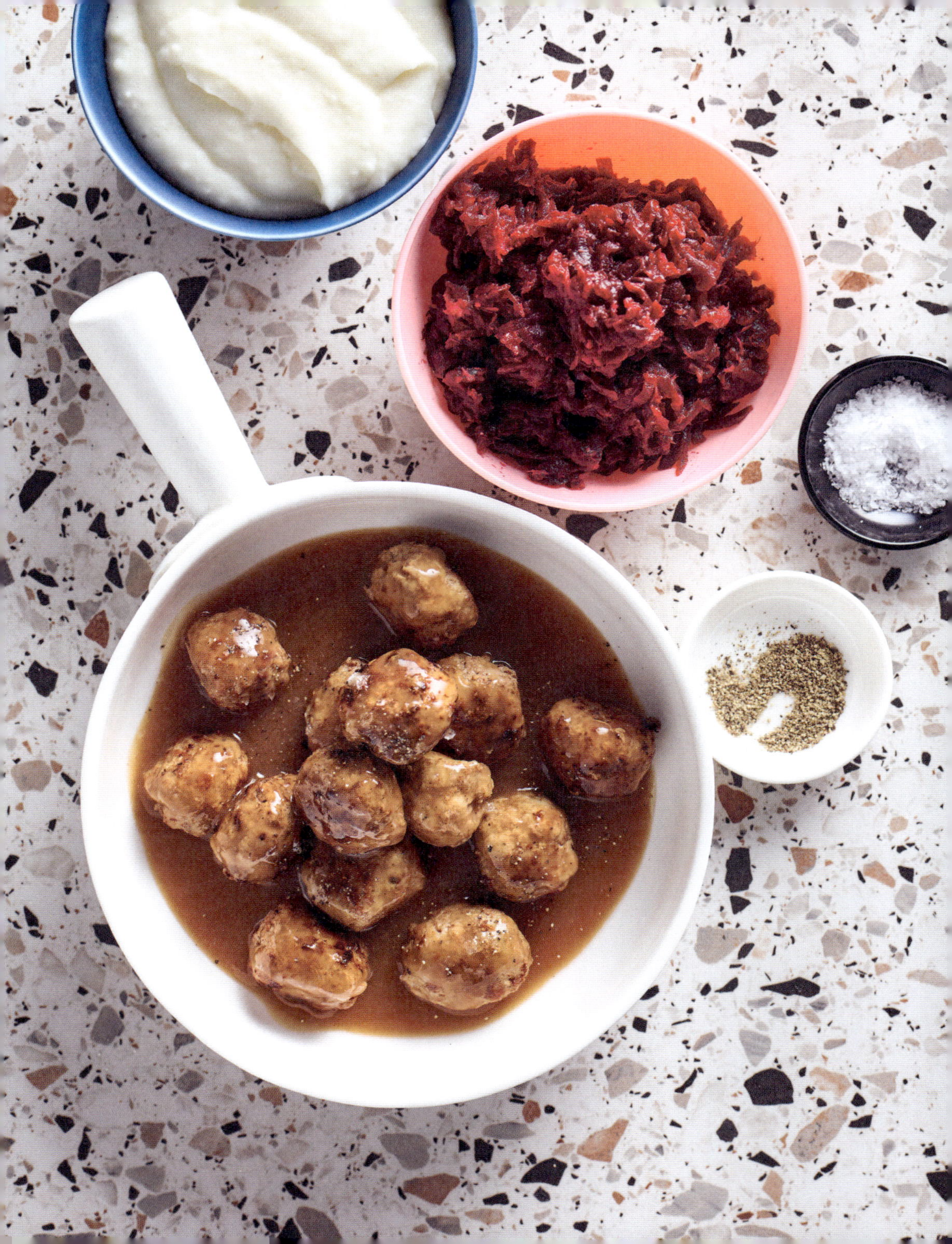

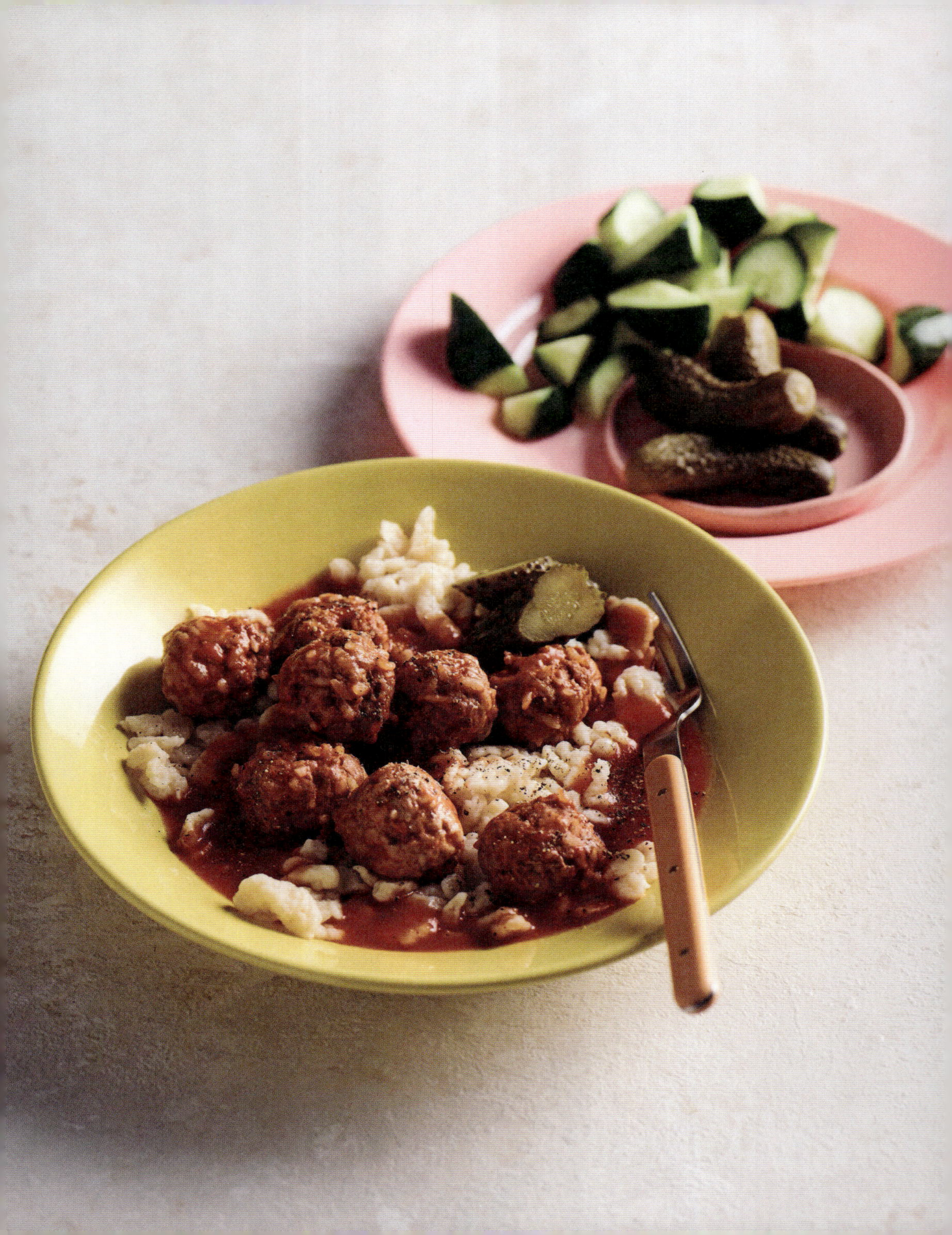

70
HUNGARY

Most children have a mixed relationship with vegetables. Geza Reisinger, born in Germany to Hungarian parents, took particular offense to capsicums (bell peppers), which is something of a problem in a country where toltott paprika, aka stuffed peppers, is an iconic national dish and a staple of most households.

Geza's mum, Maria, had a simple solution. Like many Hungarian mothers faced with paprika-resistant progeny, she would set aside a portion of the pork and rice mixture used in the dish and form it into meatballs. Maria, a chef by trade, had learned her craft under the tutelage of the former chef to Franz Joseph I, emperor of Austria and king of Hungary. So, you could say that Maria's toltott-paprika-hold-the-paprika meatballs have slightly imperial top notes. But rest assured, these meatballs are not in the least bit haughty and maintain their appeal long after you've learned to love your veggies. They're often served with another Hungarian staple, nokedli: small, simple dumplings also popular in Germany, where they're known as spatzle.

Fasirozott with nokedli
MEATBALLS WITH TINY DUMPLINGS

SERVES 4-6

- **Meatballs**

250 g (9 oz) minced (ground) pork
250 g (9 oz) minced (ground) veal
1 small onion, finely diced
60 g (2 oz) white medium-grain rice
½ teaspoon Hungarian paprika
½ teaspoon salt
¼ teaspoon freshly cracked black pepper

- **Sauce**

295 g (10½ oz) tinned condensed tomato soup

- **Nokedli**

300 g (10½ oz/2 cups) plain (all-purpose) flour
1 teaspoon salt
2 large eggs

- **To serve**

gherkins (pickles)
cucumber, chopped

Combine the pork, veal, onion, rice, paprika, salt, pepper and 60 ml (2 fl oz/¼ cup) water in a large bowl. Mix until well combined. Shape the mixture into meatballs about the size of golf balls and place them in a large saucepan.

Pour the condensed tomato soup over the meatballs. Cover the saucepan with a lid and bring to the boil over a medium-high heat. Reduce the heat to low and simmer for 45-50 minutes, stirring occasionally and gently to prevent the meatballs from breaking apart.

To make the nokedli, mix the flour and salt in a bowl. In another bowl, beat the eggs with 185 ml (6 fl oz/¾ cup) water and add to the flour mixture, stirring until smooth. Drop small spoonfuls of the batter into a large pot of boiling salted water and cook until the nokedli float to the surface, about 2-3 minutes, then drain.

Serve the meatballs and sauce atop the nokedli, with gherkins or chopped fresh cucumber on the side.

71
CHINA

Do your balls hang low, do they wobble to and fro, do you tie them in a knot, do you tie them in a bow? To this schoolyard rhyme, let's add 'do they bounce?', as a key characteristic of these meatballs is their springy, buoyant quality. The most important element for a proper bouncing ball is the temperature of the meat; your mince must be partially frozen at the outset or the balls won't form and cook properly. If sufficient bounce is achieved, you could conceivably undertake a very messy game of pickleball, but eating them is a much better idea.

Gongwan
CHINESE MEATBALL SOUP

SERVES 4

- **Meatballs**

1 kg (2 lb 3 oz) minced (ground) pork
ice-cold water, as needed
6 dried shiitake mushrooms, rehydrated in hot water, destemmed and finely chopped
1 teaspoon white pepper
1 tablespoon Chinese rice wine
1 tablespoon sesame oil
2 tablespoons cornflour (cornstarch)
1 tablespoon sugar
1 teaspoon salt
1 spring onion, very finely chopped
2 teaspoons fresh ginger, minced
1 tablespoon fresh celery, minced
½ teaspoon bonito fish powder (optional)
1 egg white

- **Soup base**

3 spring onions (scallions), minced
7 g (¼ oz/¼ cup) coriander (cilantro) leaves, chopped
½ teaspoon white pepper
1 teaspoon sesame oil
30 g (1 oz/¼ cup) fried shallots (store-bought is fine)
½ teaspoon salt
1 tablespoon chicken stock (bouillon) powder
3 celery stalks, finely diced

Divide the pork between two zip-lock bags, flatten it, then place in the freezer for 30 minutes to 1 hour (see Notes).

Remove the meat from the bags and break it into rough chunks. Transfer to a food processor and pulse briefly, adding a few teaspoons of ice-cold water to loosen the mixture. Continue pulsing for 1 minute, or until the mixture is very smooth and resembles a paste.

Place the pork meat into the bowl of a freestanding electric mixer fitted with the paddle attachment. Add the remaining meatball ingredients, then mix on medium speed for 20 minutes, scraping down the bowl occasionally.

Remove the bowl from the mixer, cover and refrigerate for 30 minutes.

While you wait for the meat to chill, make the soup base. Combine all the soup ingredients, except for the celery, in a saucepan with 2 litres (68 fl oz/8 cups) water. Bring to the boil then reduce the heat and simmer for 15–20 minutes.

Take the pork mixture out of the refrigerator. Using two spoons, scoop out 1 tablespoon of the pork paste at a time and shape it into a rough ball. Drop the meatball into the barely simmering broth (see Notes). Continue with the remaining mixture (you may have to do this in two batches). Once the pork balls float to the top, simmer for 30 seconds to 1 minute, then bring the soup to the boil and cook for another 10–15 seconds. Remove one of the pork balls from the soup, cut it in half and check that the inside is no longer pink. Remove the remaining pork balls with a slotted spoon to a bowl or plate and set aside.

Bring the soup back to the boil and add the celery. Cook for 10–15 seconds, then turn off the heat.

To serve, place a few of the pork balls into each serving bowl and ladle in some of the soup. Serve hot.

- **Notes**

Make sure you keep the pork cold at all times, until it's time to cook. Partially freeze the ground pork before you begin; it should be neither a hard nor a soft freeze. You can also refrigerate the pork mixture overnight before cooking.

Do not boil the pork balls, as this will ruin their bouncy texture. Keep them on a low simmer and bring them to the boil only during the last 10–15 seconds of cooking.

72

MALAYSIA

Simple to prep and simpler still to scoff by the dozen are these deep-fried potato and mince balls. If time is on your side, take an authentic cruise through the Strait of Malacca and prepare them with soto ayam, a spicy chicken soup commonly served in South-East Asia.

Begedil
FRIED POTATO MEATBALL PATTIES

SERVES 4–6

- **Begedil**

500 g (1 lb 2 oz) minced (ground) beef or chicken
4 potatoes, peeled and cut into chunks
1 onion, finely chopped
2 garlic cloves, minced
1 teaspoon freshly cracked black pepper
½ teaspoon ground white pepper
2 tablespoons finely chopped coriander (cilantro) leaves
salt
1 egg, beaten
olive oil, for pan-frying

- **Coating**

2 eggs, beaten

- **To garnish**

bean sprouts, blanched
2 hard-boiled eggs, halved
fried shallots
fresh coriander (cilantro) leaves, chopped
lime wedges
sambal oelek (chilli paste) (optional)

Bring a saucepan of salted water to the boil and cook the potatoes until tender, then drain and mash them. Set aside to cool.

To make the begedil, combine the meat, onion, garlic, black and white pepper, coriander and salt in a large bowl. Add the cooled mashed potato and mix until evenly incorporated. Add the egg and mix well to bind the ingredients together. Take a small portion of the mixture and shape it into a ball about the size of a golf ball then flatten it slightly to form a patty. Repeat with the remaining mixture.

Heat enough oil for pan-frying in a deep frying pan over a medium heat. Dip each patty into the beaten egg, ensuring it is fully coated. Carefully place the coated patties in the hot oil and fry until golden brown and fully cooked through, about 3–4 minutes per side. Remove the begedil from the oil and place on paper towels to drain the excess oil.

To serve, garnish the meatballs with bean sprouts, halved eggs, fried shallots, chopped coriander, lime wedges and sambal oelek, if using.

73
AUSTRALIA

This collaborative contribution was borne of two friends, Olive McCrae and Helen Angwin-Sato, duking it out over whose mother made the best porcupine meatballs. And to clear up any confusion, these meatballs do not contain the flesh of any adorably waddling, spiked critters; the name references the soft 'porcupine' spikes that pop out thanks to the addition of rice.

'Both our mothers were busy women and excellent cooks who took pride in the meals they made for the traditional sit-down evening meal,' says Helen. 'For women who cooked nightly as well as worked, it was a convenient option for a quick but really delicious meal.'

Porcupine meatballs originated in the United States during the Great Depression; tinned soup was cheap and rice helped to extend the meat. It took off in Australian households in the 1970s after it was featured in the iconic and widely circulated *Women's Weekly* magazine. Helen and Olive's recipes differ only in that Helen's mum sometimes used Worcestershire sauce rather than nutmeg. 'She might have preferred something more complicated and fancier for dinner,' says Helen, 'but believe me, my three brothers and I loved these meatballs.'

Porcupine meatballs

SERVES 6–8

- **Meatballs**

1 kg (2 lb 3 oz) minced (ground) beef
220 g (8 oz/1 cup) white long-grain rice
1 large onion, finely diced
1 egg
1 heaped tablespoon plain (all-purpose) flour mixed with 250 ml (8½ fl oz/1 cup) water to make a slurry, plus extra flour for rolling
1 teaspoon salt
1 teaspoon freshly cracked black pepper
2 teaspoons freshly grated nutmeg
1 tablespoon dried parsley

- **Simmer sauce**

1 kg (2 lb 3 oz) tinned condensed tomato soup (see Note)
salt and freshly cracked black pepper, to taste
sugar, to taste

- **To serve**

mashed potato
steamed vegetables

Combine the beef, rice, onion, egg, flour slurry, salt, pepper, nutmeg and dried parsley in a bowl and mix well. Shape into about twenty meatballs, then coat them in flour.

For the simmer sauce, bring the tomato soup and 60 ml (2 fl oz/¼ cup) water to the boil in a large saucepan. The pan needs to be wide, not necessarily deep. Season with salt, pepper and sugar to taste.

Once the sauce is bubbling, reduce the heat to low. Add the meatballs to the sauce, cover and simmer for 35–40 minutes. The meatballs are cooked when the rice starts to protrude.

Serve with mashed potato and steamed vegetables.

- **Note**

For a fancier version, use passata (pureed tomatoes) rather than condensed tomato soup. However, if you want the true taste of seventies Australia, stick with the tinned soup.

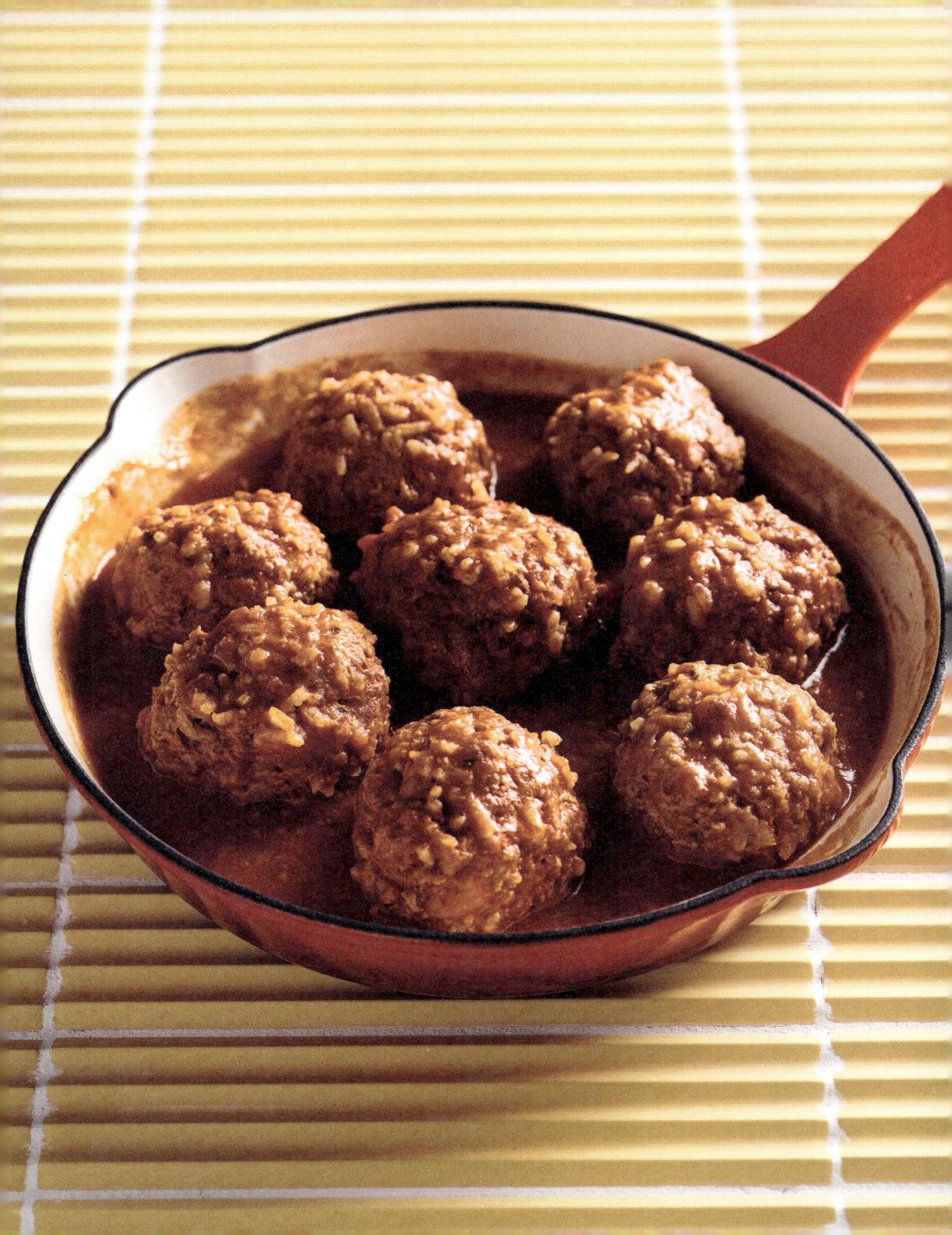

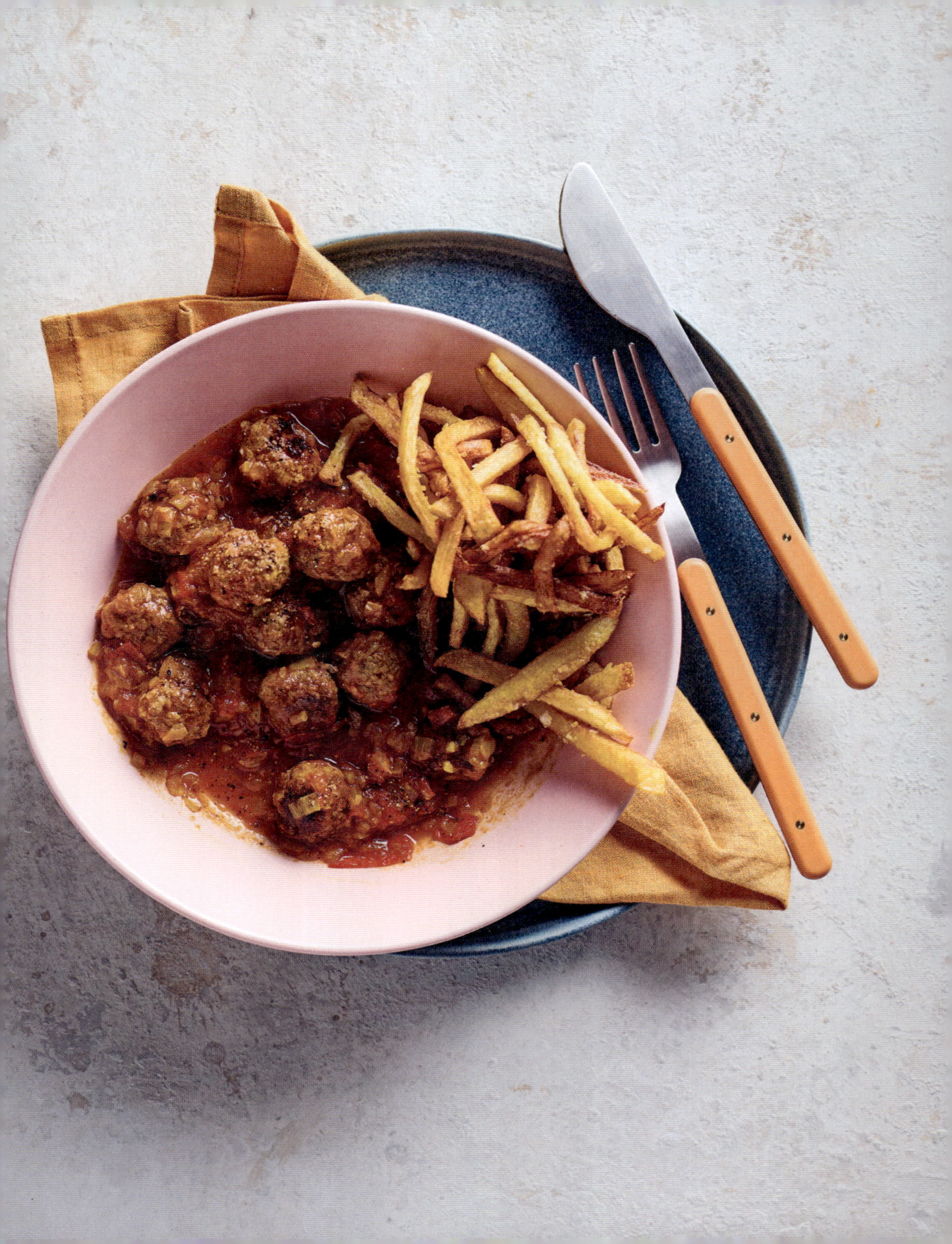

74
IRAN (PERSIA)

By now, you may have noticed that Iranian/Persian meatball recipes occupy a fair slab of real estate in this book, and that is because a) the Persians invented them, and b) they have an exceptionally diverse range of meatball recipes, as you would well expect.

Kal-leh gonjishki translates to 'little bird's head', a playful nod to the tiny, delicate nature of these meatballs. Served with roasted turmeric potatoes, in a tomato broth, these Lilliputian balls are among the most child-friendly of the bunch, and a cute eat at any age.

Kal leh gonjishki
SPARROW-HEAD MEATBALLS WITH FRENCH FRIES

SERVES 8

- **Meatballs**

900 g (2 lb) minced (ground) beef or lamb
2 small onions, grated
2 teaspoons salt
1 teaspoon freshly cracked black pepper
1 teaspoon ground turmeric
½ teaspoon ground cinnamon
80 ml (2½ fl oz/⅓ cup) olive oil

- **Sauce**

80 ml (2½ fl oz/⅓ cup) olive oil
2 large onions, diced
8 garlic cloves, minced
2 teaspoons ground turmeric
60 g (2 oz) tomato paste (concentrated puree)
4 large ripe tomatoes, diced (peeling optional)
80–160 ml (2½–5½ fl oz) fresh lemon juice
2 teaspoons salt
1 teaspoon freshly cracked black pepper

- **Potatoes**

4 large potatoes, cut French fry-style
160 ml (5½ fl oz) olive oil
1 teaspoon salt
1 teaspoon ground turmeric

- **To serve**

steamed basmati rice

To make the meatballs, combine all the ingredients, except the oil, in a large bowl. Mix well and then shape the mixture into small meatballs.

Heat the oil in a large frying pan over a medium-high heat. Sauté the meatballs for about 10 minutes, turning them as necessary to brown on all sides. Remove from the pan and set aside.

To make the sauce, heat another 2 tablespoons olive oil in the same pan and sauté the diced onion over a medium heat for 15 minutes, or until light golden brown. Add the garlic and turmeric to the onion and sauté for another 2 minutes. Add the tomato paste and sauté for a further 2 minutes. Add the diced tomatoes, lemon juice, 750 ml (25½ fl oz/3 cups) water, salt and pepper, then bring to a gentle simmer.

Return the meatballs to the pan, cover and cook over a low heat for 45–55 minutes.

Preheat the oven to 190°C (375°F).

While the stew is cooking, combine the sliced potatoes with oil, salt and turmeric. Roast for 30 minutes, or until fully cooked. Arrange the stew on a serving platter and place the roasted potatoes on top.

Serve with steamed basmati rice.

75
RUSSIA

Chalk it up to the abundance of Russian and Ukrainian blood running through my veins: these are some of my very favourite meatballs. While 'grechanyky' translates as 'patty' rather than 'meatball', these warrant inclusion for the simple reason that they are too good not to share – and what is a meatball but a patty reshaped into a ball? They can, of course, be rolled into meatballs if you are a true ball purista.

What makes these patties really sing is the inclusion of a beloved Russian staple: buckwheat (aka kasha). Under-appreciated in Western cuisine, and often mislabelled as a grain, buckwheat is in fact a seed, and a member of the superbly named pseudo-cereal family. The addition of the cooked buckwheat, which itself has a texture not unlike minced meat, makes for a super juicy patty with a lovely, nutty depth. Mushroom sauce is optional; they're also amazing with sour cream or tomato sauce (ketchup).

Grechanyky with mushroom sauce

SERVES 4–6

- **Meatballs**

170 g (6 oz/1 cup) cooked buckwheat groats, cooled
1 onion, very finely chopped
600 g (1 lb 5 oz) minced (ground) beef
60 ml (2 fl oz/¼ cup) full-cream (whole) milk
½ teaspoon onion powder
½ teaspoon garlic powder
1 teaspoon salt
¼ teaspoon freshly cracked black pepper
1 egg

- **Mushroom sauce**

450 g (1 lb) Swiss brown mushrooms, rinsed and patted dry
250 ml (8½ fl oz/1 cup) dry sherry
pinch of salt, or to taste
3–4 parsley stalks
3 black peppercorns, lightly crushed
1 bay leaf
1 tablespoon salted butter
1 tablespoon plain (all-purpose) flour
375 ml (12½ fl oz/1½ cups) thick (double/heavy) cream
⅓ teaspoon ground white pepper
¼ teaspoon freshly grated nutmeg

To make the meatballs, combine the cooked and cooled buckwheat, onion and beef in a bowl. Add the milk, onion powder, garlic powder, salt and pepper. Crack the egg into the bowl and mix until well combined.

Shape the mixture into meatballs about the size of golf balls, then flatten them into patties. Alternatively, form them into large meatballs and flatten the tops slightly.

Pour enough oil into a large skillet or frying pan to coat the bottom. Heat over medium heat until hot, then place the patties in carefully. Cook the patties for about 6 minutes on each side, or until browned and cooked through. Set aside.

To make the mushroom sauce, separate the mushroom caps from the stems. Set the caps aside and coarsely chop the stems. Bring the sherry to a simmer in a small saucepan and add the mushroom stems. Boil until the liquid has reduced by about two-thirds, then reduce the heat to a simmer and add a pinch of salt, the parsley stalks, peppercorns and bay leaf. Cover with the lid and steep over a very low heat for about 1 hour. Strain, discard the solids, and keep the liquid warm.

Melt the butter in a frying pan over a medium heat and sauté the mushroom caps until the liquid from the mushrooms has completely evaporated, about 25 minutes. Sift the flour over the mushrooms and cook, stirring frequently, for another 20 minutes over a low heat.

Slowly pour in the reduced sherry, and then the cream, whisking vigorously. Cover the sauce and let it simmer over a low heat for 30 minutes. If it's too thick, dilute it with a bit more cream. Finish with the white pepper and a pinch of nutmeg.

Ladle the mushroom sauce over the meatballs before serving.

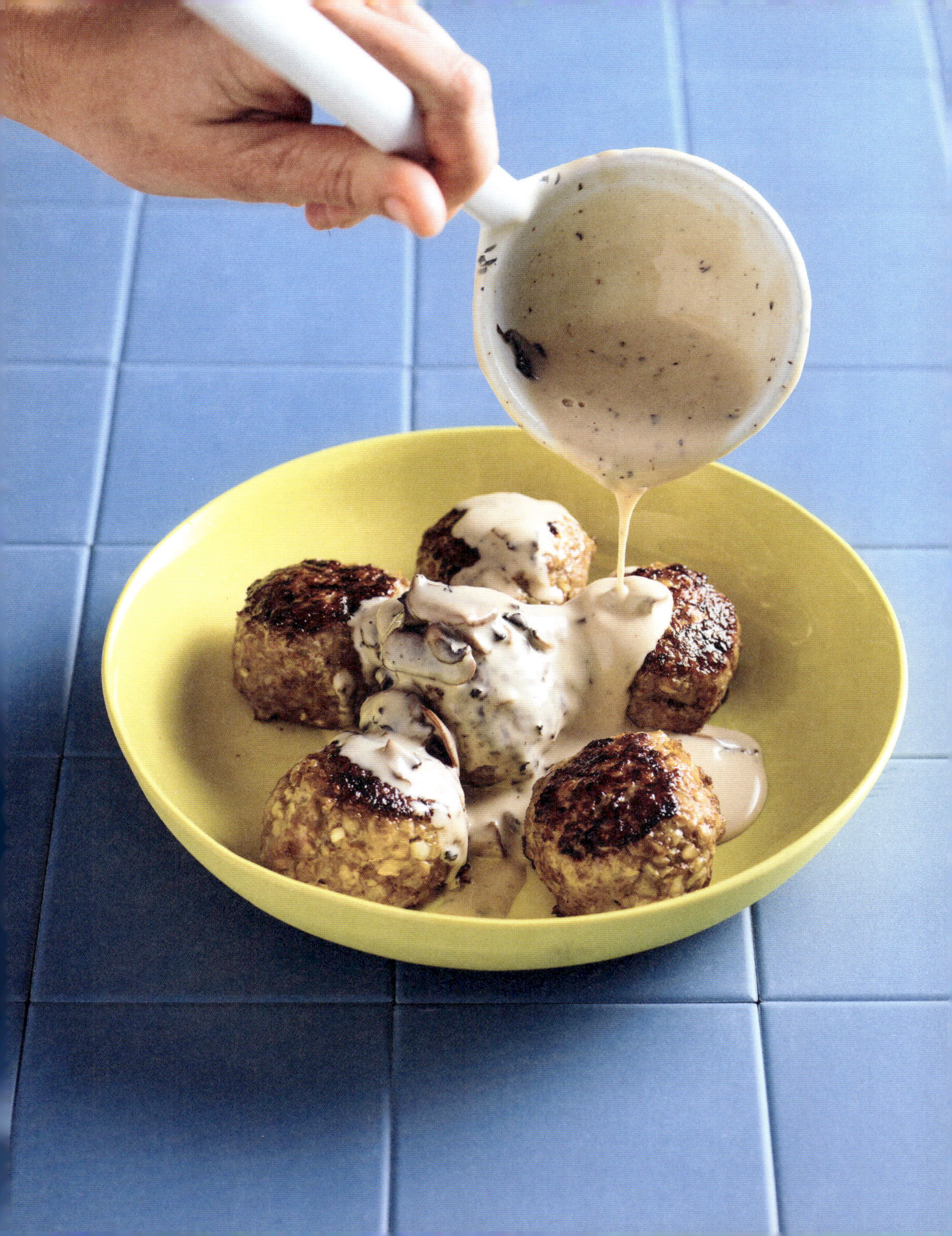

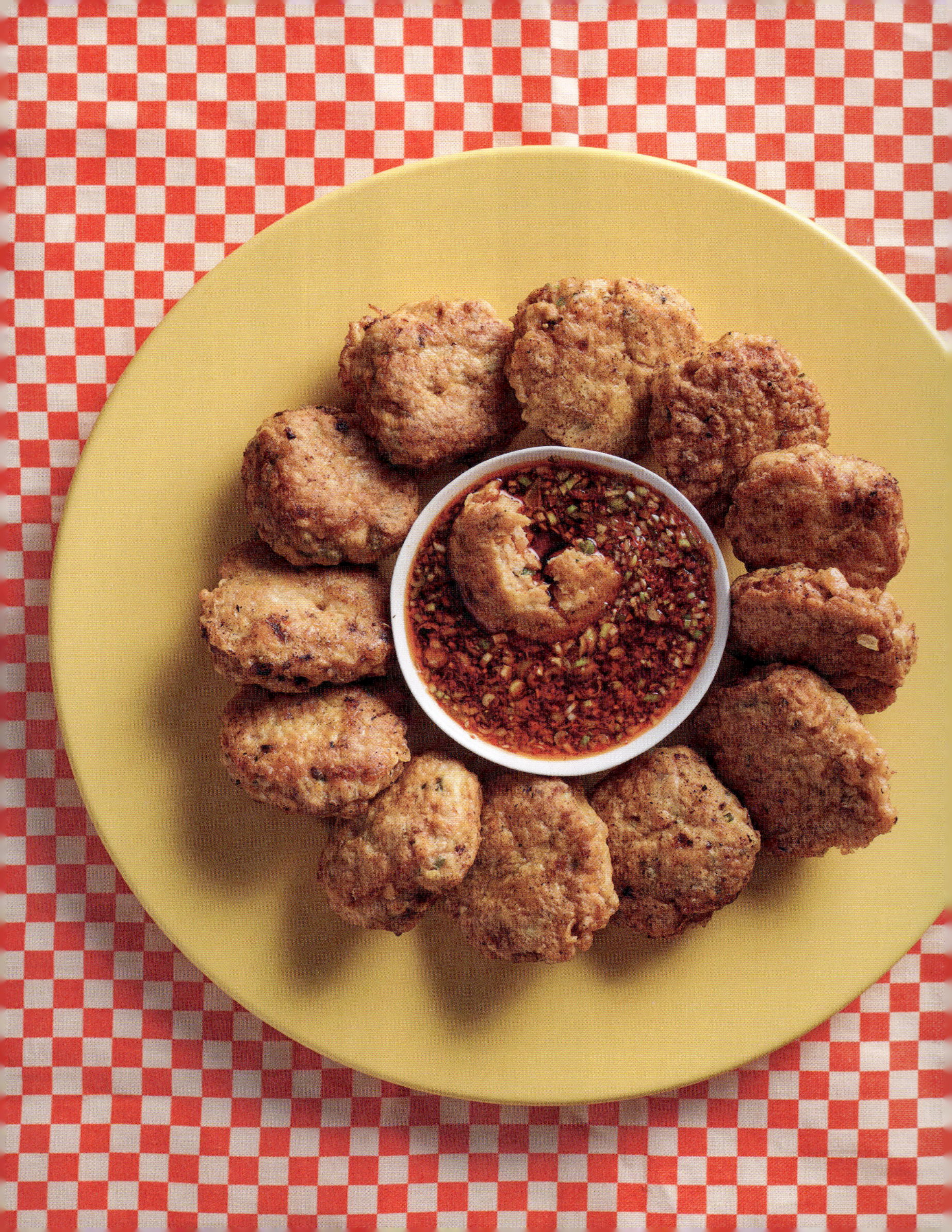

76
KOREA

Making goji-wanja-jeon, aka meatball pancakes, immediately summons the past for Robbie Yoon, along with a flood of nostalgia for the extended family he left behind in his birthplace of Seoul after immigrating to Australia in 2006. Now a chef at a popular inner-city Melbourne pub, the recipe Robbie shares here mirrors the one his mum used to make on Chuseok (Korean Thanksgiving), using a recipe passed down from her own mother. Robbie recalls the smell of the oil permeating the house as his mother, uncles and aunties prepared all the Chuseok dishes; meatballs, being a low-risk undertaking, were the dish Robbie was assigned to help with as a small child.

Don't be fooled by the 'pancake' bit here; like lion's head meatballs (see pages 150–152), the name is a cute misnomer. 'Pancakes' refers simply to their shape, which is flatter and more fritter-esque than your standard meatball.

Robbie tells me that when he makes goji-wanja-jeon for his young family, he finds it difficult not to eat them all, and you'll likely agree; they are some of the brightest stars in the meatball constellation.

Goji-wanja-jeon
FRIED MEAT PATTIES WITH GOCHUGARU DIPPING SAUCE

SERVES 6–8

- **Meatballs**

1 kg (2 lb 3 oz) minced (ground) pork
1 small onion, finely diced
120 g (4½ oz) carrot, finely diced
20 g (¾ oz) fresh ginger, finely chopped
50 g (1¾ oz) garlic, minced
3 spring onions (scallions), white and green parts separated and finely chopped
30 g (1 oz) Chinese rice wine or white wine
50 ml (1¾ fl oz) soy sauce
1 teaspoon Korean chilli powder (gochugaru)
1 teaspoon sesame oil
100 g (3½ oz/⅔ cup) plain (all-purpose) flour, for dusting
3 eggs, beaten, for egg wash
1–2 tablespoons vegetable oil

- **Dipping sauce**

white part of 3 spring onions (scallions; see above), finely chopped
50 ml (1¾ fl oz) soy sauce
1 teaspoon Korean chilli powder (gochugaru)
1 teaspoon sesame oil
50 ml (1¾ fl oz) rice vinegar or balsamic vinegar

To make the meatballs, combine the pork, onion, carrot, ginger, garlic, green parts of the spring onions, rice wine, soy sauce, chilli powder and sesame oil in a large bowl. Mix until well combined.

Portion the mixture into about 25 balls, each weighing approximately 60 g (2 oz), then flatten each ball slightly. Dust the flattened balls with the plain flour, then coat with the egg wash.

Heat the oil in a large frying pan over a medium–low heat and pan-fry the meatballs for 3–4 minutes on each side, or until golden brown and cooked through.

While the meatballs are frying, prepare the dipping sauce. Combine the white parts of the spring onions, soy sauce, chilli powder, sesame oil and rice vinegar in a small bowl and mix well.

Serve the meatballs hot with the dipping sauce on the side.

- **Note**

These meatball pancakes are delicious on their own, or served over steamed white rice.

77
SPAIN

Fernando Vidal Garrida's memories of making albondigas with his late, much-adored grandmother, Pepa, could fill a book all of their own. 'My grandmother raised me and adored me from the day I was born. Her kitchen was the perfect refuge for a hyperactive but sickly child, too exuberant for most people.' Fernando, originally from Andalusia in southern Spain and now an Australian resident, continues, 'My grandmother always tasked me with shaping the meatballs. She would pretend they were beautiful, saying "It's almost sad to eat them."' All these years later, with Pepa long gone, Fernando says, 'Eating meatballs for me is almost like Communion. It's a journey through space and time, straight to my grandmother. It is a date for both of us, and the only way I have to feel her by my side again.' A word on serving: 'My grandmother didn't put the slightest effort into presentation; she would unceremoniously dump the albondigas on a platter, or even just put the frying pan on the table.' Inspirational words for the unfussy home cook.

Albondigas Mama Pepa in white wine sauce

SERVES 4

● **Meatballs**
250 g (9 oz) minced (ground) beef
250 g (9 oz) minced (ground) pork
2–3 garlic cloves, minced
7 g (¼ oz/¼ cup) parsley, finely chopped
3–4 slices crustless white bread
80 ml (2½ fl oz/⅓ cup) full-cream (whole) milk
1 egg yolk and a little bit of the white
20 g (¾ oz/¼ cup) fresh breadcrumbs, plus extra if needed, soaked in water
tiny pinch of ground cumin (optional)
salt and freshly cracked black pepper
olive oil, for deep-frying

● **White wine and almond sauce**
1 teaspoon olive oil
1 small ripe tomato, chopped
2 onions, chopped
500 ml (17 fl oz/2 cups) white wine
40 g (1½ oz/¼ cup) almonds, finely chopped
40 g (1½ oz/¼ cup) pine nuts, finely chopped
ground white pepper, to taste
freshly cracked black pepper, to taste

● **To garnish**
1 handful parsley, chopped

Start by making the meatballs. Without mixing yet, add the beef, pork, garlic, parsley and some salt and pepper to a large bowl. In a separate dish, soak the bread slices in the milk. Mash the bread with a fork until the mixture forms a textured paste. Add this to the meat mixture, along with the egg yolk, a bit of the egg white, the breadcrumbs and the cumin, if using. Mix carefully to keep the meat in small chunks. If the mixture is too runny, add enough extra breadcrumbs until you have malleable consistency.

Oil your hands to prevent the meat from sticking, then shape the mixture into meatballs slightly smaller than ping-pong balls. Roll the meatballs in the breadcrumbs and place them on a plate.

Heat enough olive oil in a deep frying pan to submerge the meatballs, about 8–10 cm (3¼–4 in), over a medium–high heat. When the oil starts to smoke slightly, add the meatballs. Deep-fry until golden brown on all sides, moving them often. Remove and set aside.

To make the sauce, heat the olive oil in a frying pan over a medium heat and sauté the tomato and onion until golden. Add the wine and simmer until reduced by half. Transfer the mixture to a blender and blend until smooth. In the same frying pan, toast the chopped almonds and pine nuts over a medium–low heat until slightly browned. Add the blended sauce and the meatballs, and slowly allow the sauce to return to the boil. Season to taste with the white and black pepper, then remove from the heat.

Serve the meatballs in the white wine and almond sauce, garnished with a handful of fresh parsley.

● **Notes**
Fernando also likes to bake the meatballs and says, 'This method results in delicious meatballs, though it's not 100 per cent traditional. Preheat the oven to 200°C (390°F). Place the meatballs on a baking tray lined with baking paper and bake for 10 minutes, then lower the temperature to 180°C (360°F) and bake for another 15–20 minutes. The baked meatballs won't be perfectly round like their fried cousins but set them aside once they are golden and pretty.' Continue with the recipe, adding the meatballs to the sauce.

78
PALESTINE

A simple bake with a bit of pleasing bite and tang via the addition of tahini and lemons, this is a great recipe to try if you've got tomato-resistant mouths to feed. Pulsed pita in the meatballs and potato wedges give this bake a hell of a lot of oomph; you won't leave the table with looser trousers than when you sat down. A simple Palestinian salad helps lighten things up.

For those with no fear of a triple-carb threat, steamed Lebanese vermicelli rice, a simple three-ingredient dish, is a fine accompaniment – plenty of recipes can be found online.

Kafta and tahini bake with Palestinian salad

SERVES 6–8

- **Kafta**
800 g (1 lb 12 oz) minced (ground) beef or lamb
100 g (3½ oz) pita bread, torn into rough pieces
1 tomato, quartered
1 small onion, roughly chopped
2 garlic cloves
2 tablespoons finely chopped coriander (cilantro) leaves
2 tablespoons finely chopped flat-leaf (Italian) parsley
1 tablespoon salt
1 tablespoon baharat or seven-spice
1 kg (2 lb 3 oz) potatoes, cut into thick wedges

- **Sauce**
270 g (9½ oz/1 cup) hulled tahini
125 g (4½ oz/½ cup) plain yoghurt
80–100 ml (2½–3½ fl oz) lemon juice
1½ teaspoons salt

- **Palestinian salad**
4 large, firm tomatoes, finely chopped
2 Lebanese (short) cucumbers, finely diced
1 lemon
6 spring onions (scallions), finely chopped
6 g (¼ oz) finely chopped mint
80 ml (2½ fl oz/⅓ cup) olive oil
80 ml (2½ fl oz/⅓ cup) lemon juice
1 teaspoon salt

- **To serve**
toasted pine nuts
parsley leaves

To make the kafta, preheat the oven to 220°C (430°F). Set aside about one-quarter of the meat in a large bowl. In a separate bowl, soak the pita in water and set aside.

In a food processor, combine the tomato, onion, garlic, coriander, parsley, salt and baharat. Pulse until a coarse paste forms. Drain the bread, squeezing out the excess moisture with your hands, and add to the food processor. Pulse to evenly combine.

Pour the mixture over the quarter of meat in the bowl and mix with a spoon or your hands until well combined. Add the remaining meat and mix gently using your hands until evenly incorporated. Do not over mix. Shape the mixture into 14–16 koftas. Arrange the meat and potatoes in a single flat layer on a baking tray lined with baking paper and cook in the oven for 15–20 minutes, or until the meatballs have started to brown.

While the meatballs cook, whisk together all the sauce ingredients with 750 ml (25½ fl oz/3 cups) water in a bowl, then set aside. Remove the kafta from the oven and transfer into a large ovenproof dish along with any juices from the tray. Add the potatoes and arrange the meat and potatoes upright and angled. Pour the sauce over the kafta (not the tops of the potatoes), and return to the oven for about 15 minutes, or until the potatoes begin to turn golden brown in patches.

To make the Palestinian salad, add the tomato and cucumber to a bowl. Slice the lemon into thin rounds, discarding the top and bottom rounds and any seeds. Chop each round into small cubes and add to the bowl with the spring onion and mint. Drizzle with the olive oil and lemon juice, and sprinkle with the salt.

To serve, lightly toss the salad and serve alongside the kafta bake. Top with toasted pine nuts and roughly torn parsley leaves.

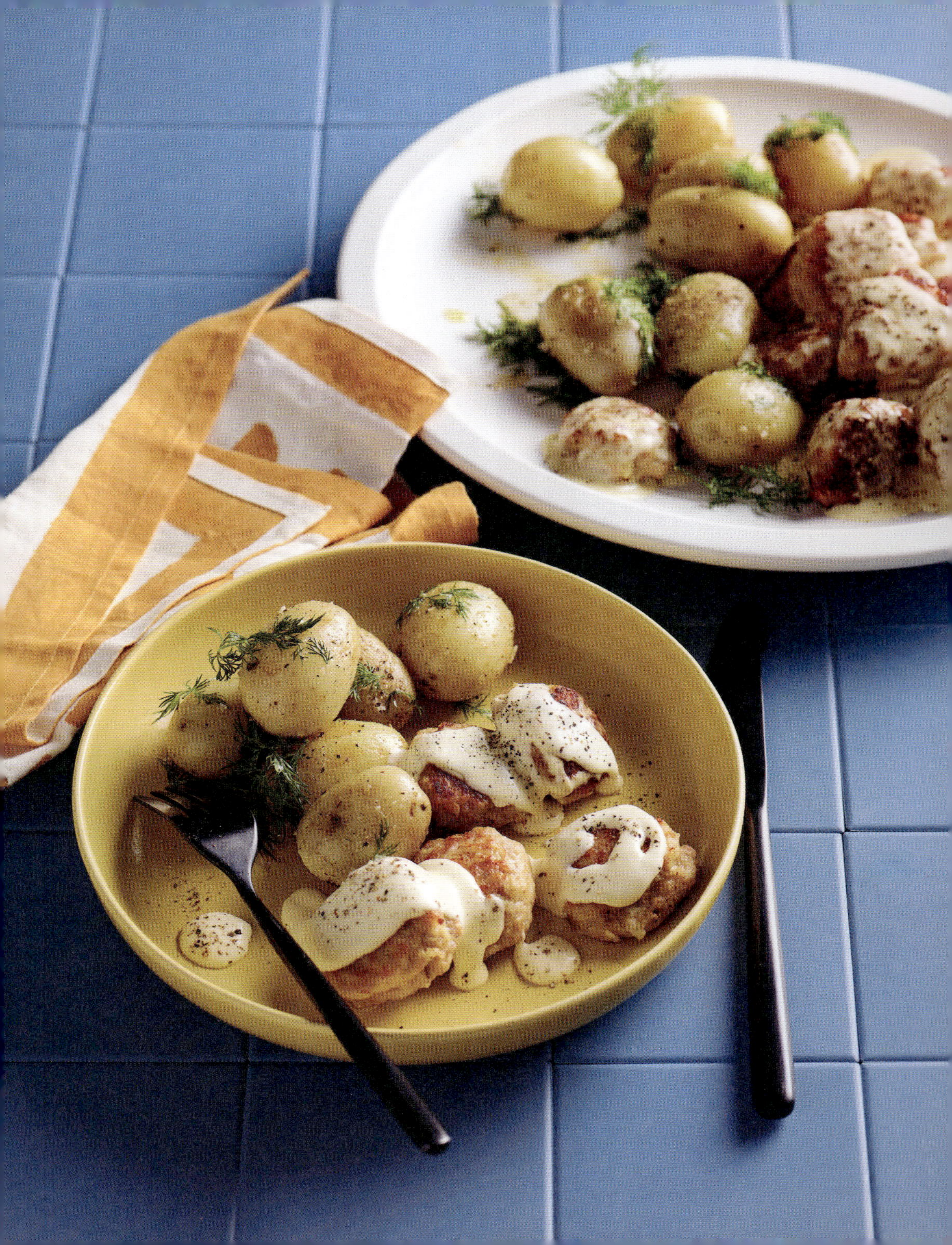

79

SWEDEN

Subtly adjusted iterations of this kottbullar recipe have passed through James Irving's family since the late 1800s; if your immediate reaction to this is 'James Irving may be the least Scandinavian name I have ever heard', rest assured that James's mother, Marie, was born and raised in Nyköping, in south-eastern Sweden. No disrespect to IKEA, but you won't want a bar of the flat-pack variety once you've given this recipe a go.

James's kids love this recipe, just as their antecedents did in the time before BILLY bookshelves, and it's on regular rotation in the Irving kitchen. James occasionally plays around with the recipe, adding a tablespoon of teriyaki sauce to the cream sauce, and piling them onto pasta; here, they're served with the more traditional accompaniment of dill potato salad.

Kottbullar

SERVES 6–8

- **Meatballs**

20 g (¾ oz/¼ cup) dry breadcrumbs, soaked in milk or cream
125 ml (4 fl oz/½ cup) pouring (single/light) cream
3 teaspoons potato flour (see Note)
60 ml (2 fl oz/¼ cup) full-cream (whole) milk
125 g (4½ oz/½ cup) salted butter
1 onion, grated
375 g (13 oz) minced (ground) lean beef
375 g (13 oz) minced (ground) pork
1 egg, lightly beaten
250 ml (8½ fl oz/1 cup) thick (double/heavy) cream
salt and freshly cracked black pepper

- **Dill potato salad**

900 g (2 lb) new potatoes, washed and unpeeled
60 g (2 oz/¼ cup) salted butter, cut into tablespoon-sized pieces
2–3 tablespoons chopped dill
salt and freshly cracked black pepper

To make the meatballs, combine the breadcrumbs, pouring (single/light) cream and potato flour in a large bowl. Mix well, adding milk until the mixture reaches the consistency of thick porridge. Set aside for 5–10 minutes.

Melt 20 g (¾ oz) of the butter in a small frying pan over a low heat and soften the grated onion for 2–3 minutes, ensuring it doesn't brown. Leave to cool.

Add the cooked onion, salt and pepper to the breadcrumb mixture and mix well. Add the beef, pork and egg to the bowl. Mix well with your hands, adding a little more milk if the mixture is too thick. Refrigerate for about 30 minutes.

Preheat the oven to 180°C (360°F).

Shape the mixture into meatballs about the size of golf balls and lay them on a tray lined with baking paper until you're ready to cook them.

Heat the remaining butter in a frying pan and brown the meatballs (you may need to do this in batches to avoid overcrowding the pan). When nicely browned, place the meatballs on a clean baking tray lined with baking paper and bake for 20 minutes.

Add the thick (double/heavy) cream to the pan with the reserved butter and pan scrapings, season to taste with salt and pepper and heat gently, until just warmed through, to prevent the sauce from splitting.

To make the dill potato salad, place the potatoes in a large saucepan and cover them with cold salted water by 5 cm (2 in). Bring to the boil over a high heat, then reduce the heat to medium, maintaining a rolling boil. Cook the potatoes until tender, about 10–18 minutes. Transfer the potatoes to a colander or strainer to drain.

Add the butter and chopped dill to the empty pot along with the drained potatoes. Gently toss the potatoes until they are evenly coated with the butter and dill. Season to taste with salt and pepper.

To serve, arrange the cooked meatballs on a serving platter and pour the sauce over them. Serve with the dill potato salad.

- **Note**

Potato starch can be used instead of potato flour, as it is easier to find and works well in this recipe.

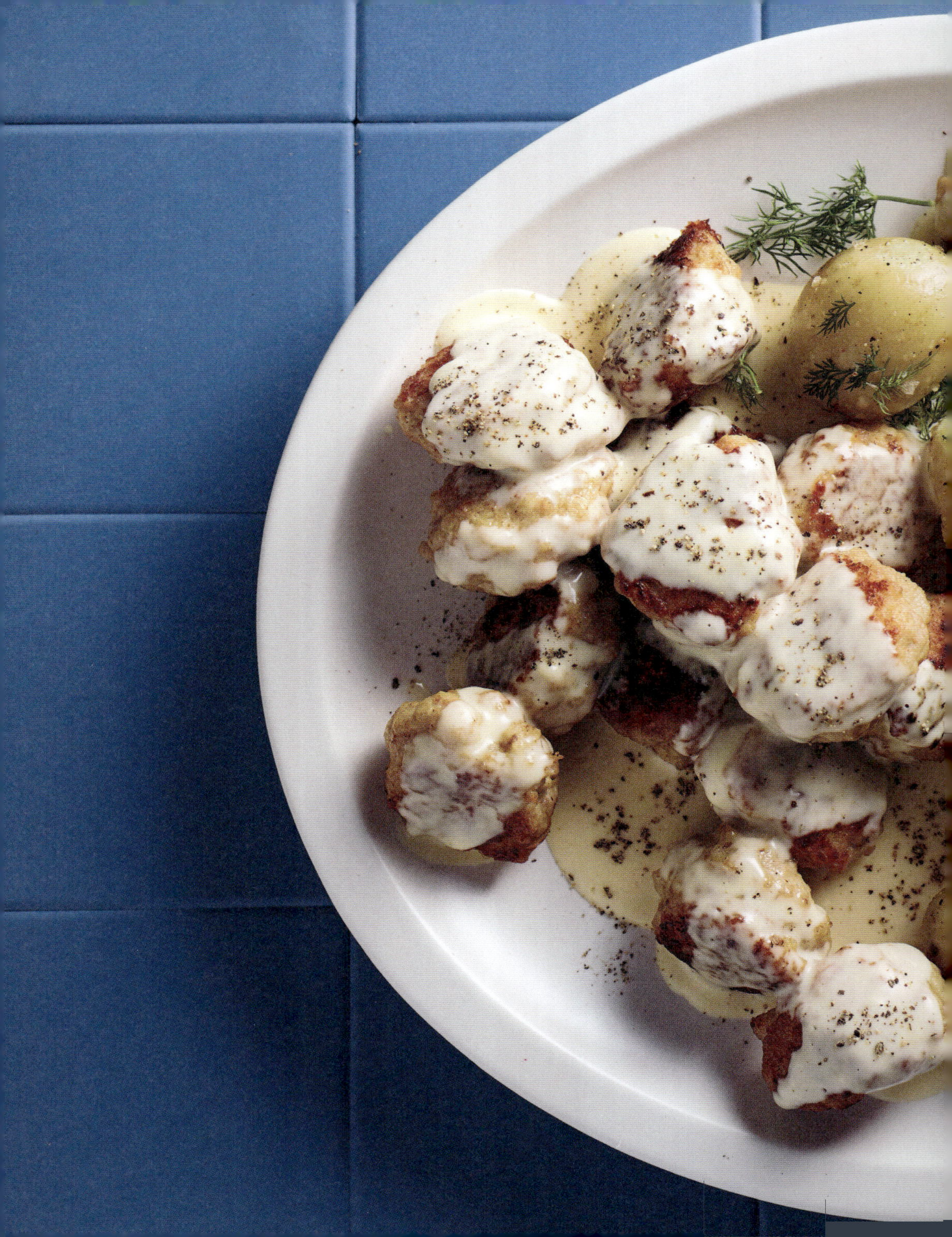

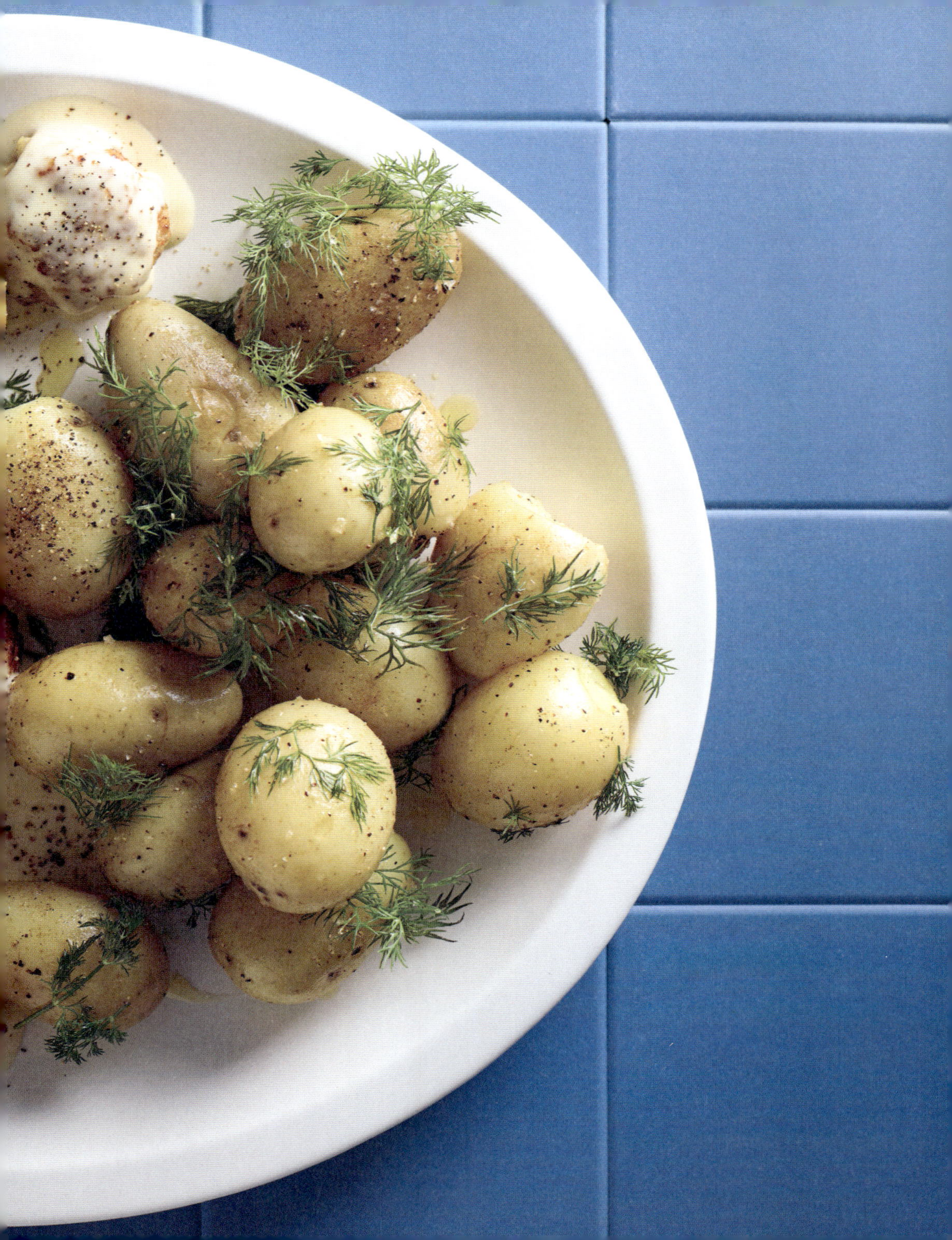

80
TIBET

Tibet's high altitudes and harsh climate demand warming, nutrient-dense foods, and this simple soup is just that. Historically, Tibetan cuisine has relied heavily on yak meat, mutton, dairy and barley – vegetables being a somewhat scarce resource due to the climatic conditions and geographical isolation.

Testament to the resourcefulness of the Tibetan people, this meatball soup is proof that beautiful things can be born of necessity. Thanks to the killer altitudes, Tibetans have genetic adaptations correlated with very high infant survival rates and unusual resistance to chronic mountain sickness. I can't promise that this soup will alter your genetic make-up for the better, but it's certainly a step in the right direction if robust good health is what you seek.

Tibetan meatball soup

SERVES 4

- **Meatballs**

350 g (12½ oz) minced (ground) beef
1 egg
½ small red onion, finely chopped
1 large garlic clove, finely chopped
½ teaspoon crushed sichuan peppercorns
1 teaspoon ground coriander
1 teaspoon salt, plus extra to taste
plain (all-purpose) flour, for dusting

- **Soup**

1 litre (34 fl oz/4 cups) boiling water or beef broth
125 g (4½ oz) baby spinach leaves

- **To garnish**

coriander (cilantro) leaves

To make the meatballs, combine the beef and egg in a bowl and mix well. Add the onion, garlic, sichuan peppercorns, ground coriander and ½ teaspoon salt and mix until well combined.

Sprinkle a little flour onto a chopping board. Shape the mixture into meatballs about the size of golf balls, then lightly roll each meatball in the flour on the board, then between your hands again, and through the flour once more. Set aside and repeat with the remaining meat mixture, adding more flour to the board as needed.

To make the soup, pour the boiling water into a large wok over a medium heat. Bring the water back to the boil, then add the meatballs. Stir them gently, adding a little more water if the meatballs are not fully covered.

Add the remaining ½ teaspoon of salt, increase the heat to high and simmer the meatballs for 5 minutes, stirring occasionally. Add the spinach 1 minute before the end of the cooking time. Cut a meatball open to check that it's cooked all the way through. Taste and adjust the seasoning if needed.

To serve, ladle the soup into serving bowls and garnish with coriander leaves.

- **Note**

This soup is often made with the addition of noodles.

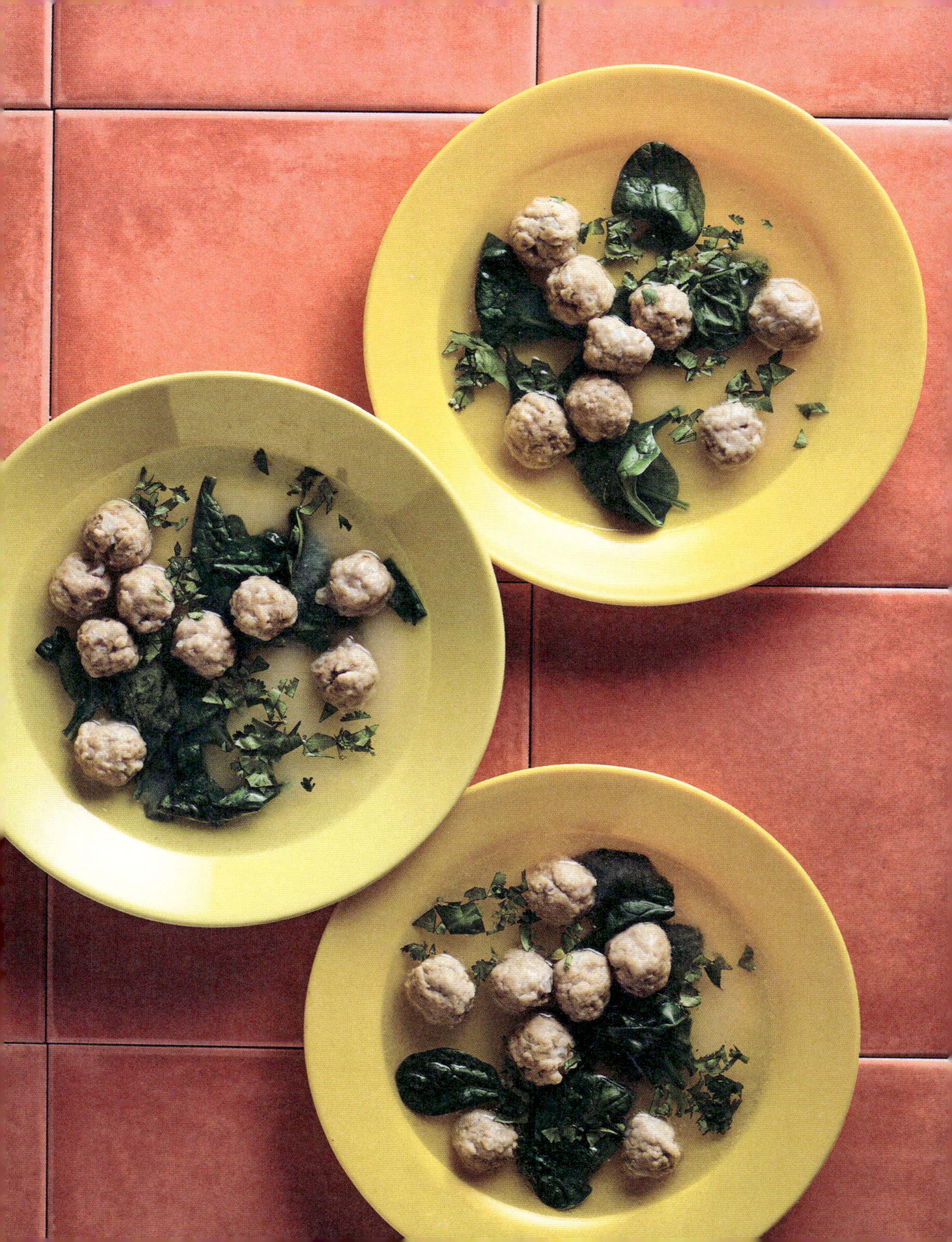

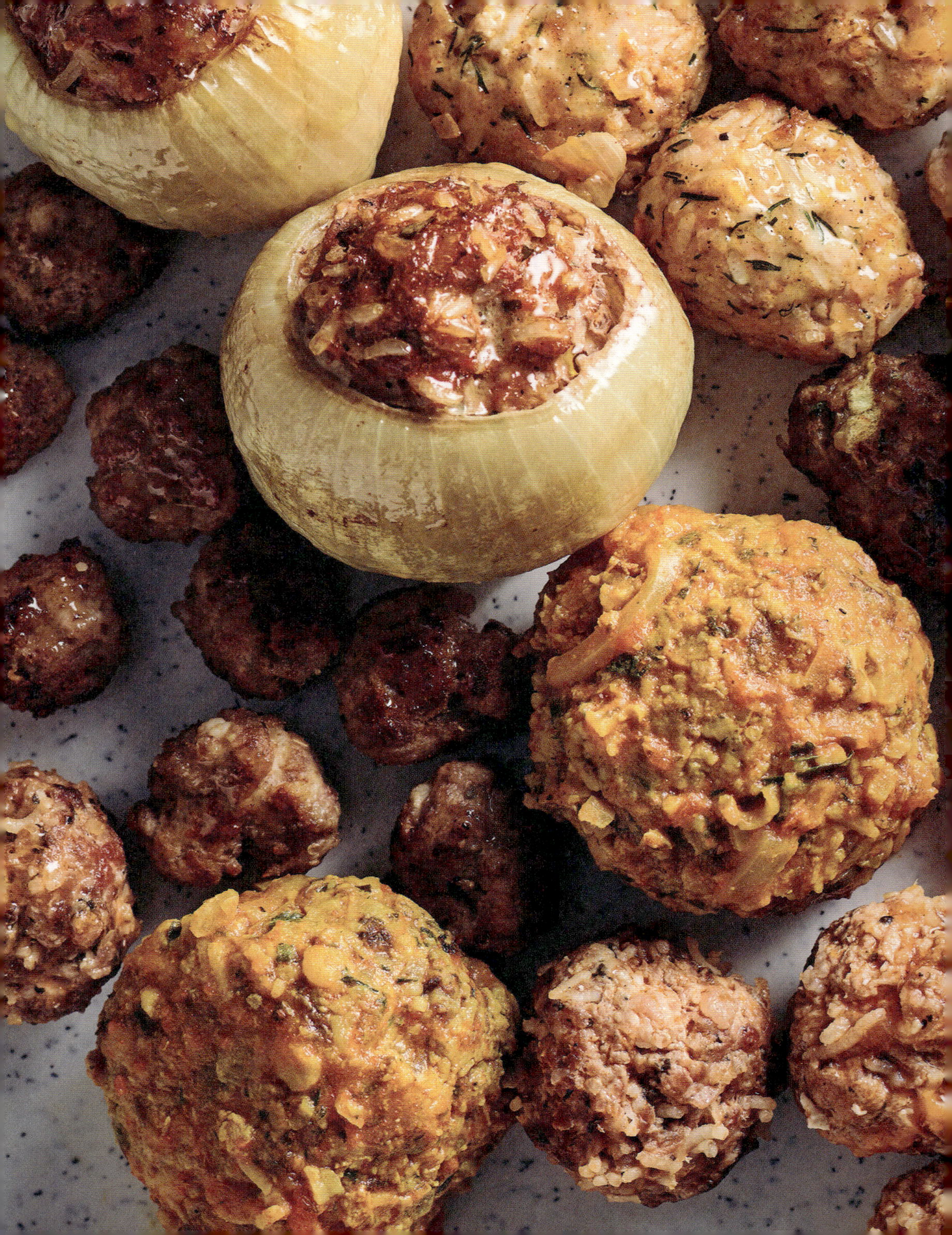

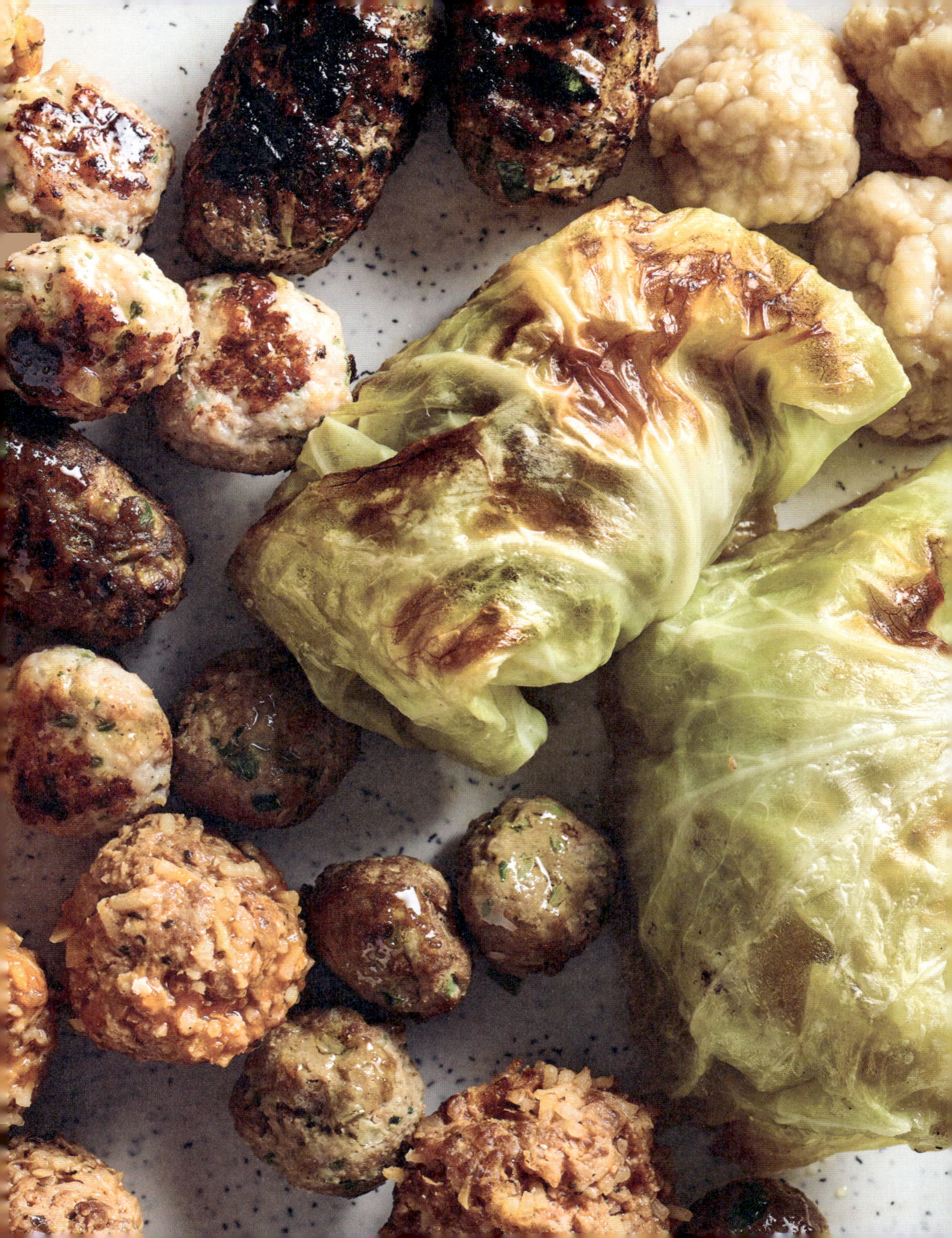

Index

• A

Adele's koftas 34
Afghanistan: Korme kofta 141
ahogada sauce 30
Albondigas 30
albondigas, Sopa de 109
Albondigas Mama Pepa in white wine sauce 172
Algeria: Meatballs with olives 140
almond sauce, White wine and 172
Almôndegas de bacalhau 82
Ash-e anar 119
A-thar-lohn-hin 116
aubergines *see* eggplants
Australia
   Porcupine meatballs 164
   Rissoles with gravy and minted peas 39
Austrian meat patties 131
avgolemono 36
avocados: Sopa de albondigas 109

• B

bacalhau, Almôndegas de 82
Baked meatballs in tomato sauce 54
Bakso 127
bechamel sauce, Meatball bake with 85
beef
   Albondigas 30
   Baked meatballs in tomato sauce 54
   Beef and potato meatballs 35
   Boulet with Haitian epis 74–5
   Burghul and beef meatballs 92
   Burmese meatball curry 116
   Cabbage meatballs 64
   Eggplant casserole 78
   Fried potato meatball patties 163
   Fried potato sandwiches with meatball filling 110
   Ghanaian meatball stew 67
   Gola kabab with charred onions 106
   Grechanyky with mushroom sauce 168
   Herbed green meatballs 95
   Indonesian meatball soup 127
   Israeli-style meatballs 51
   Kafta and tahini bake with Palestinian salad 173
   Kafta with tarator sauce and tabbouleh 133
   Keftedes with fried potatoes 46
   Kotletai in dill-spiked broth 68
   Lemony meatball soup 36

Lentil soup with meatballs 33
Maltese meatballs and meat broth 155
Meatball and potato casserole 53
Meatball and potato curry 48–9
Meatballs and creamed spinach 25
Meatballs in tomato soup 156
Meatballs in yoghurt sauce 90–1
Meatballs with baked eggplant 146
Meatballs with horseradish beetroot 158
Meatballs with olives 140
Meatball-stuffed baked onions 128
Mira's meatballs 43
Nordic baked meatballs 112
Pomegranate and herb soup with meatballs 119
Porcupine meatballs 164
Rissoles with gravy and minted peas 39
Sour soup with meatballs 57
Sparrow-head meatballs with French fries 167
Spiced beef meatballs with tomato sauce 100
Tibetan meatball soup 178
Turkish meatball soup 52
Vermicelli meatball soup 130
see also pork and beef
beetroot
   Meatballs with horseradish beetroot 158
   Pulpety with cold beet salad 26
Begedil 163
Belgian meatballs with onion gravy 77
bell peppers *see* capsicums
bok choy
   Indonesian meatball soup 127
   Lion's head meatballs with thick sauce 152
bola-bola, Misua with 83
Bosnia: Meatball-stuffed baked onions 128
Boulet with Haitian epis 74–5
Boulette de bœuf 35
Brazil: Burghul and beef meatballs 92
buckwheat
   Grechanyky with mushroom sauce 168
   Kotleti 59
Bulgaria: Meatballs in tomato sauce 72
burghul
   Burghul and beef meatballs 92
   Meatballs in yoghurt sauce 90–1
   tabbouleh 133
Burmese meatball curry 116

• C

cabbage
   Cabbage meatballs 64
   Lion's head meatballs with cabbage 150
cacik 149
Cambodia: Num pang with pork meatballs 97
Canada: French-Canadian meatball stew 134
capsicums
   Adele's koftas 34
   Albondigas 30
   Baked meatballs in tomato sauce 54
   Boulet with Haitian epis 74–5
   Eggplant casserole 78
   Ghanaian meatball stew 67
   Lentil soup with meatballs 33
   Meatball and egg tagine 29
   Meatballs in tomato sauce 72
carrots
   Chicken meatball hot pot 86
   Danish fish cakes 89
   Herbed green meatballs 95
   hutspot 40
   Israeli-style meatballs 51
   Italian wedding soup 139
   Maltese meatballs and meat broth 155
   pickled carrots 97
   Sopa de albondigas 109
   Sour soup with meatballs 57
   Turkish meatball soup 52
casserole, Meatball and potato 53
celery
   Chinese meatball soup 162
   Italian meatballs in tomato sauce 121
   Italian wedding soup 139
   Maltese meatballs and meat broth 155
   Meatballs in tomato sauce 72
   Sopa de albondigas 109
   Sour soup with meatballs 57
chana pulao 48
Chanko nabe with tori dango 86
Chebtiya 95
cheese
   Italian wedding soup 139
   Little lemony meatballs 157
   Maltese meatballs and meat broth 155
   Meatball and potato casserole 53
   Meatball bake with bechamel sauce 85
   Meatballs with baked eggplant 146
chicken
   Chicken meatball hot pot 86
   Chicken meatballs with teriyaki sauce 71
   Fried potato meatball patties 163
   Kotletai in dill-spiked broth 68

182   Around the World in 80 Meatballs

Kotlete in gravy 124
Meatballs with horseradish
    beetroot 158
Mira's meatballs 43
chickpeas
    chana pulao 48
    Herbed green meatballs 95
China
    Lion's head meatballs
        with cabbage 150
    Lion's head meatballs with
        thick sauce 152
    Meatballs in broth 153
    Vermicelli meatball soup 130
Chinese cabbage: Chicken
    meatball hot pot 86
Chinese meatball soup 162
Christmas
    French-Canadian meatball stew 134
    Norwegian pork meatballs 58
cilantro see coriander
Ciorba de perisoare 57
Cod balls 82
cold beet salad 26
Colombia: Albondigas 30
congee, Rice, with pork meatballs 113
coriander
    Albondigas 30
    Burmese meatball curry 116
    Fried potato meatball patties 163
    Fried potato sandwiches with
        meatball filling 110
    Korme kofta 141
    Lentil soup with meatballs 33
    Meatball and egg tagine 29
    Meatball and potato curry 48–9
    Num pang with pork meatballs 97
    Pomegranate and herb soup
        with meatballs 119
    Rice congee with pork meatballs 113
    Rice meatballs in spiced
        tomato sauce 115
    Sopa de albondigas 109
    Tibetan meatball soup 178
    Yoghurt sauce 91
    courgettes see zucchini
creamed spinach 25
cucumbers
    cacik 149
    Num pang with pork meatballs 97
    Palestinian salad 173
Ćufte 100
Ćulbastije 85
curries
    Burmese meatball curry 116
    Korme kofta 141
    Meatball and potato curry 48–9
Cyprus: Keftedes with fried potatoes 46
Czech Republic: Mira's meatballs 43

● D
Denmark: Danish fish cakes 89
dill
    Danish fish cakes 89
    dill potato salad 175
    Herbed green meatballs 95
    Israeli-style meatballs 51
    Kotletai in dill-spiked broth 68
    Kotlete in gravy 124
    Kotleti 59
    Pulpety with cold beet salad 26
    Rice meatballs in spiced
        tomato sauce 115
    Sour soup with meatballs 57
Dutch meatballs with mash 40

● E
eggplants
    Eggplant casserole 78
    Meatballs with baked eggplant 146
eggs
    Fried potato meatball patties 163
    Lemony meatball soup 36
    Meatball and egg tagine 29
    Sour soup with meatballs 57
    Turkish meatball soup 52
Ekşili köfte 52

● F
Faggots/savoury ducks with gravy 101
Faschierte laibchen 131
Fasirozott with nokedli 161
Fesenjoon 118
Finland: Nordic baked meatballs 112
fish
    Cod balls 82
    Danish fish cakes 89
Fiskefrikadeller 89
Fistkili kebab 149
France: Beef and potato meatballs 35
French-Canadian meatball stew 134
Fried meat patties with gochugaru
    dipping sauce 171
Fried potato meatball patties 163
Fried potato sandwiches with
    meatball filling 110
Frikadellen and rahmspinat 25

● G
Gehaktballen with hutspot 40
Germany: Meatballs and
    creamed spinach 25
Ghanaian meatball stew 67
Goji-wanja-jeon 171
Gola kabab with charred onions 106
Gongwan 162

gravy
    Belgian meatballs with onion gravy 77
    Dutch meatballs with mash 40
    Faggots/savoury ducks with gravy 101
    French-Canadian meatball stew 134
    Kotlete in gravy 124
    Meatballs with horseradish
        beetroot 158
    Mira's meatballs 43
    Rissoles with gravy and
        minted peas 39
Grechanyky with mushroom sauce 168
    Greece: Lemony meatball soup 36
green beans: Israeli-style meatballs 51

● H
Haiti: Boulet with Haitian epis 74–5
Hasanpasha köfte 53
Herbed green meatballs 95
horseradish beetroot 158
hot pot, Chicken meatball 86
Hungary: Meatballs with
    tiny dumplings 161
hutspot 40

● I
Indonesian meatball soup 127
Iran
    Meatball stew with pomegranate
        and walnuts 118
    Pomegranate and herb soup
        with meatballs 119
    Rice meatballs in spiced
        tomato sauce 115
    Sparrow-head meatballs with
        French fries 167
Iraq: Eggplant casserole 78
Israeli-style meatballs 51
Italy
    Italian meatballs in tomato sauce 121
    Italian wedding soup 139
    Little lemony meatballs 157
    Meatballs with baked eggplant 146
Izmir köfte 54

● J
Japan
    Chicken meatball hot pot 86
    Chicken meatballs with
        teriyaki sauce 71
Jok moo 113

K

kabab, Gola, with charred onions 106
Kafta and tahini bake with Palestinian salad 173
Kafta with tarator sauce and tabbouleh 133
Kal leh gonjishki 167
kebab, Fistkili 149
Kefta b'zeitoun 140
Kefta mkaouara 29
Keftedes with fried potatoes 46
Kibbeh labanieh 90–1
Kibe 92
Kjufteta po Chirpanski 72
Klopsiki with cwikla z chrzanem 158
kofta, Korme 141
kofta, Shorbat adas bil 33
Kofta aalu 48–9
koftas, Adele's 34
köfte, Ekşili 52
köfte, Hasanpasha 53
köfte, Izmir 54
Koofteh berenji 115
Korea: Fried meat patties with gochugaru dipping sauce 171
Korme kofta 141
Kotletai in dill-spiked broth 68
Kotlete in gravy 124
Kotleti 59
Kottbullar 175

L

lamb
Adele's koftas 34
Burmese meatball curry 116
Eggplant casserole 78
Fried potato sandwiches with meatball filling 110
Kafta and tahini bake with Palestinian salad 173
Korme kofta 141
Lentil soup with meatballs 33
Meatball and egg tagine 29
Meatball stew with pomegranate and walnuts 118
Meatballs in yoghurt sauce 90–1
Pistachio lamb patties 149
Rice meatballs in spiced tomato sauce 115
Sparrow-head meatballs with French fries 167
Latvia: Kotlete in gravy 124
Lebanon
Kafta with tarator sauce and tabbouleh 133
Meatballs in tomato soup 156
Meatballs in yoghurt sauce 90–1
Shorba hamra 156

lemons
Danish fish cakes 89
Kafta and tahini bake with Palestinian salad 173
Lemony meatball soup 36
Little lemony meatballs 157
Sour soup with meatballs 57
Sparrow-head meatballs with French fries 167
tabbouleh 133
tarator sauce 133
Turkish meatball soup 52
Lentil soup with meatballs 33
Libya: Fried potato sandwiches with meatball filling 110
Lihapullat 112
Lion's head meatballs with cabbage 150
Lion's head meatballs with thick sauce 152
Lithuania: Kotletai in dill-spiked broth 68
Little lemony meatballs 157

M

Malaysia: Fried potato meatball patties 163
Maltese meatballs and meat broth 155
M'battan 110
Meatball and egg tagine 29
Meatball and potato casserole 53
Meatball and potato curry 48–9
Meatball bake with bechamel sauce 85
Meatball noodle soup 83
Meatball stew with pomegranate and walnuts 118
Meatballs and creamed spinach 25
Meatballs in broth 153
Meatballs in tomato sauce 72
Meatballs in tomato soup 156
Meatballs with baked eggplant 146
Meatballs with garlic dipping sauce 94
Meatballs with horseradish beetroot 158
Meatballs with olives 140
Meatballs with tiny dumplings 161
Meatball-stuffed baked onions 128
Medisterkaker 58
Mexico: Sopa de albondigas 109
Minestra maritata 139
mint
Burghul and beef meatballs 92
Lemony meatball soup 36
Lentil soup with meatballs 33
Num pang with pork meatballs 97
Palestinian salad 173
Pistachio lamb patties 149
Pomegranate and herb soup with meatballs 119
Rissoles with gravy and minted peas 39
tabbouleh 133

Mira's meatballs 43
Misua with bola-bola 83
Moldova: Meatballs with garlic dipping sauce 94
Morocco: Meatball and egg tagine 29
mujdei 94
mushrooms
Chicken meatball hot pot 86
Grechanyky with mushroom sauce 168
Vermicelli meatball soup 130
Myanmar: Burmese meatball curry 116

N

Netherlands: Dutch meatballs with mash 40
nokedli 161
noodles
Indonesian meatball soup 127
Meatball noodle soup 83
Meatballs in tomato soup 156
Vermicelli meatball soup 130
Nordic baked meatballs 112
Norwegian pork meatballs 58
Num pang with pork meatballs 97
nuts see almonds, peanuts, pine nuts, pistachios, walnuts

O

olives
Meatball and egg tagine 29
Meatballs with olives 140
onions
Belgian meatballs with onion gravy 77
Burmese meatball curry 116
Ghanaian meatball stew 67
Meatball-stuffed baked onions 128
Oumense onder die komberse 64

P

Pakistan
Gola kabab with charred onions 106
Meatball and potato curry 48–9
Palestine
Kafta and tahini bake with Palestinian salad 173
Lentil soup with meatballs 33
Parjoale with mujdei 94
parsley
Adele's koftas 34
Boulet with Haitian epis 74–5
Danish fish cakes 89
Herbed green meatballs 95
Kafta with tarator sauce and tabbouleh 133
Kotletai in dill-spiked broth 68
Lemony meatball soup 36
Lentil soup with meatballs 33

Maltese meatballs and meat broth 155
Meatball and egg tagine 29
Meatballs in tomato sauce 72
Meatballs with garlic dipping sauce 94
Pomegranate and herb soup
   with meatballs 119
Rice meatballs in spiced
   tomato sauce 115
parsnips: Austrian meat patties 131
pasta
   Italian meatballs in tomato sauce 121
   Italian wedding soup 139
   Maltese meatballs and meat broth 155
peanuts: Num pang with
   pork meatballs 97
peas, Rissoles with gravy and minted 39
peas, split *see* split peas
Persia *see* Iran
Philippines: Meatball noodle soup 83
pickled carrots 97
pine nuts
   Kafta and tahini bake with Palestinian
     salad 173
   white wine and almond sauce 172
Pistachio lamb patties 149
Poland
   Meatballs with horseradish
     beetroot 158
   Pulpety with cold beet salad 26
Polpette in sugo 121
Polpette with melanzane
   alla sassarese 146
Polpettine al limone 157
Pomegranate and herb soup
   with meatballs 119
Porcupine meatballs 164
pork
   Burmese meatball curry 116
   Chinese meatball soup 162
   Faggots/savoury ducks with gravy 101
   Fried meat patties with gochugaru
     dipping sauce 171
   Lion's head meatballs
     with cabbage 150
   Lion's head meatballs with
     thick sauce 152
   Meatball noodle soup 83
   Meatballs in broth 153
   Meatballs with horseradish
     beetroot 158
   Meatballs with tiny dumplings 161
   Norwegian pork meatballs 58
   Num pang with pork meatballs 97
   Rice congee with pork meatballs 113
   see also pork and beef
pork and beef
   Albondigas Mama Pepa in
     white wine sauce 172
   Austrian meat patties 131
   Belgian meatballs with onion gravy 77

Dutch meatballs with mash 40
French-Canadian meatball stew 134
Italian meatballs in tomato sauce 121
Italian wedding soup 139
Kotleti 59
Kottbullar 175
Little lemony meatballs 157
Meatball bake with bechamel
   sauce 85
Meatballs and creamed spinach 25
Meatballs in tomato sauce 72
Meatballs with baked eggplant 146
Meatballs with garlic dipping sauce 94
Meatballs with horseradish
   beetroot 158
Pulpety with cold beet salad 26
Sopa de albondigas 109
Portugal: Cod balls 82
potatoes
   Adele's koftas 34
   Baked meatballs in tomato sauce 54
   Beef and potato meatballs 35
   Cod balls 82
   dill potato salad 175
   Eggplant casserole 78
   Fried potato meatball patties 163
   Fried potato sandwiches with
     meatball filling 110
   hutspot 40
   Kafta and tahini bake with Palestinian
     salad 173
   Keftedes with fried potatoes 46
   Maltese meatballs and meat broth 155
   Meatball and potato casserole 53
   Meatball and potato curry 48-9
   Meatballs in tomato sauce 72
   Meatballs with baked eggplant 146
   Sopa de albondigas 109
   Sparrow-head meatballs with
     French fries 167
   Turkish meatball soup 52
Pulpetti tal-laham and
   brodu tal-laham 155
Pulpety with cold beet salad 26

● **R**

Ragoût de boulettes 134
rice
   chana pulao 48
   Lemony meatball soup 36
   Porcupine meatballs 164
   Rice congee with pork meatballs 113
   Rice meatballs in spiced
     tomato sauce 115
   yoghurt sauce 91
Rissoles with gravy and minted peas 39
Romania: Sour soup with meatballs 57
Russia: Grechanyky with
   mushroom sauce 168

● **S**

salads
   cold beet salad 26
   dill potato salad 175
   Palestinian salad 173
   tabbouleh 133
sauces
   ahogada sauce 30
   bechamel sauce 85
   gochugaru dipping sauce 171
   mujdei 94
   mushroom sauce 168
   tarator sauce 133
   teriyaki sauce 71
   white wine and almond sauce 172
   yoghurt sauce 91
   see also gravy
sauerkraut 59
Serbia
   Meatball bake with bechamel
     sauce 85
   Spiced beef meatballs with
     tomato sauce 100
Shorba 156
Shorbat adas bil kofta 33
Sogan dolma 128
Sopa de albondigas 109
soups
   Chinese meatball soup 162
   Indonesian meatball soup 127
   Italian wedding soup 139
   Lemony meatball soup 36
   Lentil soup with meatballs 33
   Maltese meatballs and meat broth 155
   Meatball noodle soup 83
   Meatballs in tomato soup 156
   Pomegranate and herb soup
     with meatballs 119
   Sopa de albondigas 109
   Sour soup with meatballs 57
   Tibetan meatball soup 178
   Turkish meatball soup 52
   Vermicelli meatball soup 130
   see also congee
Sour soup with meatballs 57
South Africa: Cabbage meatballs 64
spaghetti *see* **pasta**
Spain: Albondigas Mama Pepa
   in white wine sauce 172
Sparrow-head meatballs with
   French fries 167
spinach
   Herbed green meatballs 95
   Italian wedding soup 139
   Meatballs and creamed spinach 25
   Tibetan meatball soup 178
   Vermicelli meatball soup 130

split peas, yellow
   Korme kofta 141
   Pomegranate and herb soup
     with meatballs 119
   Rice meatballs in spiced
     tomato sauce 115
Sweden: Kottbullar 175
Syria: Adele's koftas 34

• T

tabbouleh 133
tagine, Meatball and egg 29
tahini
   Kafta and tahini bake with Palestinian
     salad 173
   Kafta with tarator sauce
     and tabbouleh 133
tarator sauce 133
Tepsi baytinijan 78
Teriyaki tsukune 71
Thailand: Rice congee with
   pork meatballs 113
Tibetan meatball soup 178
tofu
   Chicken meatball hot pot 86
   Chicken meatballs with
     teriyaki sauce 71
   Vermicelli meatball soup 130
tomatoes
   Adele's koftas 34
   ahogada sauce 30
   Albondigas 30
   Baked meatballs in tomato sauce 54
   Burghul and beef meatballs 92
   Eggplant casserole 78
   Italian meatballs in tomato sauce 121
   Kafta and tahini bake with Palestinian
     salad 173
   Meatball and egg tagine 29
   Meatball and potato curry 48-9
   Meatballs with olives 140
   Sparrow-head meatballs with French
     fries 167
   tabbouleh 133
   Vermicelli meatball soup 130
   white wine and almond sauce 172
Tunisia: Herbed green meatballs 95
Türkiye
   Baked meatballs in tomato sauce 54
   Meatball and potato casserole 53
   Pistachio lamb patties 149
   Turkish meatball soup 52

• U

Ukraine: Kotleti 59
United Kingdom: Faggots/savoury
   ducks with gravy 101

• V

veal
   Italian meatballs in tomato sauce 121
   Italian wedding soup 139
   Little lemony meatballs 157
   Meatballs with tiny dumplings 161
   Mira's meatballs 43
Vermicelli meatball soup 130

• W

walnuts, Meatball stew with
   pomegranate and 118
wedding soup, Italian 139
white wine and almond sauce 172
wombok *see* Chinese cabbage

• Y

yoghurt
   cacik 149
   Kafta and tahini bake with Palestinian
     salad 173
   Meatballs in yoghurt sauce 90-1
Youvarlakia 36

• Z

Zhou rou wan 153
zucchini
   Lentil soup with meatballs 33
   Maltese meatballs and meat broth 155

Acknowledgements

Khassandra Yianni, for being the spiritual midwife of the book. Karen Banyai, for endless, high-level recipe testing. Tina Grundmann, for invaluable support in recruiting contributors; ditto Ben Foster and Larissa Dubecki. Tom and Beatrix Carlyon, for pushing through meatball-fatigue, and keeping the Sunday test kitchen rolling for three months straight. Belle Galloway and Sandra Mason for general assistance, recipe testing and cheerleading. Tim Evans for life-altering admin coaching. Clementine Hall, for occasionally putting her clothes in the laundry basket. Simon Davis, for being the kindest and most encouraging of publishers. Maddie Dobbins, Kirsten Jenkins, Mark Roper and Rosheen Kaul for their brilliant work bringing the recipes to life and achieving the near-impossible: making the meatballs look as good as they taste. Celia Mance for her beautiful book design, Lauren Carta and Andrea O'Connor for premium editing prowess.

I am deeply indebted to everyone who put their hand up to test a recipe and who provided such valuable feedback: Dan Smith, Adam Hutterer, Sally O'Brien, Kym Smith, Holly Marshall, Liz Bradie, Francine Kuiper, Katy Reed, Luke Fraser, Tracey Lam, Rachel McKibbin and Annabel McKibbin.

Finally, greatest thanks to all the wonderful contributors who so generously shared their stories and prized family recipes with me.

About the author

Bunny Banyai is a freelance writer and the author of non-fiction books *Sh*t On My Hands: A Down and Dirty Guide to Parenting*, *100 Aussie Things We Know and Love*, and *Anxious Girls Do It Better*. Born and raised in Melbourne to a Hungarian father and half-Russian mother, Bunny spent her childhood rejecting almost everything on her plate, meatballs being one of the few exceptions. *Around the World in 80 Meatballs* is her first foray into food writing, inspired by her intercultural love affair with the universally beloved, globetrotting meatball.